THE OUTSIDE

THE OUTSIDE

Cheating death, chasing waves
and growing up in one of Australia's
most notorious crime families

LARRY BLAIR & JEREMY GORING

PENGUIN BOOKS

UK | USA | Canada | Ireland | Australia
India | New Zealand | South Africa | China

Penguin Books is part of the Penguin Random House group of companies
whose addresses can be found at global.penguinrandomhouse.com

Penguin Random House Australia

First published by Penguin Books in 2024

Copyright © Larry Blair and Jeremy Goring 2024

The moral right of the authors has been asserted.

All rights reserved. No part of this publication may be reproduced, published, performed in public or communicated to the public in any form or by any means without prior written permission from Penguin Random House Australia Pty Ltd or its authorised licensees.

This book is a memoir. It reflects the author's present recollections of experiences over time. In some instances, events have been compressed and dialogue has been recreated. Some names and distinguishing details have been changed throughout.

Cover photography by Mikhail Dudarev/Bigstock
Cover design by Design by Committee © Penguin Random House Australia Pty Ltd
Typeset in 12.5/17.5 pt Minion Pro by Midland Typesetters, Australia

Printed and bound in Australia by Griffin Press, an accredited
ISO AS/NZS 14001 Environmental Management Systems printer

A catalogue record for this book is available from the National Library of Australia

ISBN 978 1 76134 500 5

penguin.com.au

MIX
Paper | Supporting responsible forestry
FSC® C018684

We at Penguin Random House Australia acknowledge that Aboriginal and Torres Strait Islander peoples are the Traditional Custodians and the first storytellers of the lands on which we live and work. We honour Aboriginal and Torres Strait Islander peoples' continuous connection to Country, waters, skies and communities. We celebrate Aboriginal and Torres Strait Islander stories, traditions and living cultures; and we pay our respects to Elders past and present.

*In memory of Fat Larry,
and all those who charged
over the ledges before us.*

Contents

Prologue: The Banzai Pipeline		1
1.	Baldy	7
2.	A Thief's Apprentice	18
3.	The Red Rocket	26
4.	Billy and the Pom	37
5.	The Great Idea	45
6.	In the Caves	54
7.	Bent Coppers	66
8.	The Toe Cutters	68
9.	Running from Planes, Climbing Down Drains	79
10.	Baldy's War	93
11.	Melody Street	100
12.	Young Offender	110
13.	Shaka	130
14.	The Kangaroo Girls on Tour	148
15.	Down and Out in Darwin	157
16.	In the Jungle with Gerry	164

17.	The Last Queen of Hawaii	175
18.	Undercurrent	177
19.	Fast Eddie's Kingdom	182
20.	The Sunset Stray Dogs' Home	194
21.	Take-off	201
22.	A Haunting	219
23.	Pipeline Master	223
24.	At the Peak Looking Down	240
25.	Over the Falls	258
26.	Return to Melody Street	269
Epilogue: Floating Back to Shore		285

Co-author's Note	305
Acknowledgements	307
About the Author	309

Prologue:
The Banzai Pipeline

Hawaii is world famous for its warm welcome, but don't outstay it.

December 1979

The sand on the slope at Ehukai Beach Park appears honey-gold. It's an illusion; if you look closely, every grain is a different colour. Bleached coral chips make up most of it but there are also worn-out shell fragments, specks of black lava and every shade in between. It's up to you what colours you see.

I'm studying the stuff closely while shuffling my feet about in it. The large particles feel good between the toes: not too fine and sticky, not too coarse. My stomach is a knotted mess, as if I'm waiting in that dark-wood-panelled school corridor. I'm thinking of Mum, who does miracles. Mum can make anything disappear – this is her job. She did it with my baby sister Kellie and me when Dad's friends were hunting us.

But she isn't here. And she can't help.

So God bless you, Mum, wherever you are on this earth.

And Dad, buried under Sydney Airport.

And me, here on the North Shore.

Ψ

This breezy, blue-green and gold heaven has been my second home since 1973 when I was fifteen and needed to leave Australia in a hurry. A very long surf trip to the most remote islands on earth offered me the best way to do it. I got a decent start, making some friends and even earning a little cautious respect from the big guys out in the sea. The ocean had terrified me at first but after a while I became almost at ease among the marching mountains of water – almost. I even started to believe I'd found a niche for myself. But standing here now in front of the simmering mob, I am about to be announced as the winner of the 1979 Banzai Pipeline Masters, and things are going to get very awkward.

People like me aren't popular in these parts, mostly because of the shit that comes out of our mouths. We've also had the brass to enter – and sometimes win – the surfing contests that Hawaiians have always dominated. This has been an insult. The riding of waves was invented here and Hawaii is the spiritual home of world surfing. These are warm-hearted people with a long and fiercely proud history deeply entwined with the ocean. That ocean, and those who live on it, demand respect.

Hawaiians had the sport to themselves for centuries, even after a British sea captain arrived in 1778 and documented locals paddling about on timber planks. Despite a crew member aboard HMS *Resolution* sketching this other-worldly 'dance', no *haole* (Hawaiian slang that more or less means 'gringo') actually got on a board and rode it standing up until pretty recently. I've often wondered why it took us so long.

Once foreigners discovered surfing, however, they made up for lost time and the sport grew fast, with the side effect being a foreign invasion here on the island of Oahu over the last few years. It has led to a steadily thickening, toxic undercurrent, concentrated on the North Shore. Things started getting menacing a few years ago, when hot shots like Rabbit, Shaun and Mark arrived. This trio, along with a few others, rewrote the book on what was possible in our sport. They caught the eye of everybody on their way to six world surfing titles between them, and their ever-increasing media profiles wound up tensions even further. Finally, a few faux pas in the press proved to be the last straw and a local posse felt they had to step in – physically.

I tried, I really tried to lie low these last few northern winters. But they got me in the end. I'm a runner-away, but sometimes there isn't anywhere to run. A lieutenant gave me a violent warning almost as soon as I got back to the island. My attacker was not a big man – shorter than me and of slight build – but he was made of steel wire. In my mind he's an abused bull terrier fresh from the pound – I've always been terrified of him. His physique and angry eyes remind me of my father's best pal Fletcher, and Fletcher has done some terrible things to people. On the day the man caught up with me, there were too many people watching for me to run, so I just let the blood dribble down my face and kept my fists to myself.

Now, everywhere I go feels tense, inflammable, on edge. Especially out in the water, especially here at Pipeline.

The Banzai Pipeline is the jewel in the crown of North Shore surfing and is still to this day the most famous wave in the world. 'Pipe', as it's colloquially known, has taken more lives than all of the world's waves combined. It's one of the most dangerous, snarling, tubular masses of water on the planet, and for many years it was considered unrideable; a perfectly shaped, beautiful blue suicide mission that surfers gawped at and then just walked right past. For this reason, it attracts a curious selection of mongrels, many with a point to prove.

It is a sacred site with its own set of modern-day gods. Gerry 'Mr Pipe' Lopez, Rory Russell and up and comer Dane Kealoha are the most revered. All of these great men are proud that Hawaiians have always 'owned' the Pipeline Masters, which was, and still is, the most sought-after trophy on the professional world tour. Two of these surfing deities are standing next to me right now doing the same sandy shuffle while we await the judges' verdict. I already know that I've knocked them both out of the competition.

My fellow interlopers, Shaun and Mark, are also in this little group of six expectant finalists, as if it needs to get any more tense.

Dane is fidgeting and hopping about like a boxer limbering up for a fight. If we ever came close to friendship, it ended this morning out there beyond the breaking waves. First when we came to blows during the warm-up period and Dane ripped my lucky Buddha off my neck, and then during the grand final itself just now. I don't know if relations, or my silver chain, can ever be repaired.

It's an awkward fact that I pipped him and a few other demigods to the title here last year. It sent shockwaves through the islands. *The nasty little* haole *criminal breezing in and upsetting the natural order . . . and only nineteen etc. etc.* My mouth, which I don't always keep under control, made things even worse. Giddy with victory, I imagined a certain picture as the words came tumbling out during the post-contest press interview, but when those same words floated up off the page a few months later and struck the eyes of my Hawaiian hosts, that picture seemed very different. I sounded like a massive arsehole.

For all these reasons, a second victory is not going to be palatable. Hawaiians do not like second comings of any kind, whether by gods or mortals, as Captain Cook himself discovered on his fateful final voyage, which ended so abruptly right across the straits from here 200 years ago, almost to the day.

Dane Kealoha is far and away the locals' pick; he is truly of here, like a deep-rooted trunk of dense hard *koa*, the majestic native hardwood that was once used to make surfboards ridden by the Hawaiian kings. As for me, I'm just some Aussie tumbleweed who blew into town to get away from the New South Wales police.

I am also the uneducated, handsome, blond and very lippy son of two of Australia's most notorious criminals.

Ψ

Here on the beach surrounded by the lowing crowd and the crush of cameras, Dane is avoiding my gaze. He's still fidgeting and hopping, looking everywhere but at me. Thank Neptune for that. He's not going to like what's about to be announced. Neither are the men in the black shorts.

A low hum from the mob tells me the judges are ready. I pray that if I win and the inevitable fallout ensues, Lucky Buddha can still keep watch over me from the bottom of Pipeline reef.

1.

Baldy

You can't choose your family.
– Dad, 1966

Maroubra in Sydney's east, or 'the 'Bra' as the place was called by the old tattoo-footed surfer gangs, is our home, not that we're ever in one place for very long.

Frank 'Baldy' Blair is my new dad. Ink, scars and a shiny head. I first meet him when I'm a boy of seven. I've never known any other father and so it is immediately understood that this man is now exactly that. Frank is a violent drinker and lives with my mother and me, but he has a second residence at the Oshey – the Oceanic Hotel – on Arden Street, Coogee. He holds court there most days on its wide, concrete front steps overlooking the Pacific Ocean.

My beautiful mum, Patricia, loves Frank even though his short thick legs and veiny arms host tangled tattoos of other women. He loves her too – I know this – but his demonstrations of love depend on the day.

When Frank exploded into our lives it quickly became clear that he was the boss. He brought blitzkrieg, a cycle of short bursts of anger, enthusiasm or excitement followed by periods of unexplained, peaceful absence. The fighting and shouting between my parents is relentless, because Mum is beautiful and refined, a princess in all but circumstance, and totally dedicated to me, her only child. Frank is a gnarled bundle of scar tissue who has already crammed a whole lifetime of terrible violence into his brief existence. He is a fighting dog, a pit bull always ready to snap, and prepared to hunt anything down at any moment if it catches his attention. Sometimes this is my mother, whom he often chases around the living room.

ψ

My new dad arrived with no fanfare, and little explanation from Mum, but that wasn't unusual. Life with Mum had always been an adventure, a series of delightful journeys and surprises of which this I guessed was just another. We were a kind of mobile unit, and she'd never had a long-term partner as far as I could recall. Frank was the first, and so that was that, as she always liked to say.

To his credit, Frank indulged me as his son from day one. I both loved him and feared him. No matter how bad things got, he always seemed to redeem himself. Embarrassingly magnificent gifts would often appear, including on one occasion a huge toy boat covered in flashing lights that he bought at the Easter Show in Moore Park. I was too frightened to go and float this crazy device in public and it never got the use it deserved.

Many of my most vivid childhood memories of Frank involved gifts. A brand-new skateboard, which I used to transport the mountainous family laundry stack to and from the laundrette, is another. I bloody loved that set of wheels but don't remember actually ever riding it standing up. Then came Joliette, the little white poodle that was promptly lost during a game of hide and seek out the front of our house. It was hardly a tough guy's dog, and so perhaps it felt out of place and took its chance to cut and run to a more genteel family hearth. Dogs and cats never lasted very long in our house and a beautiful glossy golden labrador had a similarly short spell as my favourite pet. If you must know the truth, I don't even remember that dog's name and there's hardly anybody left to ask.

Ψ

I played my part in our new family trio and learned to do my household duties properly and unswervingly without being asked twice. I had two reasons for being such a good little boy: I loved my mum an awful lot and, as I say, I feared my new dad just as much. This double-sided management method was very, very effective; I am still an excellent housekeeper and an absolute stickler for the neat and tidy, to the point that every girlfriend I ever had thought I was weird. Many did sharp U-turns.

I always knew that Frank didn't have a normal job like the parents of my schoolmates at Coogee Primary. He would disappear for days without warning. Years later I discovered he was usually off either philandering or wrongdoing – he did a lot of both – but at the time I was told he was away 'working', and I believed it.

I choose to forget most of the fights my parents had. Fights that I saw, fights that I heard, and fights that I only learned of years later when I twigged that they were the only possible explanations for all the broken stuff around the house. But Mum wasn't always the victim. My parents didn't need a reason to fight, but Priscilla was a big one. Dad's lover was a tall, beautiful black princess from a far better place than him. It's fair to say that they were a total mismatch in looks, height and class. I will never figure out how or why my father was attractive to either Priscilla or my mother.

When Mum found out about Priscilla vicious battles ensued and a few times I feared for Frank more than Mum. At one point my mother actually bought a doll, applied make-up to it, and attempted to voodoo the sad little thing with pins and chants. I don't know if it was a warning to Frank, or just a joke, but underneath Mum's grace and finesse, perhaps there was something harder, something she didn't want me to see.

Ψ

Shortly after Frank showed up we moved to Curtin Crescent, Maroubra, where, for a while, everything felt settled. Sort of. I hoped that we'd be there for good, but it would turn out to be temporary. Over the next few years, my parents' varied activities meant that one or both of them was regularly packing up to leave, with or without me. They must have cared about my education, though, because I was always starting at a new school or returning to an old one.

One of these, a boarding school named after a saint far inland at Campbelltown, was – and still is – one of my least favourite places. I was packed off there soon after Frank's arrival because he had business to attend to around the country, and my mother couldn't look after me because she too had to hit the road.

I strained against it with all my will. Being removed from home was unsettling and a little grim but it wasn't the end of the world – wherever we ended up I always had a second home to fall back upon in the form of the sea. But now, for the first time, I was being ripped away from that as well. Hot and dusty Campbelltown felt so far west that it could have been the desert.

I hated the thought so much that I ran away from home just as Mum and Dad were rounding me up to stuff me in the car and deliver me for my first day. I think I was on the run for quite a long time, maybe minutes or possibly even an hour. When they caught up with me and I was cornered, I started throwing rocks at them. They eventually disarmed me and took me to my temporary prison. It was a sorry state of affairs to see them working as a team just this once, for the sole reason of sending me away to boarding school.

There is much to say about that school, but thankfully much more has been forgotten. Campbelltown is a burning-hot mirage, blindingly bright in the summer midday heat, but the school itself was one long dark corridor that stank of crops left in the field at one end, and of dark brown oak panels and desks pickled in a hundred years of sweat and tears at the other. The school entrance was a bastion of sandstone topped with liver-red brick, ensuring that no light could get in and no pupils could get out. We had to pray a lot about all sorts of things but I'll bet that under their breath, most of my fellow students muttered exactly the same prayers as me: escape, escape, escape.

Unfortunately, whoever was listening to our prayers skipped past our little prison each morning and went on to attend to more pressing world problems. We were in for the long haul.

I slept in a massive dormitory with about sixty other little shits and a group of teachers. Some of them had an unhealthy interest in us boys but at seven years of age I was unable to put a name to the weirdness. Of course I now know that these men were just plain old paedophiles.

Luckily, I avoided being molested, apart from the regular smacks on my backside which I have no doubt were well deserved. It may have been about the 'skills' I was learning from Mum and Dad, as I would sometimes sneak around the dorm in the middle of the night pilfering lollies from under my schoolmates' pillows while they slept.

It wasn't all lost time – I had another string to my bow: swimming. In this regard we were lucky – the school had one redeeming feature in the shape of a massive swimming hole. I loved water and all the activities you could do in it, and so I spent every available minute diving in and out of that thick, green soup of algae and boy piss. It may have been a cold, neglected, dirty old pond of unknown depth (I certainly never saw the bottom) but when I gazed across the expanse of water to the far end, I swear I could see proof that the earth wasn't flat. For one full year, that view would be the horizon at the edge of my world.

I'm happy to say I survived Campbelltown and, eventually, without warning or fanfare, like a dazed pit pony staggering into the light, I was released.

Or at least that's what I imagine happened. While many people remember leaving school, I do not. I would go on to leave so many different schools that first and last days cannot be reliably reconnected to any particular place. Nor can the various uniforms, teachers and, in many cases, friendships.

Whatever it is that I learned at my various childhood schools, I'm sure that only a small portion of it is the stuff they tried to force into me in the classroom. You could say that due to these wanderings, I had a broad education, although my spelling is lasting proof that it wasn't very effective.

The same uneasy feeling of blurred place and time is true of many of the houses we lived in. Our centre of gravity was Sydney's east, suburbs like Maroubra, Coogee, Paddington, Redfern and Bronte. But Frankston, Elsternwick, Kensington (both the London one and the Sydney one), Coober Pedy, Barcelona and even Amsterdam were also places I would sometimes call home.

A favourite occasional bolthole was Bertie Burwick's, right across from the beach at Maroubra. Bertie was an SP bookie and Eastern Suburbs identity for whom I added up numbers, wrote down winnings and performed all sorts of chores in return for bed, board and some pocket money. It was a handy second home as what I learned there made up for the maths lessons I missed at school.

At any given time I knew who owed what to who around town and it was often my additions and subtractions that would dictate who was in trouble over which unpaid debt. I've often wondered if any of my errors, probably made because I was in a hurry to get away and into the surf on one of those perfect offshore days, ever resulted in anybody being beaten up or killed.

I somehow avoided getting drawn into gambling. I just never got the bug and Bertie, who always had my welfare at heart, certainly never tried to give it to me. I've often wondered about that.

The one reassuring constant that emerged over the period you could call my boyhood was our second home at Sandy's, my de facto aunty who lived just around the corner in Queen Street, Coogee. We must have slept there more than in any of our own homes. Queen Street was my life before, in between and after almost everything else that happened back then.

Aunty Sandy was an indulging relative and Mum's closest pal, the provider of the warmest welcomes, the best crumpets and cakes, and some of the most far-fetched tales a child could ever want to hear. Sandy and Pat were as thick as thieves. When I was a kid I knew little about the Sydney otherworld they inhabited.

Ψ

Meanwhile, back at Curtin Crescent, life was hectic. The family front room with its musty sofas and brown wall coverings hosted a lot more than just the horrible rows between my parents. The house was never empty, it seemed to me, with that inseparable little group of Mum's friends always around, and occasionally Dad's associates. The sparkling goodies that were often on display made the place feel like Harrods or Saks Fifth Avenue. When I was a kid, I thought all these visitors were just friends and family. Some of these 'family' members were a bit like our pets, entering our lives without warning, then suddenly leaving on the same carousel they arrived on.

My amazing, affectionate, but to some terrifying Lebanese 'Grandma' was one such unexplained, flying visitor. She just appeared one day shortly after Dad's arrival, and in much the same way. 'Nanna' could cook like a pro, told disgusting jokes that made grown-ups (and me) either recoil or blow up in laughter, and was not to be fucked with under any circumstances.

Mum's friends (and possibly Dad) revered and feared Nanna in equal measure, but I never felt uneasy in her presence. This being said, I do wonder if the pair of frayed, wooden-handled cook's knives that she always used, one for skilful paring and the other for fast and furious chopping, hadn't on occasion seen lethal action outside of the kitchen.

Regardless, Nanna was the woman most often entrusted with looking after my cousin Mark and me. Mark needed more attention, having a harelip and various associated difficulties but, more critically, having Unc as his dad. Unc, my mother's brother, was away a lot pursuing his business, which was heroin. His real name isn't of much interest to anyone else and in any case he had several different ones over the years; this is why I have always referred to him as just plain Unc.

My only real aunty, Unc's wife Kay, would sometimes look after us at their house in Redfern. One of their favourite hangouts was a notorious corner pub just up the road on Walker Street. One night Kay went out and didn't come back for a few days. It turned out she got into a fight, I know not what about, and was shot in the face. As a result she was terribly disfigured for the rest of her life, and cut a frightening figure as a part-time babysitter for Mark and me.

Poor Aunty Kay's face was also an untaken hint that my parents' lifestyle was relentlessly closing in on us all.

Ψ

At Curtin Crescent, while it felt like we were just a big happy family having a hoot most of the time, I soon started to twig that secret dealings were afoot. Conversations were rarely matter-of-fact local gossip or discussions about housekeeping jobs or schoolwork. We never sat about and had tea as a family of three. And I knew implicitly that I couldn't mention what was talked about at home with my schoolmates or surfing buddies.

When there was a 'mothers' meeting', there might be eight people in our front room. Men could be present but had to stay in the background, and the atmosphere was humorous and buoyant. I was rarely shooed away from these séances; in fact, I was welcome to hang around and be cooed over by Mum's friends. I may not have mentioned yet that she was quite proud of me. I had no idea these meetings were where Mum and her mates hatched new business ideas that would eventually take her, and sometimes my little sister and me, around the world.

Occasionally, my father's friends would also stop by and they too would gather in the front room. Dad's world ran parallel to Mum's but seemed much darker – during his shifts with his best mate Fletcher and their fraternity, plans were laid for more sinister activities. A 'dad's meeting' was a different kind of deal, and not for my pricky-up little ears. The room where Frank planned some of his biggest and most audacious adventures was strictly off limits when he and his mates were in session.

Looking back, I can remember countless joyous moments, jolly laughs, jokes of all colours, stupid conversations and stupid stories coming out of the mouths of my mother's glamorous, noisy, ever-present friends. I can even close my eyes and see the treats that accompanied the endless pots of tea – Battenberg cake, Victoria sponge, Ladyfingers – always decorated with laughter.

Of my father's meetings, however, my only memories are of mumbling, craggy, smoky faces, the suits, the nose-searing aftershave lotion. And the knowledge that they were in there, talking secrets all night long with the door sealed shut.

2.

A Thief's Apprentice

*There's not much you can't achieve with a
ball of string and some brown paper.*

I'm in the local corner store with Mum. Fruit, veg, hams, and cans of everything. We're shopping.

My mother has been trialling a new variant of a familiar gismo. I don't know if she invented it herself or just upgraded somebody else's idea, but basically it's a cardboard box, wrapped in brown paper. On the box is a stamp, an address and string. It's as though we're on the way to the post office. The difference is this particular box has a flap cut out and my mother's beautiful fingers can open and close this flap under the knotted string in order to insert anything the shopkeeper might not need.

Mum's face is radiating pure joy. Joy that she can induct me into a system she's been perfecting for years, and joy that one day I might carry on the family tradition and follow in her footsteps. For my mother is a virtuoso thief. We are walking the aisles selecting the best ham, pâté and smoked salmon, then secreting it all into the box. She finds this side-splittingly funny but we're still on manoeuvres, and so her face is cordial, expressionless; a regular shopper's face. 'Remember,' she always tells me, 'the hand is quicker than the eye.'

She chats to anybody who passes, sometimes at length. Nobody guesses a thing, and soon we are sauntering off past the till and out the door, which has a shrill set of bells hanging from it. Outside, during her regular debrief session, she explains the technique in more detail. Never walk fast. Smile at everyone. Make eye contact. Buy something, but not always. Stay for a chat – especially with the staff. And always wear a fresh shirt and spotlessly clean shoes.

My mother has a number of brilliant shoplifting techniques, which I know all about thanks to the many hours spent as her lookout and faithful accomplice. The cardboard box is perfect for the big stuff: hams, sides of Paramount salmon and so forth. Cardigans and other small items of clothing can also be quickly rolled up using a special wrist-flicking technique and stuffed inside.

Tights, sticky-taped around the calves, are also useful, especially for everyday goods. Mum wears one pair of tights over the other for extra strength, and the tape wound around her legs would prevent things getting out of shape or falling down to her ankles. There are times when she looks like a tin soldier barely able to bend her knees or walk.

ψ

For the first seven years of my life, it was just Mum and me. I have no memory of ever meeting my biological father and he was certainly never discussed. I don't remember any other partners who may have been in my mother's life. So it's no wonder we were so tight. While our house was always packed with people, at the centre of it all there was just the two of us. There were moments when it felt like we were simply two best friends, accomplices sharing a secret.

But when the chips were down, I knew that she was first and foremost my protector. When I was little I didn't know how dangerous the people in our orbit were, but Mum certainly did, and even though it was never discussed, I think she felt guilty bringing me into that world; a world she could neither change nor escape. But it was also a world to which she'd adapted with ease, using her extraordinary senses and keen supernatural gifts.

This situation, and my lengthy spell as an only child before my sister came along, were probably why I was horribly indulged. I was a revoltingly spoilt boy for as long as I can remember but even more so after everything went wrong. Mum often took me to lunch at upmarket restaurants, including Doyles in Watsons Bay – the best seafood restaurant in town. Doyles is on Sydney Harbour and has spectacular views across the water towards the Harbour Bridge. In those days, some of the outside tables were on the sand itself, with the water almost lapping at your feet. We'd eat a spread of Sydney rock oysters, then have a gargantuan seafood feast that could include a whole grilled whiting or flathead, topped off with an outrageous dessert and an unnecessary Tia Maria coffee and whipped cream. Mum used to say that Sydney rocks were the best oysters in the world but we both knew that at this point she'd never been anywhere else to check, and as things stood, in all likelihood neither of us ever would. We must have made for a curious sight; beautiful Mummah and little old me, living it up on the waterfront like upstanding citizens.

We'd regularly make ourselves naughty gourmet late-night snacks using the dubiously sourced top-grade produce that was often found in our little kitchen and stay up till midnight watching the *Deadly Earnest Horror Show*. Quite a lot of attention to detail, even passion, would go into these gourmet collaborations, and the pair of us would usually be terrified by these shoddily made B-movies.

Mum was horridly afraid of heights but would take me on wonderful adventures to Luna Park all the same. The pleasure she took in my laughter outweighed anything else. The most deadly and terrifying ride was the Rotor, but the Ferris Wheel was worse in that it was more rickety. When we got to the top, in our rusty little basket suspended by a kind of lavatory chain, I'd shake it furiously and she would scream in terror, which I couldn't believe was real at the time. It was, though.

I was in many ways an accidentally but absolutely horrible son, yet she always forgave me. In fact, I have no memories of her ever being genuinely angry with me, no matter what awful things I did. I guess she knew that she had my total devotion and respect and that I'd absorb whatever she said without the need for her to lace the message with acid. She could also sense that lurking beneath the layers of insolence, I had a very soft heart and always would. I hope I'm right about all of that, because even though it could have been summed up in a moment, we always seemed to run out of time to exchange the right words.

Pranking around at the seawater swimming pools down at Maroubra or Coogee was one of our favourite pastimes.

It was free and Mum loved the water. For quite a while she was a much better swimmer than me. I'm sure our play fights must have terrified the old ladies at the Coogee Ladies Baths.

One day – and I'm jumping back in time to perhaps the age of eight or nine here – we were watching TV and the Aqua Dancing came on. This weird and wonderful, ridiculously glamorous synchronised swimming show was prime-time television in those days, and the sport itself was taken very seriously, to the point of being a major Olympic event.

Mum was right there, prancing and swooshing about inside our little goggle box like a dolphin, and diving through fiery hoops with her glittery mates. She'd given me no warning about it, nor had she ever told me that she'd been an accomplished performer and TV star when I was little. Mum was many things, but this might have been when I first realised that she had abilities that other humans did not.

She could have done so much with her life if she'd wanted, but she chose her own special way. A love of freedom was at the heart of it, and the ferocious determination never to be contained by anybody or anything. In another life, she could have become any kind of superstar. I wonder if she'd already taken the wrong fork in the road before I was born, or whether my arrival had removed all other options.

Most of the time, like everyone else in those days, we had very little money. But there were other times, always fleeting, when it seemed as though we were rich. Regardless of this, my mother denied me nothing, no matter how good or bad our fortunes were. In fact, our fortunes had little to do with the gifts she lavished upon me because if we had no cash, she would just steal things or acquire them in other, usually quite ingenious, ways. And so I was usually decked out in magnificent cashmere jumpers, well-cut alpaca cardigans and quality silk shirts. Mum was always a stickler for presentation, especially when it came to her only son.

My first stereo is a good example of how she could laugh at the impossible. One day, while out shopping like normal citizens, she asked me what I thought of a rather nice record player and amp combo in the window of an electrical goods store. It was an absolute beauty, of course. Mum knew all the best brands; it didn't matter what the product was. I said I really liked it; it was an enormous pile of business-like brushed metal boxes bristling with inexplicable knobs and switches. And so, she duly went in and had a conversation with the staff. Paperwork was filled out and various forms were produced.

A few days later she took me to a house a few hundred yards away from our own home. Inside this house, there it was: the impressive pile of stereo equipment we'd seen in the shop window. The house was abandoned and Patricia and her friends had been using it to get all sorts of fabulous items delivered – without any intention of paying for them. The rundown property actually had no back rooms at all, these having been half knocked down and covered up with plants and a sort of curtain. It was in the middle of being demolished in what was probably the first, completely failed attempt at scrubbing up our suburb. Mum and her sisterhood used this old wreck to appropriate goods for quite a while. They'd even put some furniture and a rug in the hall to make people think it was inhabited.

As usual, Mum giggled her socks off at this complicated and absurd surprise – almost everything we did had fun as the main ingredient, in those days at least.

Above all else, my mother believed in me and was my biggest supporter, especially when I announced that I wanted to be a professional surfer before such a career had even been invented. In those days surfers were vagrants, wasters and the people most likely to be taking all the most noxious drugs. The idea that you could be sponsored to surf, that people would come to the beach and watch you compete against each other, or that you might represent anybody or anything people could aspire to, would have seemed like madness to any normal parent.

Yet my mother's support was outspoken and real, not just when I was a boy but all the way through to the days when I should have known better. In later years she would never miss a surf competition I was competing in if it was in Australia. And she would delight in telling her loyal gaggle of lady friends about my exploits, even asking me to recount various surfing adventures and mishaps for their amusement.

Mum once admitted that the only time she thought I was truly safe was when I was out in the water. It was only then that she didn't feel she had to worry about me. I'm glad she never made it to Hawaii, which would have changed her mind.

Ψ

My mother's uncommon good looks and sparkly openness, allied with resourcefulness and guile, made her very good indeed at many things, but especially thievery; you could say it was her calling. She was a brilliant thief, which in turn meant that she would become an extremely sought-after shoplifter to order. During the late 1960s and early 1970s, this trade had developed into an enormous, gang-controlled industry across dozens of Australian towns, and so Mum's talents soon launched her conspicuously into the orbit of the most notorious criminal organisations of the day.

At her peak she would become the queen of the business, but it would not be enough. Back then, criminals were ranked in strict levels of seniority: petty thief; burglar; specialist shoplifter; drug trafficker; safe-cracker; bank robber; gangster. Mum would never give up shoplifting (whether for the gangs, for her family or simply for fun), but in truth she was set on working her way up the underworld hierarchy towards greater things.

3.

The Red Rocket

Apparently the world changed at the end of the 1960s – it certainly did for Mum, Dad and me.

We've had a few days of screaming and shouting. Dad at Mum, Dad at me, Mum at Dad. Whenever I've glimpsed him going in and out of the living room he's been red-faced, the sweat beading and rolling down his cheeks and onto the fading monochrome people staring out from his forearms.

But today none of this matters because he's come home with a gift. And it's nothing like his usual apology offerings. Giving me this gift is one of two things Frank did that changed the course of my life.

Up until this moment, the most dedicated grommet in Sydney's Eastern Suburbs has had to refine his art on an eclectic quiver of old, frayed, sun-browned and borrowed boards. I've been borrowing other people's boards because my own canvas-topped, wobbly, rubber Narm Super Six is more like a toy. It's an embarrassment that I try to hide from the real surfers when I'm stranded on the beach waiting for a ride home. It has no fins and it bobs like a cork. It won't duck dive, won't turn, and it definitely hasn't made me a better wave rider. In fact, up till now, I don't think I've really understood what surfing is about at all.

But on this momentous day, as I enter the Curtin Crescent front room, sand still grating between my toes from a fairly ordinary session in the tiny ripples at Coogee's little Point, Dad is glowing red-hot in a good way, trying to stopper his excitement.

'I got you this.'

In front of me is a gleaming, seven-foot six-inch red spear-shaped plank. Even to this day, it's still the finest thing I've ever owned and the only inert object I've ever truly loved. Apart from my two kids, it's also the thing I've been most proud to be seen with. It's a Shane double-ender pintail. And I can't quite believe it's mine.

Shane Stedman is the top board shaper in New South Wales. The man who makes surfboards that win world titles. And I now own one shaped by his fabulous, celebrated hands.

There are times when I'm not entirely sure what my relationship with Dad is. But today I'm sure that I love him. I love him for being a hero, for giving me this gift, for knowing it would be perfect, and for taking hours out of his day to drive the old wagon across the Harbour Bridge, across the Spit, and all the way down Sydney Road to Manly. At this stage in my life Manly is another country – but the surf shop at North Steyne Beach is the only place that sells these boards. So that's where Frank went.

And so I put aside my doubts about Frank. He's the only dad I've got, and this brand-new board is The One. I guess his occasional spasms of kindness and generosity sometimes do work.

Ψ

The surfboard that Frank blindsided ten-year-old me with that afternoon had an immediate and far-reaching effect. For one, it meant no more sneaking about with borrowed boards or, worse, that garish plastic plaything (good riddance). Trivial, maybe, but from that moment on I was no longer just a kid playing in the sea – I could now strut and sit in the sand with a proper tool of the trade by my side. With the arrival of the Red Rocket, I turned a corner. I became a surfer.

Over the next few years, that board was like an extra limb. Armed with the glossy new device, my confidence out in the water grew apace. So much from those days has faded from memory, but my first surf on that beautiful thing is still crystal clear in my mind. That stick could do two things that I'd previously considered incompatible; it could paddle fast *and* it could turn. This allowed me to ride waves from the top to the bottom due to the speed of attack made possible by the board's perfectly straight rails and particular deck profile. I could turn, pivot, speed up, slow down and be where I wanted to be. This made a big difference. Everything I'd ever ridden till that point could either do one or the other: turn a bit, or proceed out of control at ramming speed straight down the line.

Over time, I started catching lots more waves and finding myself in better positions, with more speed, and the ability to do more moves. Speed fed confidence, which in turn fed more skill. By the age of twelve or thirteen I was getting pretty handy at this surfing gig. It seemed to offer a niche into which I could wedge myself.

Most importantly, with my new tool, I was able to reach the place every surfer seeks – the elusive, short-lived, partly mythical wormhole at the centre of the surfing psyche: the barrel (also known as the keg, tube, shack . . . and so on). This miraculous, turbulent, unstable phenomenon is only possible on certain waves – the most powerful type. It's the place of maximum steepness and danger, and it must be navigated at top speed to avoid being swallowed up and driven at an awkward angle into the seabed. Entering the tube takes commitment, and exiting it (which is never guaranteed) takes perfect positioning and not a little bit of luck. The prize is a few ecstatic seconds in another universe, followed by a glorious ejection – often accompanied by a cannon-like cracking sound as the wave shuts down on itself behind you.

Being inside the tube is the best feeling in surfing. Many surfers never get near it, and I was obsessed by it.

I practised my stupid hobby non-stop and it quickly became an obsession. I'd be out there for hours on end. Often an entire day from dawn till dusk would pass by with just a pie break in the middle. The pie is, after all, the unsung engine of Australian industry and creativity, and the X factor that has traditionally helped us punch above our weight in the world. It's why my country, with only twelve million people in those days, was able to deliver three cultural heavyweights – Paul Hogan, Dame Edna and Rolf Harris – all in the same decade.

Those magma-hot, salty-brown, sludge-filled pastry fat-bombs were often my only nutrition over the course of an entire weekend, if there were waves, that is. The pies were disgusting, but they enabled me to avoid squandering valuable ocean time on the pointless act of nourishing myself.

Soon enough, other surfers started noticing. Some even asked me how I was doing what I did. Of course, I didn't have a clue and I still don't. It would have been easier to explain how I breathed. So I was rarely asked twice. A thickset frame acquired at an early age helped me bulldoze my way out of froth and trouble anyway, and perhaps that was the real magic ingredient.

The Red Rocket had another important effect on my life. In my early childhood, surfing was mainly for drop-outs, drug takers and unemployed losers. The equipment and clothing generally matched the personality type (scraggy, daggy and brown). It wasn't something parents encouraged, and it didn't gain you entry into any school cliques. Proper competitions were still a way off in the future. This all meant that there just weren't that many other wave riders at my school. Greg Day in the year above, his younger brother Terry, and Mick Power, both in my year, were the only other surfers anywhere near my age at Coogee Primary. With the Red Rocket I could maybe become their equal, or even their friend. I wouldn't be alone in the sea anymore.

Greg and Terry would soon start surfing seriously, and getting a lot of attention from it, but for me at that point it was just about having fun. The sea was my release from Dad's dark world. Riding waves was exhilarating, and I realise now that it was also deeply cleansing; whatever shit was going down at home, being out the back on my beautiful new board always washed it away.

No matter the conditions, when I went through that foamy portal and felt the cold, slap-in-the-face moment of that first duck dive on the way out beyond the mush, I became untouchable. Did I surf more on days when others wouldn't brave the onshore winds and woolly conditions *because* of the atmosphere at Curtin Crescent? Did my weird family set-up make me a better surfer than I would otherwise have been?

All I know is that I always came out of the ocean feeling way better than when I went in.

So, Dad – Frank – Baldy – thank you for that too.

ψ

In time, with a little help from the Red Rocket and the irresistible pull of the ocean, Terry, Mick and I found each other. I can't remember when or where it started, but it was probably at the promenade at the back of Coogee Beach after a session riding the little waves there one summer.

That promenade, which was in reality a broken pier from the 1800s that had been partly turned into a lifeboat store, was many things to us. Most memorably, it was the location of my first experience with a girl. One sultry summer's afternoon, beautiful Tracy gave me lessons in kissing. Tracy's mouth and her mum's laundry powder delivered sweet tastes and fragrances I had never experienced before and that I would never forget – although at the time I didn't see the purpose in skulking about in the dark grappling with girls.

The promenade was also the boys' headquarters when there wasn't any rideable surf, which was most of the time. We would even sleep out under it in order to get into the surf before dawn. When the sea refused to deliver, we'd spend our days annoying passers-by from our little hideout by throwing whatever glass or metal would make enough noise to startle them. Or we'd feed seagulls with anything we could find, and lounge about in the sea pools.

On unsurfably big days we'd amuse ourselves by crouching down on the concrete behind the line of huge rocks at the end of Gilesy's Baths and letting the waves wash over us, creating a sort of waterfall that we could pretend was a proper barrel ride. Our first barrels.

Terry, Mick and I extracted an awful lot of juice out of that place over the years. By the time I grew up a bit and hit double digits, we had become the best of friends and partners in crime (often almost literally – flat-spell boredom is a dangerous thing). We had a plan for all types of weather. Most afternoons would kick off with a stroll from school to Terry's house, which he shared with his two brothers at the top of Arden Street. We'd retrieve our boards and carry them on our heads down to the Point at North Coogee. Mick's board probably weighed more than he did but bloody hell could he ride it.

We'd hop across the concrete and boulders that border the sea pools, jump off the ledge and paddle out through the rocks. The left-hander was usually pathetically small, but it peeled perfectly if it was in the mood. Most of the time it was a lazy ripple but every so often it would awaken and re-form off a break wall halfway across the bay, doubling in size. This crooked and difficult wave then threaded itself between various rocks, which was probably why nobody else was ever dumb enough to take it on. This meant we had this little pig's ear of a spot to ourselves, and once we'd made it a silk purse, it became our own private world for the latter part of our childhood.

If conditions weren't quite right for the Point, or the tide was too low, we could sometimes get peaky, unruly little waves over at the main beach, or dare ourselves to venture out to the distant reefs off the Ladies Baths at the southern end of the bay. Looking out at those open ocean waves breaking halfway to the horizon would terrify me and I often chickened out of throwing myself into the sea and paddling out towards them.

On huge days, the Tooth, as us kids reverentially referred to it at the time, much further out to sea round the headland, would be breaking. Only the big boys would ride this terrifying wave, usually wearing motorbike helmets. To tackle the Tooth you had to take off next to a big spike of rock, and then hope to get around it rather than get smashed up on it by the face of the breaking wave. We worshipped this older gang of five or six very skilled, fearless surfers, and dreaded the day it'd be our turn to take on this mutant wave. At least I did.

Dickie Williams, Greg Zoulos, John Day (Terry and Greg's eldest brother – there were a lot of Days in that house!), Norm Moore and Steve Hickmont were our local heroes back then. They were what you'd call 'hell men'. We would never have done what those guys did and they had no reason to do it other than pure fun. Professional wave riding just wasn't a thing in the early 1970s. There wasn't even an official world championship.

Some of those men had psychedelic artwork painted onto their helmets and we guessed they must have added the art while high on the LSD which washed around our neighbourhood. I wonder now whether they needed the acid to actually want to ride that terrifying and death-defying wave. But they were good blokes who cared about our community.

One day, the wave inside the Point mutated during a massive swell and the boys and I quickly found ourselves in over our heads. There were torrents of water going in all the wrong directions. I thought we would drown. Dickie and Greg spotted us, jumped in the water and dragged us back to safety.

They probably saved our lives, these counterculture surf bums who parents taught their kids to avoid.

If the waves were too big to surf, we'd go up to the cave on the headland and watch the mystical Bommie in all its majesty. The offshore bombora reef here kicked up unimaginably huge waves when the southerly storm swells were at their peak. They were the biggest I'd ever seen.

When I look back, I realise that whatever mood the sea was in, she'd always give us salt-encrusted kids *something*. Someone should have sat us down and told us we were living in paradise. Eventually, the time would come for us all to graduate from the comfort of Sydney's Eastern Suburbs and its collection of messy beach breaks, and look for something more.

Ψ

I took those first steps when I was not even twelve years old, falling in with Doug and his South Coast crew. I'd developed a nod and grunt relationship with these fully grown men out in the sea at North Maroubra, where I was now an accepted local grom (an annoying but tolerated junior surfer). Eventually we graduated to actual conversation, and all they could talk about was a mythical wave way out to sea down in the far south, that broke in big winter Southern Ocean swells and worked perfectly when everywhere else was a filthy and chaotic onshore mess. Very few surfers ever took on this solitary, cold water open ocean creature but somehow I was invited to go down there with them and take a look. Impulsively, I said yes.

A few days later, the boys picked the Red Rocket and me up from outside the Oshey in their aged brown Volvo wagon and took me on what seemed like a ride to the very end of the continent. We spent hours in that car driving down south until we got deep into a national park. Finally we jumped out, untied our boards from the roof racks and hiked through the forest for an age. We eventually came out on the white sandy shores of a lagoon dotted with islands. Doug and his mates jumped into the water and started paddling so I followed timidly. We went out across the lagoon and seemingly towards nowhere. It felt like we were paddling forever and it was frankly quite spooky – everyone knows that river mouths and lagoons are the favourite feeding places for bull sharks and that when bull sharks are confused they sometimes eat human legs.

We soon made it out of the river mouth, and a tiny island came into view way out to sea. Peeling around one side of it was a dark, towering wall of water that seemed to stretch across the horizon. It was the longest, most perfect wave I had ever seen, and I suddenly knew that from this day on, the world had more to offer than Coogee Point.

The wave petered out into a deep channel outside a boulder-lined lagoon that the men called the shark pit. Of course they did. These were the days before leg ropes, so if you fell off, it usually meant that your board would drift away in the current and end up in that dark ominous pool, where you would have to take a long, lonely swim to retrieve it. I was terrified of being left alone with the sharks and so I dreaded falling off anywhere near there.

That year, I hung out with Doug's crew as much as I could. Sometimes they picked me up in the Volvo, other times I'd take the train to the end of the line at Nowra. My surfing went to the next level as a result of the kind acceptance of these grown-ups.

I can't recall the first wave I rode down at the island, but I have faint visions of streaking at high speed through the spray and across infinite walls of water. I know for sure that it was on this lost piece of Australian shoreline that I discovered what surfing could be.

Ψ

Dad delivered one other big surprise that year. It wasn't life-changing, but it was pretty awesome all the same, and it created a rare, joyful but intense moment of family togetherness that I can still reach back through time and feel. Kellie, my baby sister, came along. I probably should remember being told she was on the way. I probably should remember my mother's pregnancy. But I don't. My first memory of Kell is her arriving home with Mum from hospital, just like that. About as expected as a brand-new red surfboard.

4.
Billy and the Pom

*People say Maroubra had a violent edge in the 1990s.
They should have been there when I was a kid.*

The Oceanic Hotel, Coogee. If ten-year-old me needs to get attention, answers or taxi money from Dad or one of his mates, then this is where I must come. It's the key staging post on my way home from school.

Inside, the Oshey has seen better days. It's all sticky floors and sticky doors. There's a sticky bar, sticky tables and cloudy, sticky schooner glasses. You have fair warning on the way in because you can smell the soured, congealed cask beer that the whole place has been marinating in since 1927, from out on the street. Calling a dank and sweaty pub a 'hotel' is a uniquely Australian thing. I guess it comes from our sense of defeatism and irony, also known as our 'dry Australian humour'.

Dad has a lot of pals, comrades and friends, and I can't always tell which dog belongs to which pack. The members of his court come to meet him here, often arriving in foreign cars and wearing suave Italian-style suits.

Dad meets up with Billy and a gentleman they call 'Jimmy the Pom' most days from around noon. Sometimes you'll find them propping up the enormous bar that skirts the back wall and looks out over the road to the sea, but they usually congregate at the top of the front steps, on the expansive brushed concrete terrace. This is Dad's perch but I can share it with him sometimes. He always lights up with genuine delight as I hop into view; I think he likes showing me off to these smoky gentlemen.

Mum insists that I always look perfect before leaving the house. She is obsessed with my clothes, my grooming and my overall appearance, sparing nothing to supply me with the finest in European fashion. Shoes are the key to it all: improperly cleaned footwear signals the impending end of civilisation, while a flawless shine means we are all going to be okay. I'm often humiliated by such eccentricities but I love her for it with all my heart.

Arriving in this manner at the Oshey, wearing either my school uniform or a silk shirt and a cashmere cardigan, tends to amuse Dad's crew, most of whom are usually camped on those concrete steps, surveying the Coogee seafront, all cigarettes, beer and menace.

They've given me a nickname; Fauntleroy (thank you, Mummah).

I ask Dad for five bucks. Today, as always, I'm only really interested in what's happening out in the surf. Surfing is my second great love, with Mum being the first.

Our little Point at Coogee is usually too small to surf. This is a shame because it's right by my school. If I run across the grass and paddle out, I can eke out an extra half hour in the sea before it gets dark. When the Coogee Public School bell rings on those rare but glorious big swell days at the Point, the only obstacles between me and the surf are the paedophiles in the public loos at Giles Baths, which sit halfway between the schoolyard and the jump-off spot into the line-up.

But today, there just isn't enough juice here and I need to escape the Oceanic Hotel, fast. I have to get my skates on and make it home to Maroubra, a full five kilometres away, before it gets too dark to be out in the sea. Northeast winds and a smaller swell will make for perfect conditions down there off the more exposed expanse of beach. The place is a magnet to most groundswell marching past, depending on where it's coming from, and so that's the spot for me. It might even be hollow enough for a cover-up or two. The dazzling whitewash surrounding Wedding Cake Island, just visible over the bus sheds across the street from our vantage point on the Oshey's front steps, suggests the waves will probably be three feet plus.

In English, a three-foot wave means five-foot wave faces – easily enough to get barrelled. And these glass-roofed cylinders of moving liquid are (in case I didn't mention it) my obsession.

But I have to get there first and there's only one way to do it. The bus will be too slow. I need that taxi. And I know that Dad'll fund it if he's in a good patch, which is about fifty per cent of the time.

I ask again.

'Dad, do you have five bucks on you?'

Dad's mate Billy turns around and cuts in on Dad's behalf. The afternoon sun shines at an angle and when it hits his face it lights his eyebrows up as if they're on fire. Orange on orange.

'I'll give you a fiver, Fauntleroy. For a yarn, that is.'

Luckily, I've anticipated this – it's pretty much a daily request – and I've come prepared with a theatrical story just long enough to earn my money, yet short enough to minimise the loss of surf time. I might not have learned much at school, but I do know about the sea, and I can make most adults laugh doing voices and funny movements.

A crowd favourite is my 'Ultimate Toob Ride', a made-up tale performed in a sort of singalong ballet which I duly perform, right in the middle of the smudged-schooner and fag-ash-littered terrace. 'Ultimate Toooob Riide!' is the shout, in a cowboy singsong accent, legs spread far apart and hips gyrating as if being buffeted by the wave, with a leading hand pointing at each audience member one at a time as the words, the rest of which I can no longer remember, are yelled.

It works. Billy smiles and claps his chubby, fur-clad hands. A note is produced with a pull and a push. I grab it and run down the steps, over the road to the taxi stand. I stuff my board in through the back window in the tried and tested manner, then jump into the back seat next to it. We're off, up over the hill towards Maroubra.

I'm thinking about Billy's red face and rusty wire-for-hair as we descend Maroubra Road. The ocean comes back into view and I can see corrugations of the waves all the way to the horizon – a fresh, clean swell is arriving. Peaks are already visible far out to sea, lit up burnt orange in the late afternoon sun. Something tightens in my stomach. A light offshore breeze is grooming the lines, organising them perfectly for me and the handful of wasters, thieves and thugs I'll be jockeying with in just a few moments.

That sight, and the familiar, involuntary tensing up of the midriff that always accompanies it, mean that I'm out of the back door of the taxi before old matey even comes to a stop, my board under my arm, scrambling through the scrub and down the rocky cliff like a goat on speed. With a carefully timed jump off the slimy green slab, I'm into the rip and being transported seaward in the channel between the rocks and the sandbank. Thank Neptune there's still a couple of hours of light left.

No matter the conditions at home at Curtin Crescent, out here I'm in a place of absolute calm. Some people meditate on the loo, others in bed or in the bath. For me it's in the ocean. That short paddle out from the beach to the line-up is like a voyage to a world where fear hasn't yet been discovered.

I know I have a lucky life. Dad is generous; I have very smart clothes and enough 'stuff'. Depending on the state of our variable family fortunes, I take taxis most of the time – not the bus. And of course I now own a really good surfboard.

More importantly, I can indulge my passion every day after school if the conditions are right. If the waves are too big everywhere else, I can surf the little ones off the Point in Coogee. Most days, though, I can surf here in my home patch of Maroubra. When the southerlies come through it's perfect down at the south end by the shark hatchery. The banks there can fire up with super-fast, hollow tubes. But when the regular afternoon north-easterly winds blow, the north end is the place to be, which is why I'm here today. Out here, beyond the white, where I don't need to think, life is rich.

Although. Sitting on my board waiting for a wave, looking down at my feet and beyond to the turquoise-tinted sand on the seabed, I can't shut out the thoughts.

Out of all Dad's crew, Billy Maloney, the affable Irish sheep, is the most interested in me. Billy's a follower who laughs at any joke. His hair seems too small for his head, sitting on top of rather than surrounding it, as if it's a feature that was somehow added afterwards. Billy laughs and goes along with whatever Dad says, and usually gives me money with a smile. It's just his smiles never quite fit his face.

Dad's other mate, Jimmy the Pom, is more aloof. The story goes he was a somebody in Melbourne. He came to Australia from Ireland via London and still has a lyrical accent. He never has much to say, though, tending just to grunt and mumble from under the front curtains of his sweeping mullet. You could say Jimmy the Pom's a watcher.

Fletcher, a boxer who came up from Melbourne at the same time as Dad, is usually right there at my father's side too, twitching, gnawing at the knuckles of his hairy fists, always shifting about from one foot to the other. They match each other in height but Dad is the better-fed bulldog. At times they seem leashed together.

Steve Nittes, aka 'the Bomber', is quite well known around town, with a big rap as a bare-knuckle prize fighter. He's new to the scene at the Oshey. The others reckon he's knocked out half of Melbourne's fighting fraternity at one time or another, and that he once blew up a nightclub. The Bomber is a jittery, spindly, mousey bloke with a small face, so I don't really understand how he did it. He shifts about, skulks and hides, keeping his distance from any debate. His talks with Dad always involve hunched backs and the flicking of cigarette ash onto the ground. They tend not to laugh.

Pals, friends, mates and comrades. There are so many of them in the entourage and in 1970, who can know which face is thinking what?

ψ

A dark line forms out to sea towards the horizon and I know that a set is coming. It jolts me away again, to the other side of the portal. From the shade on the water I can see that it'll be a solid one. There'll be a right-hander (a wave that peels from left to right when riding it) peeling into the channel, but I'm sitting close to the perfect spot for the faster left-hander that's going to form off the same peak.

I let the first one go through; two of my fellow surfers today are tempted by it and they split the wave, which suits me just fine. The second one is going to be bigger anyway, and looks like it'll be a better shape . . . It's going to be mine. I turn and paddle for the peak, and then sit back again on my board to spin it around and lunge forward.

I'm quickly at the apex of the wave, the top of which is about to throw itself up and outwards over me, and with three more strokes I'm popping up to my feet while dropping down the face and knifing my rail and single fin into the water for traction. Pumping off the bottom, I'm back in the middle of the face and gunning it fast to the left, my right foot pressing forward for top speed. I won't get tubed today but on my way across the moving wall of water I'm able to carve a few turns and I can feel the acceleration each time I come off the lip and drop down again, sometimes through the air.

When that Billabong boardshorts company said 'Only a Surfer Knows the Feeling', they didn't understand the enormity of what they were saying, or what anybody with a life like mine would be hearing.

After an hour and a half I've had about thirteen or fourteen waves and am still raring to go, but it's getting dark. I'm almost the last one out, which isn't good, given what a perfect bite-size snack I would make if a bronze whaler happened to be patrolling underneath me.

So I catch a small one in, belly the last bit of foam onto the sand and return to the world.

5.

The Great Idea

How to rob an armoured van.

My arms feel like overcooked spaghetti. A rich supply of swell, sunshine and well-directed winds have seen me and my pals spending four to six hours in the surf every day for a week. Somehow, I've managed to attend school as well, and despite the fatigue I am frothing about how good life can be.

The boys have been hanging around at ours because we've had the best of the waves over here in Maroubra, and now the full house is about to burst at the seams. Dad has been away for a couple of days with his friends and now he's suddenly back. And it's something more than the usual pandemonium – it's the return of Caesar. Frank has pulled up in a brand-new car, a misshapen glossy bright turd-coloured Valiant V8 hardtop. We know it's a V8 because he revs it three times in the driveway before turning the engine off, shouting 'V8! V8!' and waving at us to come and see it.

My dad is so excited that flames might soon come out of him. I've never seen him quite like this before.

Pretty soon, a few of his pals pull into the drive too, screaming, hooting and shouting. Dad and friends are dressed up in suits and ties, Mum and the aunties in puffy dresses, and everyone wears glossy leather shoes. We are all going out for Chinese food. The boys and I are stuffed into the car by Mum, with Dad at the wheel. What a machine, but it ain't exactly roomy.

The convoy lands at the Mandarin in Redfern. Us kids are sent downstairs where we can order whatever we want. The adult group quickly swells, and there must be at least twenty of them up above us, screaming, shouting, terrorising the staff. Prawns, pippies, roast duck, gloopy soups of every description, king crab three ways – the lot. My friends and I are hypnotised by the lazy Susan spinning condiments, cutlery and plates of food around and around until they fly off. For some reason none of the staff say anything about our despicable behaviour or the mess we're making – they just keep bringing more food so that we can make it worse.

When we leave, Dad's got to demonstrate the new machine and so we are all packed into it again. The boys and I are terrified as he speeds down Anzac Parade at 100 (miles not kilometres) per hour. Sweating, accelerating, braking, swerving and screaming at every poor soul we pass. He is intent on carrying on the celebration because something special happened today, and he is without doubt completely and utterly pissed.

Ψ

Here's what I didn't know while being carted about at high speed in my father's new pride and joy.

I realise that up until those fateful few weeks, I didn't know much about my dad's work, his various associates, the Painters and Dockers union, or any of the things he and his hangers-on were up to. Why would I, a straggly grommet of eleven?

Over the years, I've pieced it together with snippets from Mum and Aunty Sandy, and some help from other relatives who can never be mentioned by name. Elderly associates of my father who still haunt Sydney and Melbourne today, many after being released from Long Bay or Pentridge prisons having served their time, reluctantly filled in some of the remaining gaps. There were many. There still are and always will be; outlaws don't keep diaries.

As a Melbourne Painter and Docker, 'Baldy', as my father was known (all hard men must have an alias), and his comrades had their fingers in every nook and cranny of the criminal hive that was stevedoring on the docks. The Painters and Dockers were the hatchery for the vast majority of Australia's top criminals of the era. The union supplied more than just labour. It was estimated that in the late 1960s and 1970s, more than seventy-five per cent of gang murders, armed robberies and drug trafficking was carried out by its members.

This was the golden age of violent crime in Australia – if you were a criminal, that is. The Painters and Dockers imported most of Australia's heroin, hashish, marijuana and general contraband. Those were relatively genteel crimes in many ways, but the protection of this lucrative trade was at the heart of all the death and destruction.

I was always told that Dad was an honourable man and one of the few gang members to refuse to traffic heroin or cocaine:

his gang were instead specialists in Afghan hash, which they imported by the ton.

Baldy got a name for himself because of his exploits with a car stuffed with Buddha stick. He and his comrades had a thriving business taking old jalopies apart and rebuilding them, packing every cavity, whether tyres, roof, doors or floor, with vacuum-sealed top-grade drugs. Unfortunately, one evening one of these 'narco-cars' was stopped at the Melbourne docks and impounded. This wasn't the end for Dad's crew, who instead of walking away and forsaking their shipment, simply broke into the compound, overwhelmed the Customs guards and dragged the car off on a flatbed truck.

Dad's crew were good at learning from their mistakes, and they eventually cooked up a smoother, safer and generally more brilliant system: the contraband, usually bales of hash, was vacuum-packed in Afghan government-stamped one-kilogram bags and bundled into large boxes. These boxes were then loaded into the sub-compartments of shipping containers that would be identified and intercepted by Dad and his mates once they arrived on the Melbourne waterfront. In order to help the reception team quickly and easily identify which boxes to skim, the outsides were always plastered with pornographic magazine covers, usually featuring *Playboy* bunnies.

Baldy & Co. had a specific job: to retrieve the hashish from the ships and distribute it. This they achieved with astonishing success by simply tossing the boxes into rubbish trucks operated by their comrades, which were quickly driven to warehouses around town.

The system worked for a few years until a pious truck driver took exception to the boxes' lurid wrapping. He mistook the payload for actual pornography and refused to work for my father again, saying it was a sin to bring such filth into Australia. This caused the entire system to fall apart, mainly because friendly truck drivers prepared to risk prison were in short supply.

Dad was lucky not to be found out, but in all likelihood it was this hiccup, and his reluctance about the emerging heroin business, that brought him up to Sydney – and into my life. It would have all been just fine had my mother not bumped into him one night at Chequers, the gangsters' nightclub of choice, located in the heart of Sydney.

After the departure of his disposal driver on the docks, Dad quit the import–export business and became an armed robber and thief. He came up from Melbourne with a number of his Painters and Dockers comrades, all of whom were looking for richer pickings and less 'heat'.

Ψ

Baldy & Co. carried out a wide range of crimes in Sydney and across Australia throughout the 1960s and '70s. Banks, shops – anywhere you could point a gun at someone – were a target. Importantly, they had become specialists in armed hold-ups of trucks carrying cigarettes, jewellery and luxury goods.

The front steps of the Oshey was where they discussed their ongoing operations. It was where they met new recruits, unless the strictest secrecy was required. The most sensitive and lucrative jobs were discussed in our front room on that dank, stinky old sofa. It was here in my childhood home that my father and his friends plotted the biggest armed robbery in Australia's history.

Always driven to adapt and innovate, Baldy realised that sticking up trucks and shops, and even most banks, yielded a limited bottom-line profit once the goods were fenced off and everybody, including the union, got their share. It would be a much more rewarding use of his time if he were to rob an armoured van full of actual money. And he had a 'genius' friend (in Mum's words, much, much later) who had a great idea about how to get away with it. The plan involved two tactics:

1. Wait until the guards exit the van to dispose of their rubbish at the end of their lunch break.
2. Wear mirrored sunglasses and hats.

That was Dad's crew's great idea. Or so he thought. The principal architect was a well-known criminal logistician called 'the Professor' or 'Wooka' (his dull real name, Les Woon, must have been why he needed two pseudonyms). Dad's job was to lead a team of three robbers and execute the plan. This job was to be a first – in 1970 nobody had ever successfully robbed an armoured van.

Success, of course, has various definitions.

Wooka, Dad and his Melbourne crew had identified a particular Mayne Nickless & Co. truck that did the rounds of Sydney's western suburbs collecting cash from racecourses, betting shops and banks. The number and location of stops marked it out as an especially fruitful target, and Wooka had an inside source who had given him a lot of good 'hits'. The crew confirmed this by following the van for weeks, using a series of different cars to avoid detection.

Wooka had successfully pulled off a smaller yet similar job down in Melbourne. At least that's what he told my dad. He left out the part where that stick-up had gone terribly wrong for the poor fellas who had actually done the robbing. They had been caught within a day of the heist and ended up in prison for a very long time.

The most important piece of intel was that the three Mayne Nickless guards stopped at the same carpark near the Commonwealth Bank in Guildford each day to eat their lunch. They did this without fail. Their meticulous tidiness turned out to be their downfall – the foolish guards always opened the door of their van to dispose of their rubbish. I've thought about this a lot – they must have been idiots! Perhaps they thought that their guns would deter anybody from holding them up. The fact it was a sweltering day may have also sealed their fate; it would have been bloody hot in that metal truck with no air conditioning, and they would have been forced to open the doors from time to time just to cool down.

On the day in question, Dad and his two new Melbourne comrades, Steve the Bomber and Al (Alan Jones) from the Oshey, followed the armoured van to the bank then watched it stop at the usual luncheon spot in the adjacent carpark. As always, after a half hour or so the van door opened and one of the guards got out to dump the rubbish. At this point, Dad, the Bomber and Al, who had been crouched behind the van, pointed their silenced pistols at him and ordered all three guards to let them into the van or else they'd blow their fucking heads off. Luckily the guards didn't have time to loosen their own pistols from their holsters.

Dad then used his standard phrase, 'Don't let's turn robbery into murder.'

It worked. The guards were compliant and the van doors were shut, with everyone now inside. The guards placidly allowed themselves to be tied up and their mouths taped without too much complaint. The money, still in its original canvas bags, each marked 'RESERVE BANK', was then transferred to Baldy's getaway car. The only violence that occurred was when one of the guards had his glasses broken.

The proceeds of the robbery totalled $587,890 in cash, which at the time eclipsed all other heists in Australia many times over. In today's money it'd be close to $10 million. There were a few more banks the van had yet to visit later in the day, which could have increased the takings even more.

The police had no idea who the thieves were despite them being seen by several witnesses, including the three Mayne Nickless guards. The poor blokes were interviewed time and time again but couldn't identify the culprits. Why? The mirrored sunglasses and hats, of course!

Dad split the money with his fellow gang members. He, Al and the Bomber took away about $100,000 each. Wooka got the lion's share (about half the total) on behalf of the Painters and Dockers, despite not even being present. Much of that share went to the union's boss, who went by the magnificent nickname of 'the Texan'. Dad was also told that a chunk of money had to be paid to a 'steer', a Mayne Nickless employee who had provided inside information.

Baldy's share was a life-changing haul back in 1970. After acquiring it, his first act was to go and buy that stupid car.

His second was to take us all out for a huge Chinese banquet – schoolboys, aunties, uncles, robbers and all.

I didn't see a lot of him after that, and if I did, he was always surrounded by his entourage at the Oshey. I never saw Al or the Bomber on those concrete steps again.

I was only eleven or so years old and my brain has been heavily weathered during the last half century, but one thing that does help me focus my memory of this time is the pile of musty old canvas bags that were given to me by my grave-faced dad, and that only I was small enough to stuff into their hiding place.

6.

In the Caves

On a kind of 'holiday' with Mum and Dad.

We're outside our little terrace house in Curtin Crescent, wondering how all three of us can squeeze into the bloody Valiant, which is already overstuffed with bags, suitcases and a labrador. That hardtop was useless for the purpose but it had already become Dad's pride and joy. He had been so eager to show it to us in a pristine state on that special day that he'd stopped the car, left the engine running, got out and beaten a man up. Just for scratching past it while my father drove it out of the car yard.

We'll be away for quite a while it seems. In fact, we may never come back, or so I'm told. Dad has grand plans to buy a motel in Queensland – the Pink Poodle – which sits right on the highway at Surfers Paradise. He also says he wants to buy an opal mine.

Fuck knows what's going on!

In order to underline the point, the poor labrador, one of many animals unfortunate enough to be a temporary pet of ours, is dropped off at the home of a man named Jack Sparrow, much to the delight of Jack's son, Adam. The Sparrows are Dad's only respectable (non-criminal) friends. They have a name in the horse racing world, where betting is one of the only legal pursuits that offers similar returns to crime. The dog will probably survive.

With the jettisoning of our pet, any slim possibility that this all might be one big joke has now evaporated. This is *really* happening. We are *really* leaving. Worse still, there's no sign of Kellie. My baby sister was left at Aunty Sandy's a few weeks ago 'for a while'. Maybe Mum and Dad need time to get to know her before she's allowed to come on adventures. Maybe she won't fit in the Valiant. Maybe she won't fit into their plans.

I have to think of something to distract myself and push down the rising fear . . . What are the waves like at Surfers Paradise? I've heard of Burleigh, and Kirra next door, because they're the two most famous waves in Australia. These perfect, long, hollow, sand-point breaks are often featured in surfing magazines and are known all around the world. But they're right-handers and I'm not a fan of 'back-side' surfing. If, like me, you naturally ride with your right foot forward on the board (what's known as a 'goofy foot'), you have to have your arse to the wave when surfing to your right, which is not too pretty.

Anyway . . .

We are getting out of town, running away, and Mum and Dad tell me I don't need to worry about school after the Easter holidays. In fact, I don't need to worry about school for quite a while. Curiously, this is the bit that makes me most uneasy. I don't love lessons but I do like the routine of meeting up with the boys before class and running off to annoy passers-by at the promenade in the afternoon, or seeing the crew out in the water. It's a comforting ritual in a world that is far from normal.

Over the past year or so, our small group of surfing misfits has become a bona fide crew, squeezed tighter together by the shared experience of being infected by a passion that everyone else sneers at. I do everything with these two wasters, and sometimes three if the middle Day brother shows up. We nearly lost Mick at one point when his father returned to Ireland, but Mick managed to fight it and thankfully was allowed to stay put in our little beach Nirvana. I wasn't going to be able to do the same, it seemed. The other two musketeers can keep messing about in this wonderful world but not me. Our trio of pals – Terry the death-defying charger, Mick the smallest and funniest, and little loudmouth me in the middle – was to be disbanded when it had barely been put together.

If I have a home it is here. Not just in our house at Curtin Crescent, or at Aunty Sandy's in Coogee, but the whole five-kilometre strip of Pacific Ocean that connects the two. These streets, these beaches, the Point, the sea baths, the surf club, our hidden world under the rusty promenade. Even the bloody Oceanic Hotel. It's taken a forced eviction for me to realise it.

Some of my childhood feelings from those days, the days when I was uprooted before I knew about roots, are sharp prints on my memory. In truth, though, a lot of it's a blur. But one thing I know for sure is that up until the end of the summer of '69 I was just another Eastern Suburbs surfer kid. Afterwards, I was not.

Ψ

So we piled into the old Valiant V8 and set off. A caravan, attached to the towbar and also stuffed to the gills, with what seemed like everything except the Red Rocket, made me feel even more apprehensive. We looked like a snail moving to a new habitat. The last thing Dad loaded into the vehicle was a pile of green canvas bags.

'First,' he announced, 'we have some chores to do.'

Lexington Place in Maroubra was our first stop, just up the road. We pulled up outside a betting shop, but not to place any bets. I went in with Dad, and he chatted to the manager who seemed to be a friend. Then I was told to hop onto a table covered in boxes and remove some perforated polystyrene ceiling tiles. The green canvas bags were carefully handed to me one by one and I threw them up into the darkness of the ceiling cavity before putting the tiles back in place like a dutiful little helper.

I never thought twice about anything Dad ever asked me to do. He would have a reason for whatever it was and that was all I needed to know. Despite its constant presence, I'd never directly felt the force of his anger but I probably feared it all the more for that.

I don't know if the manager of the betting shop knew that most of Dad's share of the proceeds from a robbery was in those canvas bags (I certainly didn't) but he must have suspected. The heist had been on the front pages of every newspaper in the country and all over the TV, and such was the hurry of our departure that the loot was still in the original wrappers, all screen-printed with 'RESERVE BANK' in large, if faded, black capital letters.

Ψ

Once this 'chore' was completed, to my relief we then drove round to Aunty Sandy's place in Queen Street, Coogee. We were here to collect Kellie. Thank god. I'd started to think I'd lost her for good. Nothing was ever said about her absence, as far as I remember, and I certainly never dared ask. I believe now that she had been deemed a liability because, I was slowly beginning to realise, we were on the run, requiring fast escapes and fleet feet. Dad knew I was already a good runner-away, but my one-year-old sister was baggage, and a risk to us all. I guess being tucked away around the corner in the relative safety of Aunty Sandy's was better for her too.

Reunited as a family of four, we headed west on our first and last family road trip.

Ψ

The opal-mining town of Coober Pedy is way out in the South Australian desert, about 800 kilometres from anywhere. Temperatures get so hot in summer that most people have to live underground to survive. With the benefit of hindsight, I suspect Dad must have thought it would be a great place to lay low for a while until everything cooled down back home. He was also obsessed with his opal-mining plans. I wonder if he'd started having thoughts about laundering his winnings and going straight.

We had countless hours of mundane chit-chat during our never-ending time on the burning road but I was never told exactly why we were leaving Sydney in such a hurry, or about the danger we were in. I don't think that at that point Mum or Dad were fully aware of quite how much shit we were in either.

All I knew for sure was that this was quickly becoming one of the most unsettling times of my whole, short life.

It took almost three days of continuous driving in a straight line with nothing to look at except red or yellow dirt to get to Coober Pedy. The name means 'hole' in the local Aboriginal language. And Coober Pedy *is* a hole, literally. Not only because of mining, but because most of the residents really do live in holes in the ground. After discovering that our caravan was an oven rather than a dwelling, we were forced to follow the locals' lead and booked ourselves into a 'dugout' – a big cave drilled out of an even bigger boulder.

On arrival in town, we were greeted by groups of young men fighting on the streets. Apparently, it was all about drink and, as if to confirm it, most people seemed to be staggering about plastered all day long. The only exception to this rule was when they were lying unconscious in pools of piss on the footpaths. I guess relentless forty-degree heat will do that to you.

I knew I was in trouble when Mum marched me up to the local school one day and enrolled me. Surely we wouldn't be here long enough to worry about school? The thought made me quiver. I ended up spending about a month in that place. Every other student came from one or other of the local Aboriginal communities, most of whom camped in large groups on the outskirts of town. I was a prime-time curiosity, with my shock of long blond hair signalling my arrival everywhere I went. I soon got used to being hooted at in the classroom, on the way home, in the street, basically everywhere. It eventually dawned on me that they thought I was a girl, and a pretty one at that.

This awkward situation was made worse by the fact that getting to and from school was a very slow process for me.

In order to fit in I'd stopped wearing shoes in my first few days because I was the only pupil who owned a pair. Unfortunately, the footpaths around town were spiky, hot grit that baked in the sun. This made getting about very painful indeed for a city kid whose mother always insisted on excellent sartorial standards and who therefore had feet like a baby, them having always been luxuriously enclosed in cotton socks and smart clean shoes.

After a hot day at school the only respite was the neighbours' water tank. At first, I mistook it for a swimming pool and spent hour after hour splashing around because it was the closest I could get to the feeling of being in the ocean. A sorry situation for the world's most surf-obsessed grommet, perhaps, but Mum used to whoop and cheer me on when I did my 'laps'. This made me laugh till my ribs hurt since the tank wasn't much bigger than your average bathtub. My laughter in turn always set her off, and we matched each other blow for blow, upping the ante until one of us couldn't breathe and had to surrender.

I hope I never peed in that tank; in any case its owners, no doubt under Mum's spell, didn't seem too worried about contamination.

That laughter was Mum's first superpower. She could deploy it to combat any threat, or to fix any situation. It could cure anything, including my desperation at being landlocked in the desert. That she was able to use it to shield me from what was really going on over the course of that month reminds me of her extraordinarily powerful spirit, the extent of which I had little idea at the time.

Ψ

The town's lights at night are something I will never forget. There were only two sources: the local pub, and the Milky Way. I have never been as overwhelmed by nature as I was by the dazzling night sky out there in the South Australian desert. I was pretty sure that I could see to the very edge of the cosmos, which I presume meant I ought to have been able to figure out what was on the other side of it.

Of course, I never solved that pointless thought experiment, but since we didn't have a TV in our cave it was helpful to have something to occupy my mind during our dry and dusty exile. The raw, pristine beauty of the place draws a certain kind of person. The type who can see what he wants to see in its red soil and boundless, bluer than blue skies. That person wasn't me. When I looked, I just saw dust and heat shimmer.

Inexplicably, abruptly, but thankfully, this brief diversion in my life was soon over, and we were loading up the Valiant once again, preparing to leave. I didn't know why, but we were suddenly gone, heading back across the desert towards the coast.

We never did become opal magnates, although Mum spoke of it ruefully for years afterwards, usually just to tease me about how close to riches we'd been. She loved to tantalise me with her thoughts on what we might have done with all the money from the rare jewels we would have unearthed, had Dad only gone through with those plans.

At the end of our desert dream, we only had one thing to show that we'd ever been there – an enormous multicoloured opal that my father had somehow acquired. This stone was unimaginably beautiful, with too many facets to count and a near-infinity of colours that sparkled differently every time you looked. It was quite something. In the absence of Joliette the poodle or the unnamed labrador, this rock briefly became my beloved pet.

Ψ

My mother was an unusually superstitious person, a disease that I inherited. Ladders, of course, were always a big problem for her, and I had to say 'bread and butter' whenever we got near one. Scissors had to be correctly crossed at all times, and knives had to be arranged in a specific, geometrically perfect way – no arguments. Certain gemstones also, it turns out, were a red flag for Mum, who could not touch them or even look at them. It was an odd way to be for a jewel thief.

These superstitions, along with various 'feelings' she had, would turn out to be her second superpower and the one that would keep my sister and me alive. But it was not always used in my favour.

On the afternoon we left Coober Pedy, driving back along that highway of mirages, my mother plucked my glorious opal out of my hand (I was always clasping it tightly or playing with it and I still believe that it was bigger than my fist) and threw it out the car window. Within moments it was half a mile behind us. Despite Dad's and my passionate protests, Mum proclaimed that opals were 'bad luck', and that it had to go. 'And that's that.' The discussion was over and my beautiful treasure was never recovered. I was bereft.

I saw the universe in that stone, with its galaxies of reflections and colours changing with every different angle of view. Dad, I guess, saw a business opportunity and a way out of the criminal life. Maybe he even saw a way to offer his family a safer existence. Mum only saw danger.

This was the only time I can remember siding with my father, who was livid. Occasionally, Mum would shock us and put her foot down – it all depended on the cause. On that stinking hot day in the South Australian desert, her will triumphed over his, and the Valiant continued on down the highway. Underneath all the ink, sweat and snarls, he must have had some sort of respect for her, after all.

Ψ

We drove through the desert and then up and down the Pacific Highway for weeks. Every time a big truck dragging its monstrous carriages roared past in the other direction, we had to get off the road to avoid being crushed. The billowing dust and grit swirling behind those road trains took a full minute to settle before we could move. Broken Hill, Dubbo, Swansea, Coffs Harbour, Grafton, on and on it went, with us stopping at various motels on the never-ending curves of that bumpy old road.

Eventually we made it to Surfers Paradise, which seemed more like an idea than a real town, with half-finished buildings outnumbering the completed ones. I didn't get to go surfing because every time we arrived anywhere Dad was ready to leave. We barely had enough time to take a tour of that ridiculous but famous motel, the Pink Poodle – which we did as a family, without telling the bemused receptionist about my father's grand plans for the place. The delightfully effeminate neon sign outside, depicting a huge strutting poodle, is my main memory.

When I woke up the next morning Dad was gone. He'd been spirited back to Sydney by his mate Fletcher, who had materialised out of nowhere some time during the night. Mum mumbled something vague about things 'having to be sorted out' and that we were to join him later.

This wasn't necessarily cause for alarm, and we were soon back in the Valiant and on the road again, heading north, destination the insect-infested South Molle Island in the Whitsundays. I was grateful to have Mum to myself again – more or less, since Kellie didn't really count, spluttering away in the little plastic bucket thing that was her permanent mobile home.

The hilly island was hot, sandy and infested with microscopic flies that could get through any screen or netting. It was also dangerously boring. There wasn't even any surf. We languished in a caravan park, Mum busying herself with Kellie, who was under constant attack from the flies that seemed to love her, and me turning boredom into miscreant behaviour. I would steal things from the neighbouring caravans, such as milk bottles, and line them up in neat little groups on our kitchenette shelves. Then, when I was satisfied I'd got away with it, I'd realise the uselessness of my new possessions and give them all back.

It is curious how angry this made my mother, who harangued me with lectures of the type I had never heard from her before and never would afterwards. I was puzzled about what behaviour was acceptable, and what was not. I often wonder how much crime is caused by necessity, and how much by simple boredom. It was a mercy for Mum and me – and the holiday-makers and inhabitants of North Queensland – that our month on the island soon came to an end and we packed up and headed home.

There was no particular foreboding about going back to Sydney; all I could think about was surfing. I was desperate to duck my head underwater on the paddle out across the foaming no-man's-land that separated the world I loved from the diesel, dust and dirt life I had.

I can't remember the last moment I spent with my father, but our fleeting stop inspecting the Pink Poodle in Surfers Paradise may have been it. That red-brick motel with its unmissable white colonnade sitting so pretty and hard to miss right on the side of the highway would take me by surprise for many years to come, brutally interrupting my new life with old truths right up until the place was finally torn down to stop it bringing down the neighbourhood.

Years later, somebody found that neon sign and resurrected it outside a much bigger hotel a few kilometres up the road. They even featured it on a postage stamp. Almost a lifetime later, it just will not go away.

7.

Bent Coppers

Spare a thought for your poor hard-working policeman.

Visitors to Australia today often complain that the place has become a bit of a police state. There's a cop on every second corner and every small misdemeanour is punished courteously, swiftly and expensively. I tend to agree – compared to almost anywhere else in the world, there's a police presence pretty much everywhere you go. Those who aren't comfortable with this would understand the need for it had they been in Melbourne or Sydney in the 1960s and '70s.

Back then, our two biggest cities were utter bedlam. It was a fiesta of crime, with most of the crooks being armed and very ready to shoot. An awful lot of people did get shot, and not always for much of a reason. When I speak to Dad's few surviving friends, those who have served their time and have nothing to lose are quite willing to reveal who they killed, and to explain the often spurious (in my opinion) reasons why they did it. One of Dad's close mates once shot a man dead for speaking to the wrong girl. He was more than happy to talk me through his rationale years later.

For cops and crooks alike, life was cheaper than it is today. Crime was out of control and the pendulum had to swing a long way in the opposite direction; otherwise we would have descended into anarchy.

I accept that my family and their associates were part of this unbridled era, participating in violent crime with abandon and openly profiting from it. They had guns. They stole in many different ways, and whole families were involved, including wives and sisters. I don't think any of them cared how they obtained whatever loot or jewel it was that they were after, and so shops of every kind – banks, jewellery stores, anywhere you store valuables – were all legitimate targets. And it wasn't entirely their fault that the police were as corrupt as fuck, almost all the way to the top.

Back then, the police went after crooks with a fairly primitive toolkit. Proving that a suspect was in a particular place at the time of a crime wasn't as easy as looking at CCTV footage or scraping up some bodily residue and sending it to the laboratory. They didn't have mobile phones, text messaging or social media to give them any background, and criminal networks were infinitely dynamic and complicated. It must have been incredibly frustrating trying to track down the baddies and gather enough evidence to convict them. That same lack of technology also made it easier for any policeman to use 'unorthodox' methods to get ahead without anybody noticing.

And so, if I really think about it, I can almost understand why a detective sergeant of the New South Wales Police might set up his own criminal gang to pursue and murder crooks, to claim their ill-gotten gains as their own – and solve crimes.

8.

The Toe Cutters

With friends like Dad's, who needs enemies?

Aunty Sandy's, Queen Street, Coogee, on a glittering April morning. I thought we'd never escape Queensland, or that hot little Valiant. The trip home seemed to take a full week of bumping and swerving down the terrifying Pacific 'highway'. I'm glad to be back at last, reunited with the Red Rocket and my backyard full of waves.

For a little surfer kid of eleven, this is the golden time of year to be around the beaches of the Eastern Suburbs. The sea is usually still hanging on to summer warmth and everything is glitter.

I've been staying here with my oddball little sister Kellie for a week or so, since Mum turned up at Mick's parents, where us kids had gathered after school the other day, and told me not to go near our house under any circumstance. She was deadpan as usual but I think my little friends were freaked – even mad-dog Terry.

I've been getting to know what Kellie's various squeaks and gurgles mean, and we're building a sort of common language together – the start of a relationship. We haven't seen or heard from Dad since the Pink Poodle, which under normal circumstances would not be too unusual. When I see Mum, I keep asking her what's going on anyway, but she's not giving anything away.

Nor have we seen Dad's mate Fletcher, which is also odd; they're usually inseparable and it's often Fletcher's presence that alerts me that Dad is back from one of his 'excursions'. I don't like Fletcher for reasons I can't put into words, but at least he'd have some answers.

Early one morning, Mum bursts into the room without knocking and starts shaking me out of my sleepy state. She says I won't be going to school today and that we have to leave town *again*; in fact, we're heading to the airport *right now*. Apparently, Dad's in big trouble. He's been missing for three days, last seen chatting to some men in a van at the bus sheds across from the Oceanic Hotel.

My beautiful mother, who looks exhausted for the first time in my memory, is telling me in a roundabout way that my father is probably dead.

Even if a small corner of my mind has known for weeks that something isn't right, I still struggle to process what Mum's saying. But I don't doubt her for a moment. I get up, grab my things, stuff them into plastic bags and follow her into the living room.

Ψ

I've pieced together a vague picture of what happened in that grim week in 1970, although the journalists, the police and my family have offered up a diverse range of versions over the years. It is difficult to know who to pick out as the least trustworthy of these three sources.

However, everybody would probably agree that Dad was unbelievably unlucky. Baldy had found himself caught in the midst of five of the most terrible men in Australia.

The first of these men was Detective Sergeant F Kaiser. Kaiser was one of the most corrupt coppers in the country. He'd allegedly murdered a local madame, ordered a spate of other killings, and been involved in countless disappearances. He'd been a policeman since leaving school and had long-standing relationships in the underworld, most based on allowing bank robbers to conduct their trade in return for a commission on their takings.

He was also a clever, tenacious investigator with many successful prosecutions to his name, which gave criminals more than one reason to fear him. Dad's friends often talked about one of Kaiser's sidelines – a certain boutique and bric-a-brac shop in sleepy Randwick where random items from various burglaries would often show up.

Lenny 'Mr Big' McPherson, Sydney's top gangster, known for extreme violence and downright nastiness, was the second. He was a brutal standover man with several murders and rapes to his name and connections to both the mafia and the CIA. McPherson had burnished his reputation by decapitating a rabbit in front of his mum at her seventieth birthday party and tossing the head at her feet, having become sad because Mrs McP hadn't invited him to the festivities.

Then there was Kevin Gore, the safe-cracker. Gore was a member of my parents' wider underworld fraternity. He eventually married into their entourage, coming close to being my uncle. Like many of the men of that world, he was a regular on the Oceanic terrace, and I must have brushed past him more than once.

Next was Linus Patrick 'Jimmy the Pom' Driscoll, Dad's taciturn, regular drinking mate from the Oshey. He was a very bad man indeed, even worse than my parents thought, and was quietly doing appalling things for Sydney's organised crime gangs.

Last but not least was Billy Maloney. The sheep-like, carrot-topped nice guy Billy from the Oshey, who would listen to my tales and give me money for the taxi ride home. It turns out there was a bit more to old Bill than my parents or I could ever have known.

At the relatively young age of thirty-four, my father was unaware that from the moment he agreed to carry out the biggest armed robbery in Australia's history, he never stood a chance.

Ψ

When Dad and his mates had first turned up in Sydney after their Melbourne dockland schemes went wrong, the city didn't know what had hit it. The police were dazed by the crime wave at first, but they soon adapted to a point where they became accomplices. Detective Sergeant Kaiser found himself right in the middle of all this.

Dad's armoured van job attracted a lot of unwanted attention, in part because of the record-breaking amount of money. But the fact that it was also a world first – nobody anywhere had ever successfully stuck up an armed van before – must have led to some red faces at press briefings.

Also, I believe that the sheer simplicity of the plan – just sunglasses, hats and guns – had captured people's imagination. Dad and crew had apparently also donned matching butchers' overalls and so must have presented quite a comical sight. The utter silliness of the get-ups must have made it seem all the more brazen.

This all resulted in outrageous headlines blazing in bawdy capital letters across the front pages of the newspapers and in sensational reports on the television. Not just in Sydney, but right around the world. One of them read 'World's most expensive lunch break', and phrases such as 'World record breaking bandits' etc. were bandied about.

I can imagine how embarrassed the Sydney police would have felt, especially when their American counterparts started calling up to take the piss. They would have been quite bitter too. It was at this point that things started to go wrong for Baldy, Mum and me.

Detective Sergeant Kaiser was not formally assigned to the case. Dad's friends think he felt left out, and so decided to take a personal interest in it, partly for all the above reasons. This was facilitated by the fact that the authorities, who were also quite flustered, had diverted every detective in the state away from what they were doing in order to help solve the case as fast as possible. It had become crime number one in the country.

I reckon Kaiser's main motivation was the amount of money involved, none of it yet recovered, and a good chunk of it hidden away somewhere by a stupid surfer kid. The temptation must have been too great. Whatever his reasons, he called a few of his criminal contacts and asked them to track down the robbers, extract the proceeds any way they could, and share a portion of it with him. In this way the crime would get neatly solved and the perpetrators brought to some kind of justice at the same time. Kaiser was an old-timer, and he and his contemporaries had all faced some sort of corruption probe at one point or another, many of them well documented in the press. And so this would have been a reasonable plan of attack for many of the policemen of the day.

Rumours had long swirled about Kaiser's close relationship with Lenny McPherson, who had become a police informant: sort of a double agent. The pair, so said Mum, enjoyed a long-standing collaboration, and it's likely McPherson was the one who confirmed Dad's involvement in the heist, and even helped his pursuers to locate him.

The next villain Kaiser called up was Kevin Gore. Gore was known for his rare skills with his oxy acetylene torch, with which he was able to get through anything that found itself between him and whatever loot he was after. But few knew that he had turned the corner into Psychotic Street, discovering horrifically cruel new uses for his tools. I guess it would have made him a perfect hunting dog for a rotten policeman: a raggedy-eared cur rather than a pit bull. My parents' friends say that Gore eventually wanted to take over as the 'Mr Big' from McPherson and, after a failed plan to cut the big cheese's head off, realised it would be much easier to oust him by collaborating with Kaiser.

The third helper was Billy Maloney. Billy, of course, knew exactly where to find Dad most of the time, being one of his most trusted friends after Fletcher. And it turns out that Billy had a lengthy track record of violent crime, including allegedly stabbing his own mother. He'd walked a well-trodden criminal path, starting with petty theft and shoplifting, and meandering onwards and upwards to more and more bloody work. He had only ever held down one legitimate job in his life; he'd been a butcher when he first left school. Presumably he was introduced to the detective by Gore.

Both Gore and Billy would have known about the armoured van robbery: I occasionally imagine the pair discussing it with Dad in a haze of booze and fags on the Oshey steps while laughing at me dancing about and telling stories for cash.

At some point, 'Jimmy the Pom' Driscoll was also enlisted. Dad knew Jimmy from Melbourne via their mutual friends, the three Kane brothers, who were among the most awful, violent murderers in Australia. They'd all worked at the cutting edge of Painters and Dockers crime. Perhaps Dad trusted Jimmy because of their previous collaborations; perhaps because they were both out-of-towners in glitzy Sydney.

Jimmy had been a hitman for the IRA. According to the police, he'd also been a gun for hire on the Israeli side in the Six-Day War. When he got to Australia, he'd been taken on by the Painters and Dockers to pull rival gangs into line. He then moved to Sydney, where he quickly became the most sought-after contract killer in town, covering his tracks by working in the local pubs and pretending to be a normal citizen. He was literally pulling pints in a Bondi pub and then murdering people for money in the course of the same evening.

Jimmy's tough-guy reputation must have been the reason Kevin and Billy wanted him to help out. He'd already killed quite a few people, and I still get a queasy feeling when I see photos of him in the papers, peering out from under that floppy mullet with the same vacant look he used to land on me at the Oceanic.

And so Kevin Gore, Billy Maloney and Linus Patrick 'Jimmy the Pom' Driscoll were now Australia's newest gang, brought together largely through the efforts of a detective sergeant of the New South Wales police. Their union – and the conversations they had with Kaiser – lit the fuse for Australia's most deadly gang war.

Ψ

Depending on who you ask, one of the other two armed robbers, either Al (Alan Jones) or Steve 'the Bomber' Nittes, gave up my dad.

Al went to ground straight after the heist and succeeded in hiding from everybody for a while. But he then made a fairly dotty error; he went back to the Oshey for a beer. Upon arrival, he was kidnapped almost immediately by Billy Maloney and his friends. They threatened him with boltcutters and Kevin Gore's blowtorch but he escaped. A lot of people think he negotiated his escape by telling them where Dad was – and also mentioning the fact that Dad had bags of money stashed away.

The Bomber disappeared too, probably back to Melbourne with his cut, but the gang also caught up with him and demanded money and further information about Dad, using the same graphic threats.

Some think the Bomber gave Dad up, some think it was Al, but I guess it doesn't matter – who could blame either of them given the nastiness of the kidnappers?

Rumours circulated that the Bomber had held talks with Jimmy, Kevin and Billy at some point, with a view to joining them, and had even tried to recruit others to this new type of work but was scared off by a bank robber friend of Dad's.

One afternoon a couple of days later, Dad must have felt the heat was off because he too was back at the Oshey. I must have been on that fly-ridden Queensland island with Mum and Kell at the time. I don't know what Dad was thinking, going back to his old haunt at a time like this, but he was probably meeting other gangsters to discuss next steps for the loot.

Three men pulled up in a van on the other side of the street by the bus sheds. They probably waved at Dad up there on the terrace, in the customary manner. When Dad was invited to inspect some stolen goods in the back of the van, it would have seemed like a normal afternoon activity. But he was then coaxed – probably pulled – inside, and driven off to any of a number of warehouses around Botany and Kingsford. I can only imagine the moment he realised something was terribly wrong. These were people who he knew perfectly well as individuals, but not all together as the group they had just become.

They asked my father where the money was and to give up his share. Word has it that Baldy wouldn't tell them anything. To get him to talk, Kevin Gore blowtorched his testicles and other parts of him with his trusty oxy acetylene torch. He then lopped off his toes one by one with the boltcutters, while Billy held him down.

Frank 'Baldy' Blair, the womanising bully, died of his wounds, and the Toe Cutters, Australia's most murderous gang, were born: named after the manner in which they had tortured and killed the only father I'd ever known.

The elders told me that Dad's body was dissolved in a barrel of acid and his remains buried at Sydney's Kingsford Smith Airport. Apparently he now resides under the tarmac of the extension of the north–south runway that was being built at the time. Other people say he was dumped in the Harbour to be eaten by the sharks, but they weren't hungry and he was later retrieved from Botany Bay. We were never asked to identify his body so I have never believed this version of events.

Dad's toes were supposedly sent out to gangsters across Australia, including the Bomber in Melbourne, where he was lying low. Apparently this was the last straw that led to him giving up most of his share of the proceeds in return for his life. The Bomber eventually got sixteen years for the robbery. When released, he returned to his life of crime and achieved a degree of notoriety as the most prolific drug importer (by weight and value) of the 1980s. At some point, he left Australia and lived in the UK. He died old and peacefully in 2022.

I never saw him again after those few vague, half-aware moments on the front steps of the Oshey, and I certainly never knew him, but I wonder if he ever reflected on the fact that many of his friends would have been better off, or at least still alive, if he had stuck to boxing.

Alan Jones seems to have gone quietly into custody, basically telling the police everything in return for protection rather than face the torture gang again. He'd apparently already spent all his remaining loot anyway. Al was not a popular man after this sorry episode, even though he paid his dues in part by going to jail on a sixteen-year sentence for the robbery. Within a few months of his imprisonment in Parramatta Gaol, another inmate stabbed him, in all probability in an act of vengeance for giving up my dad.

The Professor, Les 'Wooka' Woon, ran off to England, partly in fear of the police, who hunted him across Europe for years. His greater fear would have been that of facing the same fate as Baldy. Wooka, after all, was said to have received half of the total proceeds of the heist; enough to purchase half a street of nice houses in the centre of town or at the beach in those days. The police were desperate to get him of course, and as a result he enjoyed a spell as Australia's most wanted crook.

He eventually returned to Australia as a very old man, and, according to Dad's old mates, planned and conducted elaborate robberies mainly for his own amusement. His reputation as the top-ranking master criminal logistician survives today with the nickname 'the Professor', although his two big operations were disasters, where the price paid by the perpetrators far outweighed anything that was pocketed.

Ψ

Baldy's sudden death was the starting gun on a terrible period of gangland murders right across the country. Ten or more people were shot dead as a result of his murder. It is fair to say that the wider underworld fraternity was enraged by what Jimmy Driscoll, Kevin Gore and Billy Maloney had done, and the repercussions rumbled on for almost a decade.

These 'friends and comrades' of my dad's were the most feared, most notorious gang in Australian history. 'Toe Cutter' became a dictionary term in itself, used to describe crooks who rob and murder fellow crooks for loot, as well as the name of a particularly nasty character in Mel Gibson's *Mad Max* films.

I wonder if any of them ever reflected on what they did to Baldy and his family, but I suspect their only feelings were fear of reprisals. In any case, Dad's murder and the fact that he hadn't given up that pile of musty old bags that I'd stuffed in the ceiling meant it was time for us to go on the run yet again.

9.

Running from Planes, Climbing Down Drains

*Boring Frankston – a perfect hiding place
for a small family on the run.*

We leave Aunty Sandy's Queen Street house in a hurry, barely packing. Our baggage does not include Kellie, who is to be left behind, again.

We're in a cab, plastic bags rustling about between us, racing to Kingsford Smith Airport. I don't think we'll be stopping off at Curtin Crescent to grab undies, pets or any other essentials – Mum doesn't want us to go near the place.

The pair of us are now on an Ansett twin-engine jet, waiting on the tarmac, about to take off for Melbourne. I'm starting to recognise a pattern and realise that the jettisoning of Kellie is a sure sign that we are in real trouble.

'We're going to see your Uncle Alfie and Aunty Joan,' Mum says.

I never knew that I had an Uncle Alfie and an Aunty Joan.

My mother has all her sensors switched on and is continually looking around her, scanning the seats in the rest of the plane. She's making me scared. I've never seen her truly stressed before, even during the bad times back at the Crescent. She just isn't the nervous type. She suddenly freezes, rigid, white-faced. The plane starts to move and I have my seatbelt on, but Mum takes hers off and stands up, so I do the same. She glances nervously around. Again, I do the same. A few rows behind us, I see the red face and rusty wire-for-hair of Dad's mate, Billy Maloney. I don't know if he's seen me. He's frowning through his fiery orange brows and chatting away to another man.

A lifetime later, I'll look back and conclude that my mum is amazing. She is full of love, can turn any grey day into a riot of laughter, she's always dazzling, and she can even tell the future. But now I can see that she is the strongest person I've ever known.

She marches right up to the cockpit and is surrounded by cabin crew. Hands are waved and faces folded around busy mouths that I cannot hear. Then the plane grinds to a halt. We're sitting in the middle of no-man's-land out on the tarmac and everybody is looking at me (and I'm looking back at everybody). Mum's in deep conversation with the cabin crew up front. Finally the cockpit door opens and the captain ushers my mother and one or two of the crew inside.

At some point there is a grinding shudder and a clunk, the aeroplane door opens and six policemen file in. They speak to Mum, who points at me, and the next thing I know we're marching down the steps accompanied by the police and crossing the tarmac back into the airport sheds.

Ψ

We reached those sheds and another group of policemen soon arrived, after which I spent quite a long time, possibly hours, sitting on a bench. Mum was in a room being questioned. I didn't know what was going on; I'd never been on a plane before, or even in an airport, so everything was a bewildering mess in my head. I didn't know at the time that you usually don't get off an aeroplane once you've boarded it.

I don't remember much of Mum's explanation, but the police organised a taxi for us back into town. Melbourne was off the cards for now. In the taxi, I was full of questions. I trusted my mother to protect me always; she was more than just a human and could defeat anybody. I'd seen her do it many times, to Dad and others. But when she froze on that plane, I was terrified. Whatever her fears had been, I had felt them too. Real, sickening, gut-clenching fear. But fear of what? I just didn't understand.

So I only mouthed one of those questions.

'Why are we going, Mum?'

'There are some people I'd rather we avoid at the moment,' she replied. And that was that. My mother's sixth sense had never been wrong, and so when she said we had best not be in a particular place, it was time to go. She saw my little upturned face with its unblinking big eyes, and added, 'We'll be okay.'

And that was fine by me – Mum had said so.

We ended up at the Esron, a crappy motel that once graced the crest of Coogee Bay Road, barely a kilometre from where we had started off this bewildering, circular day. The Esron was a place of squeaky doors, barely disinfected funk and long, dank corridors. It felt like we were its only guests.

By the time we got into our room we were exhausted. As soon as she sat down, Mum burst into tears. Torrents, sobs, bodily shaking, right in front of me. I'd never seen her cry before. I would have been less shocked if Batman himself were having a blubber, and it sent the blood draining from my face. The running, the hiding, the desert, the news about Dad, and the endless driving around the country, the being escorted off a plane – these were big events. But my mother's meltdown was the shattering of childish certainty and the dividing line between two different stages of my life. My mother was mortal, human, and as vulnerable as anyone else.

She babbled about Dad, how he'd been kidnapped, and how he was gone. She bawled about how we might have been followed onto the plane, and she blathered wildly about everything else that had happened over the last three weeks. I couldn't make sense of it all, such were the explosions of half sentences and bits of words, but I reckon this was the moment I really knew for sure that it hadn't been a dream, that my dad was dead.

The Esron had those pull-down bunk beds with dangerous springs of the kind you might find on a night train, which we had wrenched out and were preparing to get into. Out in the corridor, we heard doors opening with a squeal, and gruff male voices that seemed to hum as much as speak. Then the squeak of trolley wheels approaching; presumably housekeeping. I looked at Mum. Something was amiss; it was after midnight, too late at night for housekeepers. That squeaking sound was enough. Something twitched in her mind and ran across her face. She stood up, grabbed our bags and told me to jump out of the window, right away, and to hang on to the drainpipes.

It was blood-drainingly terrifying. But I trusted in that second sight of hers, so I did as I was told without any hesitation or doubt. It probably wasn't very far down to the ground but it seemed to take forever to climb down those pipes. I'll never forget threading my arms around them and hugging the rusty, flaky, painted metal, feeling it stick to me. I didn't know what was happening in that corridor outside our room, but my fear was visceral and Mum's voice confirmed that I was right to feel it.

We were quickly down on the concrete driveway, from where we both easily climbed over the dented corrugated-tin fence and into the property next door; an old block of flats which looked abandoned except for a tangle of overgrown bushes and some creeping lantana.

A couple of loud bangs and a *crrrunch* audible through the open window just behind the fence suggested that the trolley had been driven right into our bedroom door. There were voices, scraping, squeaking and thumping, then silence. Mum and I were as stiff as two dead things.

We remained that way, hidden in that wasteland almost all night, Mum squeezing my hand tightly, perhaps to keep me quiet, perhaps through terror. It seemed to me that every little night creature had come to life in those bushes; cicadas screeching, rabbits scratching away, even the plants trying to say something by rubbing their leaves together in the breeze. Any human noise or car anywhere made us think we were under renewed attack. I don't believe that Mum and I exchanged a single word all night.

At dawn, we made a dash for the road when Mum saw a vacant taxi. Dragging me by the collar, she stuffed me like a sack of clothes into the back seat. We drove straight to the bus station at Central and hung around till the next bus was due, which must have been around noon.

Once again, we were on the move and after an interminable bus trip, we finally made it to Melbourne. We arrived to the warmest of welcomes: Aunty Joan and Uncle Alfie greeted us like long-lost children at the terminus and instantly drove us back to their red-brick Federation cottage in the suburb of Frankston, one of those ignored districts where the inhabitants can't decide between the bush, the city or the sea. This had of course been the original plan before Billy Maloney made his guest appearance on our flight.

To this day I believe my mum saved our lives twice in the space of those twenty-four hours. I'll never know how, but she'd sensed vibrations moving through the ether, through brick walls and doors. She deciphered the invisible signals and reacted instantly to get us out of that motel. And she'd stopped a plane just as it was about to take off, willing the police to remove us while leaving everybody else on board.

Ψ

Uncle Alfie was a smiley-eyed, little brown nugget of a man who had two kids and a fluffy white cockatoo with a fluorescent yellow crest and a huge menacing beak called Louis that mostly hung about on his shoulder. Alfie would often kiss Louis on the beak, saying he loved the little fella. But sometimes the bird would bite him on the neck, lips or ear, which would send him into a terrible rage. I thought it was pant-piss hilarious.

Uncle Alfie also had a rusted, ancient shotgun, which he hid rather half-heartedly. He would do regular house and backyard walk-throughs with this old relic. He seemed to relish his new sentry-sergeant role, and I wonder if he'd been in some war or other and was missing all the shooting and camaraderie.

Alfie immediately went to work building a ridiculously high fence around the entire house and yard so that we could be well hidden and safe, and he installed a system of little bells and strings to warn us of any intruders. He even enrolled me at the local school under a false surname. Alfie and Joan took our safety seriously.

Those bells rang often, sending Mum and Alfie into high alert and leading to some of the funniest moments I can remember in my life, as well as some of the scariest. Every time we heard a *ting!*, I imagined Dad's friends stalking through the garden, heavily armed. The usual culprit, however, was a fat possum caller Poitier for whom, for reasons I can't fathom, I left out scraps of apple every night, and who then scared everybody senseless when he kept coming back for more and setting everything off.

We were primed and ready to run, at all times. I'd learned my running-away skills evading the council workers who'd corner a half-dressed little me in the Giles Baths public toilets in Coogee, but Frankston was where I refined them.

On the way to school, alone with my bag of stuff and my thoughts, I imagined Billy Maloney from the Oshey everywhere. I didn't have much else to occupy my mind other than waves that were well out of reach. There were times when I hid, crossed roads, ducked into driveways or just scarpered for no reason at all. Billy's red face was becoming an omnipresent scourge and I started to see it all around town. I believe that Mum did too.

Our new family indulged us to distraction and would stop at nothing to make us feel like this was our own home. It was the first time in my life I'd lived as part of a normal family who would sit and watch TV together, eat meals together, have tea together and enjoy regular conversations, and to me, it was almost the real thing – almost. We played canasta and gin rummy and watched absolute rubbish on the TV. *Hawaii Five-0* nights were the best. I'd look forward all week to the thumping drums and cymbals that signalled it was finally on, often waiting in my room with the door open till I could hear the theme song banging and trumpeting up the stairwell.

Columbo on the other hand was the most depressing thing I'd ever seen. I hated that show. But whenever that crumpled old man was on, Louis the cockatoo would step in to keep my spirits up – I think the show was his favourite. In fairness he had us laughing more than a parrot should, and rarely for the right reasons. He would assault any visitor, peck holes in the furniture, rootle through people's sandwiches and shit on anything, anywhere, anytime he felt like it – especially food. He was relentlessly offensive, and his misdemeanours were always accompanied by the ugliest selection of shrieks and squawks. I bloody loved that bird!

We certainly ate well down in Frankston. Mum worked her way through the extensive Lebanese repertoire she'd learned from Nanna and in this way we were at least able to contribute something to our upkeep. Mum's falafels were not a patch on Nanna's but they were still epic. I'd help by chopping up all the various ingredients for the tabouleh, overdoing the parsley to the point where the others accused me of getting it out of the back of the lawn mower. Never skimp on the parsley!

I had to take charge and cook dinner myself once a week; I relied on potato bake with a ton of Bega cheese, bolognese, pilaf rice and my favourite, chicken cacciatore. There was no end to the weird ingredients I would add into this last dish to try to surprise everybody. Sometimes it must have verged on inedible, but the process of trial and error resulted in a pretty good signature recipe in the end. I still use it today. In Frankston, close to the bay but far from the sea, messing about in that kitchen was just about the only time when I felt at peace.

I imagine that this is how most families live. I ought to have felt right at home and been a whole lot more appreciative, but for me it was cold, this glimpse of what a normal family should be, followed by the bleak realisation that we didn't have one; not before Dad's disappearance, and certainly not now. Even 'Nanna', our great leader, and the lady who first taught me to cook, was adopted. I still have no idea where she really fitted in, and eventually I ran out of time to ask.

Likewise Uncle Alfie and Aunty Joan.

Despite the kindness of our temporary family, who were probably just pals of Dad and Fletcher, down here in Frankston I felt truly displaced. I was lonely, imprisoned and lost. There were no friends to play with, no familiar routine. The worst thing was that before this exile, my relationship with my baby sister Kellie had been starting to bud. Now it had been suddenly nipped once again, and before I'd even been aware of its existence, of how much it could be worth.

To add to the discomfort, it was freezing. Autumn in Sydney is peak surf season – the Southern Ocean swells are big, the sea is still warm and the dry winds can blow offshore all day. But here in Frankston I was a long way from my home surf spots or any real ocean. It was obvious that I wouldn't last very long and I know Mum could feel it.

Waves had always been the source of my energy. I was pulled towards them and mesmerised by them, but now I'd been dragged far away. But they were never completely out of my mind. I used to go down to the Frankston jetty to watch the six-inch wind waves as they formed different shapes and broke onto the shingle. They were all that this little inland waterway could summon. I was fascinated by their geometric lines and would mind-surf them, imagining they were six-foot peelers and that I was inside their minuscule tubes. For now it was all I could do.

Waves still intrigue me now. Their hypnotic effect can't just be to do with surfing and I wonder if everyone is linked to the sea in some way. Many people are drawn to it and, without any need for mysticism, we certainly all have a physical connection to waves.

For starters, everything we see is delivered by them, as is the warmth we feel when we stand next to another human being at a bus shelter on a cold day. So too is sound, and as we now know, the force of gravity.

Freakier still, our connection to waves goes even deeper. The very smallest building blocks of everything, including the atoms in our own bodies and minds, are governed by and in a sense made of them. Without this arrangement, those atoms couldn't exist; their inner forces of attraction would make their outer parts collapse into their centres and they'd immediately self-destruct into slushy plasma. Not good news for us or anything else made of stuff, i.e. the whole universe.

The basic gist of this wave/matter ambiguity was formalised in the Wave Function, symbolised by a mysterious Greek letter, Ψ (Psi), in Erwin Schrödinger's famous equation.

That equation, probably the most important in science, has never made a wrong prediction in almost a hundred years. If it had, we wouldn't have any modern electronics (or nukes, or a periodic table, among other things). You can see that the symbol is a trident, God of the Sea Neptune's trident. I don't know if that is a coincidence or not.

So maybe it's no wonder that we are fascinated when we waste hours looking at the sea, trying to understand how ocean movements work, how waves form up and get all the way from there to here without any actual water being transported, and how those beautiful walls of water erupt so perfectly that we can ride across them. Maybe we're just longing to comprehend the system that governs us and the world around us.

At least that's one excuse for all the hours and days I've wasted checking the surf!

In any case, these thoughts offered no answers to me on those grizzled suburban streets of Frankston, whose red, grey and brown colour scheme was making my soul heavy. At the time I didn't understand why I was so saddened by the flat, windswept inland bay with its embarrassed little ripples. I now realise that thoughts of waves are never enough; if you want to fill up with their energy, you have to plunge in.

$$\psi$$

Shamefully, I recall the sadness, depression and emptiness of exile, but I don't remember how I felt about my father's death, his absence or the dawning fact that I'd never see him again. These emotions seem to have been lost. Or maybe I didn't have them at all. Maybe I didn't understand. Maybe I invested everything into Mum, where it got mixed up with everything else.

In a way our new situation was simply a reversion to what our life had been like before Dad came along. Perhaps his sudden and permanent departure was just an extension of his typical ad hoc style, where everything happened in bursts of energy that came without any reason, warning or explanation, whether they were momentous events or insignificant gifts. I wonder if this is how animals think – what a small impala feels when the patriarch of the herd is suddenly dragged down and eaten by a cheetah: it's just life on the grassy plain – we carry on, we follow the herd, we chew the grass.

I was mostly upset because of Mum and her obvious, visible, desperate grief. She was devastated, and now she would openly cry at the slightest hiccup. And her fear was new and shocking to me, coming from a superhuman. The sight of her ruffled and unsure was something I'd deemed unthinkable till all of this, and I still couldn't get used to it; her inner steel was tougher than anyone's and clad far more elegantly. But now I was seeing holes.

This is not to say that I did not have sad and anguished thoughts about my dad, Frank, himself; then, afterwards and now. I knew he was a walking contradiction, and the different feelings I have about him today are the echoes. I loved him and I hated him fully. Perhaps for this reason, the way I feel about him will never make sense. So I better just make a list and be done with it.

- He was more of a good bad guy than a bad bad one.
- He was my dad, irreplaceable.

- He cared about me but used gifts to communicate it.
- He was proud of me and I think it was genuine.
- I made him laugh whenever I wanted.
- He wasn't faithful. And I'll never understand why.
- He fought Mum and me, but mostly Mum.
- She rarely reciprocated but when she did . . .
- He fought everybody.
- He loved Mum and me, and he felt lucky.
- I wanted it to continue.

Dad lived every minute of his short life at a stupidly high speed, which was too fast for anybody else. I don't know how many people he may have killed. I hope it is none, but there are certainly many who died in connection with his activities. I honestly don't think there was a universe in which he would have lived a longer life.

I never had any conversations about this with either my sister or my mum. In fact, being constantly afraid and on the move, we never even had a chance to have a real funeral for Dad. It would have been too dangerous.

I've been asked more times than I can remember about my father's life and his behaviour, especially towards my mum. Has it affected me? I suppose it has. Do I think it was okay? I didn't like it and it wasn't okay. Frank is a part of what I became. I just don't know what part.

What I can say for sure is that at the time his behaviour seemed normal, if frightening, and that soon after he died, I realised it was not. I think he wanted to be there for me but robbing banks made it difficult. I thank Neptune that I channelled my feelings about it into a healthy, if wordy, timidity, and that I have never felt violent towards man, woman or beast. And that the whiff of violence has always made me want to run away.

Ψ

Our spell in Frankston only lasted a few months. One day, Mum received some news and announced that it was safe to go home. I had no idea what had changed, but I'd soon find out. It had nothing to do with the police, who most definitely hadn't come to our rescue or rounded up any of the horrible men who were after us. Nope. It was Dad's old mates in the Painters and Dockers union. They'd stepped in and put together a three-man 'death squad', who were on the way up to Sydney to avenge my father's murder.

10.

Baldy's War

The baffling sequence of events that took place while Mum and I were putting our feet up in sleepy Frankston

In my mind, the maelstrom that continued to swirl for several years after my father's death is still a gloriously tangled-up mess.

Some details, reported to me by my parents' friends, are disputed or unclear. Other details just don't make any sense, although often with those people it was usually only when things didn't make sense that they could be taken as truth.

What I do know is this. Having heard that Dad's Melbourne Painter and Docker mates – led by Les Kane – were on their way to Sydney with murder on their minds, Billy Maloney and Kevin Gore got themselves into a right state. When the Melbourne killers arrived, there was a skirmish, but the out-of-towners soon retreated, most likely because 'Jimmy the Pom' Driscoll turned up with his stash of automatic weapons.

Shaken and upset, Billy and Kevin hightailed it down to Melbourne and shot one of the men who they believed was involved. This was another of Dad's Painter and Docker comrades, a poor bloke named 'Cossie' Costello. Cossie might have had some vague involvement in planning the Mayne Nickless robbery, but he was really just a shoplifter and occasional tough guy. He was no murderer and no threat to any Toe Cutter. But nevertheless he was killed, blown apart by two shotguns. For some reason Billy and Kevin thought that going on the attack in this way might make all their troubles go away. It just made things worse.

During this confusing period, Kevin found the time to murder his old safe-cracking partner: another notorious, seasoned torch-man by the name of Alan Francis. This wasn't a Melbourne order, just some ongoing business requested by Detective Sergeant Kaiser, who was up to his eyeballs in everything that was happening. It was supposed to be another Toe Cutter–style rob-the-robber thing. Apparently, Francis had carried out another lucrative job and Kaiser wanted some of the money. This may not have been relevant to the reprisals that were going on, but whatever happened, it certainly had echoes of the events that surrounded Dad's abduction and another example of Kaiser's recurrent, deadly FOMO.

After Cossie's murder, a fresh face was added to the Melbourne death squad: Johnny 'the Magician' Regan. Regan was part psychotic, having nonchalantly racked up dozens of violent crimes by his mid-twenties, but he had missed out on the sharp analytical skills that make up the other half of the psychotic nature. A number of small-time criminals were accidentally caught up in Regan's pursuit of the Toe Cutters, and one of these was the hapless thief Robert Donnelly. When Donnelly foolishly borrowed Kevin Gore's car, Regan mistook him for Gore and shot him dead.

Regan eventually got his man, though, as a few days later, Gore himself disappeared and was never seen nor heard from again. I don't know if our family pal Fletcher had any involvement in the removal of the man who cut my father's toes off and blow-torched him to death, and I never asked him.

Johnny Regan's primary target was Jimmy the Pom, who was regarded as the leader of the Toe Cutters and their most seasoned killer. Regan somehow acquired the key to get into Driscoll's garage in the sleepy suburb of Oatley, and rigged up a remote detonation bomb in his car. The bomb never went off due either to some shoddy electrical work, a poor transmitter design or Driscoll's own paranoid diligence in spotting it.

In a slightly comical twist, Billy Maloney and his brother Jake may have actually helped Regan gain access to their comrade and leader Driscoll's car. Jake had been getting closer to the gang and was helping out by hiding some of the Mayne Nickless heist money they had got their hands on. He was making efforts to be seen as the new Toe Cutter. While this was happening, Driscoll had been seducing ladies all over town, including the partner of one of Jake's close friends. Rumours went around that Jake was miffed about it, and that he and Billy used this wives and girlfriends network to get their hands on the keys for Regan, to enable him to sort Jimmy out.

In any case, Driscoll came to the conclusion that it was Jake who had personally planted the bomb in his car, having discovered the affair. Their common cause now counted for nothing it seemed, and a few days later he burst into Jake's house and shot him twice in the head.

Jake Maloney, who had desperately wanted to be a real gangster and become a Toe Cutter, had now become another of their victims.

Driscoll was eventually picked up by the police, who found an arsenal of machine guns and bombs of every shape and size in his Oatley garage. He was questioned about it by infamous detective Roger Rogerson, at which point he described the cache as simply his 'tools of the trade'. When pressed about the string of murders that was getting longer by the week, he remained enigmatic, merely pointing out that 'everything's connected'. Which, in the farcical world of my father and his friends, I suppose it always was.

Driscoll did jail time for Jake Maloney's murder, sharing a wing at Pentridge with Brandon 'Chopper' Read, who it is said modelled himself on Driscoll. Chopper professed to be very impressed by Toe Cutter methods, even chopping his own ear off to make the point. The moment, which is the same moment he acquired that catchy nickname, is portrayed rather nastily by Eric Bana in the eponymous film.

Johnny Regan, who had succeeded in one contract killing and failed in another, was eventually gunned down outside a Sydney pub. His nickname had come from his ability to make people disappear, and in the end it was obviously the only trick he had. To be fair, while he was a very unpleasant man indeed, he may have saved more lives than he took: who knows how many more murders Kevin Gore might have committed with those tools, either for the police, to get Mum and me, or just because he had them in his kit bag.

Les Kane, who had ordered the death squad, soon met his

death in an equally bloody way – cut to pieces by three gunmen in a hail of machine-gun fire.

For some reason, Detective Sergeant Kaiser, who had remained in the thick of the developments and had probably driven them right from the start, seemed to give up trying to find Mum and me for now. Maybe Kaiser got spooked by the amount of death and destruction all around him or, perhaps more likely, the nasty piece of old shit just ran out of accomplices.

I wonder if Billy Maloney had phoned Kaiser in a panic from Melbourne after the police had spirited us away from the Sydney runway that day, and if Kaiser had subsequently made the call and found out where the taxi – that had after all been ordered by the police – was taking us. It was on Kaiser's orders that Maloney and Gore were chasing us down. The three men had an open business line, and the detective could easily have found out the location of our temporary hide-out. I bet Mum knew the answer to this troubling question, and maybe that's why she understood at the first squeak in the corridor that we were under attack that night in the Esron Motel.

By this stage, Billy Maloney was in and out of jail, having somehow survived the storm. Mum's intelligence network reported that he had found himself quite busy shuttling between Melbourne and Sydney, trying to kill the Kane brothers and Regan before they killed him.

In the end, the gangsters' preoccupation with slaughtering each other was good news for us. The campaign to avenge Dad's murder may not have been a complete success, but Mum and I were damn lucky that some of the country's most violent murderers had given the people who were hunting us something else to think about.

I have a strong feeling that Dad's mate Fletcher was also somewhere in the background – keeping track, pulling levers, and more – one of several figures lurking in the shadows at the time, watching over us. While I never dared ask my mother about any of this, I think their presence, and the news of Kevin Gore's shooting, gave her the confidence to end our exile, to return home, and to re-start our lives.

Ψ

I spent years trying to find out where Billy Maloney ended up, making enquiries with various shady types in between excursions to faraway places. The trail went cold after he did two separate jail sentences for unrelated crimes and then fled to the UK. In the end I gave up. I think I simply got tired of being scared, and let it go.

This is not to say that he stopped haunting me. He's still in my thoughts today. He got away with murder, with both the police and the gangsters eventually leaving him to get on with his life and no doubt plenty of other crimes. His brother, two of his associates and perhaps a dozen other people lost their lives in the backlash from the Toe Cutter murders, but he and Jimmy the Pom got away with it. I guess they were lucky because it wasn't in the interests of the police to dig too deeply into who actually orchestrated Dad's murder. Kaiser was probably not the only officer involved, and over the course of the ensuing decades, a number of his senior Sydney police colleagues were prosecuted or quietly pensioned off.

I often wonder what was going through the minds of all these criminals as they shared drinks and laughs with my dad on the concrete steps at the Oceanic Hotel. At what point did they decide they were going to kill him? And after they'd done it, did they continue hanging out there, smoking, swilling and laughing together on that sticky, rancid, beer-infused terrace overlooking the seafront as if nothing had happened?

I'm glad they pulled the place down and turned it into a big ugly tourist hotel.

11.

Melody Street

The peculiar world of my mother's back room

When I was a teenager, passers-by outside our new home at 44 Melody Street, Coogee, might have assumed from the tea, cakes and raucous female laughter coming from within that a bowling club meeting had spun out of control. But those meetings were rarely what they seemed.

Our little house, a single-storey, red-brick cottage tucked away in a quiet leafy side street up the hill from the bustling beach, signalled a fresh start. I must have been twelve or thirteen when we moved there, coming all the way over the hump from Maroubra to get away from rotten smells that hung around in the years after my father's death.

The new geography didn't lead to a change of career for my mother, however, who picked up pretty much where she had left off. Our chicken-soup-infused (Mum's signature dish at the time, which disgusted me when I was a kid since it was made with all the quivering giblets) back room became the new incubator, where supposed uncles, aunts and friends would get together to drink (tea or gin) and plot, just like when Dad was alive. Along with our occasional hideaway at Aunty Sandy's, Melody Street fast became one of Sydney's underworld hubs; the command centre for some of Australia's largest, and occasionally most outrageous, robberies.

The 'throne', from which Mum or one of the men would chair their meetings, was a black, yellow and orange velour sofa featuring psychedelic diamonds and a mismatch of other dazzling geometric shapes. Cups of tea would be constantly passed through the hatch from the tiny kitchenette that adjoined the back room, often by me. That kitchenette wasn't equipped with an oven or a reliable fridge but it was a brilliant place from which to listen to what the grown-ups were up to.

At the time, most of them didn't seem like grown-ups to me. They behaved like a naughty bunch of schoolkids. Everything was an excuse for a joke, and whatever terrible deed or complicated scheme was being dreamed up, it was always dressed with laughter. It often seemed like a celebration was taking place and sometimes it actually was; the divvying up of a pile of loot from some clever enterprise or other, or the debrief after an absurd yet successful robbery.

Despite the same old goings-on, Melody Street was a very different world compared with our life at Curtin Crescent. Unsavoury types still came and went, but our back room never suffered the chilly drafts that always came in with Dad and his pack of dogs. It was a home.

My mother's entourage loved having a little helper to goad, laugh at, perform for them or run bizarre errands around the Eastern Suburbs. I was entrusted with delivering packages and envelopes of all colours, shapes and dimensions. I never thought much about what was in these packages as I ran or biked to and from laundrettes, betting shops, private houses and cafés. And it was mostly betting shops, whose managers I would deliver the goodies to, or collect the goodies from. I guessed that some of the deliveries contained wads of money, others just messages, and thankfully none were stuffed with drugs as far as I knew.

When you consider the weeks at my on/off residence at Bertie Burwick's Maroubra flat, I probably spent far too much of my youth in betting dens. But there was one positive and unintended consequence. Knowing what I knew about that barely legal world was the perfect deterrent and I never felt the desire to gamble.

I took pleasure in being entrusted to carry out these tasks for my mother and her friends – it felt like I'd been invited to join the sixth form naughty boy's club, and it was all the more delicious for the fact that my annoying baby sister Kellie was not included. Asking too many questions might have meant being thrown out of the club, so I rarely did. Today, I remain in blissful ignorance about so much of what went on.

The regular posse at Melody Street included Aunty Sandy of course, plus a gaggle of half a dozen other 'aunties' who I can only refer to as the Tea Leaf Club in these pages if I ever want to have more kids. Gilbert and Jerome, who were what you might call the bosses, completed the core group around which a swarm of other miscellaneous ladies and gentlemen would often flitter. They had become an extended family to my sister and me, brought into our lives by a world of crime but somehow circling around us to offer protection from it. Whatever the underlying reasons, we existed much as I imagine a normal family would.

Drawn-out meals were usually at the centre of everything, often prepared by Nanna with a little help from me. Over the years, I built up a strong repertoire of dishes learned under the watchful instruction of my imported granny. She was the queen of tabouleh but she also did amazing things with lamb, which was minced by hand using those vicious old knives of hers, and turned into all kinds of aromatic, spicy dishes. Cumin was always involved, likewise tomatoes, mountains of garlic, equally large mountains of parsley to fight off the garlic, and huge, thick-skinned 'mafioso' lemons.

Nanna's baklava was celebrated throughout the Sydney underworld – delicately laminated pastry alternating with a homemade mix of different nuts, seeds and all sorts of other treats, always dripping with too much honey. It was so sweet it made your throat jangle with electricity but this didn't stop me licking our big, cracked, old brown china mixing bowl half to death every time she made the stuff. Whenever a sesame seed pops in my mouth, its minuscule release of rich nutty flavour is a trip back to our little kitchenette, where Nanna awaits with her knives.

Outside of lunch and dinner there would always be tea and crumpets, card games, cakes and laughter. At all hours, strays would 'just drop in'. Apparently you're supposed to call before you visit friends and family, or at least knock before entering someone's house. Mum's crew never did.

That crew, along with their selection of loose associates, had come to be known as the Kangaroo Gang. They both predated and outlasted my mother and father's partnership, partly because they were run like an all-star basketball team, rotating talent in and out whenever they pleased, or to suit whatever game they were playing. This meant that whoever disappeared, got caught or was injured was rapidly, readily replaced as if nothing had happened. This system made them hard to catch, helping them to become the most successful criminal gang in Australia.

The tall, dark and slender Gilbert was an incredible contortionist. He could snake his way around counters and underneath barriers, unseen, to steal money, jewels and anything worth money while the girls worked their charm. In those days, banks had simple desks with a small glass decency screen which you could get in behind, if you knew how.

Gilbert and Jerome were very clever planners and logisticians and seemed to delight in concocting ever more elaborate and outrageous ways to rob banks and shops, whose security set-ups were always one step behind, no matter what updates they installed.

In those in-between days after Dad's death, Mum had a long-running affair with Gilbert, who indulged me, spoiling me with gifts and time, and generally tolerating my presence. I knew he was a crook, of course, and so I must have known that whatever surprise came my way, usually smart jumpers and shirts, would have been stolen. He once gave me a silky pocket handkerchief and I think I may have even worn it once – a dangerous thing to do around the Eastern Suburbs in those days.

The others followed Gilbert's lead, also happy to give of their time and patience to Mum's little pride and joy. They craved her respect and knew that they would have to keep me happy if they were to earn it.

There were countless other thieves, robbers and tricksters orbiting this group, some notorious in their own right – the Kangaroos totalled about a hundred members at various times.

In some ways, they weren't even a material entity at all; they were more a process, constantly evolving and reshaping like clouds.

All the top criminals knew each other, and my mother's world was a merry-go-round of different characters who would get together when it suited them, or drift away and do their own thing for a while if the mood dictated. For this reason there can't have been any major underworld figure of the 1960s, '70s or '80s who didn't visit our back room at some point to chat, plan or just wile away an evening with the girls.

Aunty Sandy's husband and his little friend were among the first Kangaroos, many years before the group went intercontinental. Another favourite aunty, babysitter and Kangaroo was married to one of the top bank robbers and safe-breakers of the time, my mum and dad's great friend, Bert. I believe Bert the Kid, (not to be confused with Bertie Burwick, whose line of work was very different) was a good illustration of the futility of trying to get to grips with the circular convolutions of the world of my family and their many friends.

On top of the safe-cracking, he loved counterfeiting money, enjoying a short jail term after too many of his tenners were spent in the same pub (which happened to be his local). There wasn't much Bert wouldn't try his hand at, but his adventures rarely went smoothly, and he eventually became famous for an outrageous but failed mid-air robbery for which he hid in a crate in the hold of an aeroplane, in an attempt to steal the one million dollars it contained. Despite some of these disasters, he was feared by cops and gangsters alike, having allegedly shot a few of each at one time or another.

Bert the Kid had stood firm and tried to save my father's life when he was on the run from the Toe Cutters, and it was also probably he who delivered the final warning to Dad's killers to leave Mum and me alone to get on with our lives: Bert was certainly no friend of Dad's sadistic blow-torturer Gore, who had once shot his best mate in the back. That best mate also happened to be the Kangaroo's founding commander, Arthur Delaney.

When that other Toe Cutter, Gore's chum Jimmy Driscoll, told the police that everything was connected, the treacherous assassin had a point. Yet the full richness of those tangled, ever-morphing, breaking-and-remaking, often lifelong but sometimes fleeting connections was never truly understood by anybody, except perhaps my mother.

Ψ

Once the dust began to settle after Dad's death, Mum started spreading her wings. She was moving steadily up the criminal ladder, fulfilling many different roles with the Kangaroos, but the specialty for which she was most sought, even celebrated, was as a 'head puller'.

This is what I know of the typical head puller job description:

1. Look strikingly beautiful and carefree.
2. Engage in conversation with guards and staff.
3. Divert attention and block lines of sight, with props if needed.
4. Leave the scene slowly and calmly after the job is done. Never run.

Jewellery shops, department stores and banks were raided with astonishing success over a ten- to twenty-year period using this method, with my mother and her girls dazzling and confusing guards and staff to enable Gilbert and Jerome to get on with their business. Their work was always meticulously organised, and often carried out 'to order', with every object already on a list or, in the case of banks, with sums set in advance, to a detailed budget. I don't know if these were inside jobs, but given the things the Kangaroos got away with, there must have been collaboration at some level.

The family theme that permeated my mother's dusky world spread way beyond this tight group of regulars at Melody Street. Mum and her friends never had romantic liaisons or friendships with anybody outside the fraternity; marrying outside the club was unthinkable. When you did what they did for a living, it would have been hard to have a conversation with your partner over a refreshing beer or a glass of wine after work if they weren't also in the business. How else would you open a bottle, sit in the garden and hold a therapeutic dissection of your busy and stressful day without incriminating yourself?

As a teenager I already knew, without much being said, that I was a part of this 'family' whether I liked it or not and I had to keep its secrets at all cost. Whatever was discussed in the Melody Street back room was to stay in there. When I was out in the sea with Mick or Terry or any of the Maroubra crew, I only ever talked surfing and trivia, never family. When the boys came around to ours to gather for, or debrief from, the surf, they wouldn't have picked up many clues from Mum about her job. If she did ever let slip, I think they were probably too dazzled by her to notice.

Our home at Melody Street was always full of cardboard boxes containing exotic stuff. Cut crystal, fine bone china, a lot of fashionable clothes, statues or curios and, on occasion, jewels. Any burglar foolish enough to break in would have thought he'd stumbled into the secret cave of Monte Cristo Island.

On one occasion Mum and I were transporting some boxes of fabulous cut-crystal glassware from one house to another when we were rear-ended by a van (my mother always made sudden baffling driving decisions, including braking, and her negligence often led us into difficult situations). The boot of our car had caved in, causing the wheel arch to scrape loudly against one of the tyres and create billows of smoke. Mum was utterly nonchalant about the damage to the car but she cornered the terrified van driver and raged about the broken payload, which was apparently more valuable than the car.

I was a poorly educated kid with subpar literacy and very little knowledge of the world, but by the time I was fourteen I knew my Wedgwood from my Spode, my alpaca from my cashmere, and my Waterford from my Baccarat. It annoyed people, believe me!

People estimate that Mum's gang was liberating around $200,000 worth of goods every week from upmarket shops, in addition to regular bank robberies. I wonder if quite a number of the various embarrassing crime waves that were reported on from time to time in the early 1970s were, in fact, nothing more than my mum's lot having a good month. They got away with most of it, and many of their fantastic escapes were due to Mum's finely tuned senses.

'Clients' would regularly stop by to view goods or discuss orders of goods to be procured. These clients could be anybody from loose-minded civilians to senior gangsters and crooks. Some were cops. When I was younger, I thought that my family just had a lot of friends. I gradually figured it out, however, and eventually I could tell the cops apart from the crooks even before they rang the bell, because they were the only ones who didn't drive smart new cars or dress like in the movies.

On one occasion some of the girls stopped by with dozens of huge boxes containing an extensive, delicate Wedgwood dining set. They asked Mum if she wanted it. She told them that she was sorry and thanks but she was broke at the moment so please would they kindly piss off. So, they offered to flip a coin with her for it.

Mum flipped and won, and I still own what's left of this classic English bone china crockery set today. A little piece of her legacy, alongside spotlessly clean shoes you'll often see on my feet.

12.
Young Offender

Mum and friends teach me some new tricks

Once the 1970s got going in earnest, and Terry, Mick and I were fully fledged teen surfers, a singular dream preoccupied us and pretty much every other surfer we knew: Hawaii, and the Banzai Pipeline.

Our heroes were the legendary Hawaiians Reno Abellira, Rory Russell, the Aikau brothers and, most of all, the great Gerry 'Mr Pipe' Lopez. These men of *koa* ruled the mountainous waves of the gladiatorial arena that was the North Shore of Oahu. This volcano-island sat over the horizon in our very own Pacific Ocean, yet was so removed from our boundless mass of dusty red dirt that it seemed barely real. Maybe it only existed in the pages of *Tracks* or *Surfer* magazines – and in our imaginations.

I wanted a piece of the Hawaiian dream, very badly indeed. But going overseas cost money, and as a fifteen-year-old I was earning a pittance putting together telephone directories at Brooks' Phone Book factory out in the dreary (at the time) suburb of Zetland. Even with my rudimentary maths it was clear that I'd have to pack and stack an awful lot of paper to get to Hawaii.

What I needed was a little shove, and some luck. It came in the form of a 'project' Mum and one of her best friends needed help with.

Ψ

With the majority of the Toe Cutters now either dead or in jail, and police interest in the remaining tangle of loose ends, especially the loot, having (mostly) ebbed away, life had returned to what Mum called 'normal'. The only scares were the occasional newspaper articles about court cases connected with one or other of the robbery, the revenge or the loot. I imagine Mum would have been hearing a lot more about it through her contacts, but she shielded me. In this period of relative calm, she set about the complicated business of righting our finances, which were virtually shot.

This basically meant that I had to pull my weight. I can't recall if I was instructed or if anything was actually said, but I was pretty good at reading my mother's mind. With the benefit of hindsight, I think I stepped too willingly into this murky world. Maybe I didn't want to let the family down, maybe I saw it as just another adventure, or maybe I was simply blinded by the desire to get on a plane to the centre of world surfing. In any case, all the questions I should have asked myself would have to wait for later on in life.

The opportunity to be more than a messenger boy for the Kangaroo Gang presented itself in the form of John, an enormous, charming, beautifully dressed gentleman, and one of the last dandies. John's bronzing was always perfect and his hands were so tightly manicured they could have featured in a luxury wristwatch ad. Even Mum was in awe of his immaculate but sometimes mad dress sense. John called himself 'the Big Fat Poof', and in 1970s Sydney that took guts regardless of your situation, but especially when you were mingling with some of the hardest gangsters in town.

John lived over the road from us in Melody Street. He was a gifted painter, often giving away intricate, beautiful works of canvas art in return for a carton of Tooheys twist tops. He'd hang around with Mum all day, painting away while they both sang songs and quaffed (on a twenty-three-to-one ratio – Mum ate and drank like a bird but John had a huge appetite for both beer and life). His works of art littered our house; bluebell woods, still-life flower vases, blue and green splurges that may have been scenes of countryside paradise. They were everywhere, usually on the floor or leaning against the walls. I don't recall ever seeing any of them hung. Little Kellie herself soon caught the painting bug (although she didn't bother with brushes) and sometimes you couldn't tell which piece was John's and which was hers.

At one point John got bored of painting on canvas and announced he would 'do' our house. He was good for his word, single-handedly stripping down all the old doors, antique fireplaces and walls and eventually covering the entire place, inside and out, in bright white emulsion. Whenever I smell fresh paint today, my mind bypasses conscious thought and takes an instant shortcut through space and time to Melody Street.

John's arrival was always preceded by a wave of exotic musk, as if a grand Bedouin chief were making an entrance. It would then linger for hours after he left. Sometimes we all got together and danced around the living room; sadly for our neighbours, we had a massive stack of hi-fi equipment that could really pump up the volume. This must have frightened poor little Kellie, who used to run and bury her head under a cushion.

Apart from painting and drinking, John was also in charge of a very large dole office. And he had a brilliant idea.

He was a polymath; not only cultured, well read and artistic, but a gifted mathematician and logistical thinker. By combining his creativity and his ability to visualise numbers, he created one of the largest, most elaborate and most profitable scams in Australian history. And Mum and I were among its first foot soldiers.

What made the scam particularly appealing to its perpetrators, apart from a steady flow of money into our bank accounts, was that the fraud was against the government. In our opinion, this meant it was practically victimless, and almost noble! The people who were legitimately claiming their unemployment benefit cheques at the Kingsford Social Security office might not have agreed, but that was beside the point.

John's system involved the redirection of dole payments into the accounts of as many collaborators as possible; 'the more the merrier', as he put it. He set us up with various bank accounts in fictitious names, mostly stolen from dead people, and found ways for the unemployment benefits to be paid into them. At one point I had five or six accounts and a roster of different passports which were all kept in a bag under the sink in our Melody Street kitchenette.

My role was fairly minor, although I was well aware of the obvious risks we all faced if we got caught. The plus point of the scheme, however, was that it enabled me to contribute to the gang's activities and help my mum without having to do any shoplifting, help rob any banks or carry a gun. I thought that I could dip my toe – or at least wade at a safe distance from shore for a while – and still do my bit. I never believed that I might eventually get swept away in the current and into the depths.

In the meantime, money was paid into my various bogus accounts just like that, although unfortunately I wasn't allowed to keep all of it. Over time I did manage to pocket a small amount for my part as a child soldier. Here are the maths as I recall them:

Weekly payments
Larry (me): 4 accounts × $45 (average) per week = $180
Patricia (Mum): 4 accounts × $45 per week = $180
48 other participants × 4 accounts × $45 per week = $8640
Subtotal: $9000 per week
= $468,000 per year

Where did the other forty-eight helpers come from? The Coogee Bay Hotel mainly. The uneventful pub on the corner of Coogee Bay Road and Arden Street – a stone's throw from the Oshey – became John's key recruiting ground. Most of the pub's regulars were in on the deal at one time or another, and I often wondered whether scheme members drinking in the sedate, leafy beer garden knew that the people on the next-door tables were likely to be members of the same criminal club.

The program yielded lots of money and was a success right from the start, but John soon fired up his imagination even more and found a way to ramp things up. He managed to find somebody who could quietly backdate some of the payments by three months. It was this simple trick that made the scheme really pay out.

The new maths were 45×13 weeks = $2340 per member. All that was needed was a steady flow of passports.

The scheme grew apace. In a good week, thousands of dollars could appear in our accounts. I got to keep just enough of it to keep the Hawaiian dream alive, although it'd be a lie to say the whole charade didn't make me extremely nervous.

John always exuded complete confidence in his scheme and he was very convincing. He and Mum regularly laughed about how well it was all going, about the new recruits, and about the simple, brilliant mathematics behind it. Passport procurement was a hot topic and one of the most technically challenging aspects. It required a steady stream of the right kinds of deaths to happen in the right kinds of neighbourhoods.

Impersonating the dead isn't healthy, however, and it got to a point where so many names were swirling about in our heads that we sometimes forgot who was dead and who was alive. Sometimes one of our victims shared a name with an acquaintance or a local business, and it would pop up to give me a fright – a nasty electric jolt. It was horrid back then, but it's worse today. Please dear God, do not let me stumble across any of those names again in newspapers, on plumbers' vans or on book covers. The names of the departed, the dead people who we briefly became and robbed.

Ψ

During this period, my surfing buddies only knew me as the stoked grommet, maniacally buzzing about in the line-up and getting into impossible little barrels. I was part of a gang out there in the sea, and another gang on land in the underworld, but the two had to be carefully separated. I couldn't share any details of my bad life with the people from my good one.

On the water, Mick, Terry and I were improving all the time. Mick had the speed, the fitness and the quick reactions. I thought I could find my way to the good part of any wave. And Terry was just a total kamikaze in and out of the water, his flaming orange hair matching his never-say-die attitude. Both of Terry's older brothers absolutely killed it in the surf in fact, but he was the one who pushed himself the most, often over mutating ledges of water that no sane kid would go near. In fact, some of my mates were already becoming local heroes and gracing the pages of *Tracks* and *Surfing World* magazines.

We were a tight crew, eyeing up our futures as young adults, and we hoped and prayed that those futures would include surfing. Polluting our relationship with the truth about my day job was out of the question. Where on earth would I even start?

Mick: Laz, where were you yesterday? It was pumping out here!

Laz: I was at the dole office pretending to be Reggie Burns, that guy who died of a heart attack at the checkout in Coles last month.

Mick: Ha ha, great. Well, you missed some good ones. We all got seriously shacked (or barrelled, tubed, etc.).

And so on.

There was an awful lot about my family and me, both from the past and the present, that I could never share with my friends. Some of it wasn't clear to me until much later, but I knew that everything that was discussed by my family was to remain sealed within the walls of 44 Melody Street. If conversation with the boys ever veered towards my home life I would make a joke, act the fool or just run away. It goes without saying that there could be no more sleepovers at Melody Street, ever. I don't know how I evaded all their questions but I must have told a lot of lies at that time in my life.

The need to mislead my closest friends about the criminal bog I was in became a continuous, unstoppable force pushing us apart. This is not to say that my mates were angels. When we were small, our stupid behaviour had stopped at pranking people in the laundrette or calling them up from a phone box and telling them they'd won the lottery. Now all three of us were taking things too far, crossing the line that divides naughty from illegal. Yet still, my situation eclipsed everybody else's.

Newcomers, girls, jobs and real-world aggravations had also been slowly accumulating and conspiring to further disturb the clockwork universe we lived in. Inevitably, it started to unwind, and the ticks (which used to take the form of daily meet-ups before school, after school, on Saturday and Sunday mornings) were becoming so infrequent that I wondered if each one might be the last.

But while it lasted, when I did meet up with the boys, we still larked about like nine-year-olds, of course, and we had enormous laughter in the sea and on the streets. The joy I took from their company made everything all the more painful.

I don't know at what point I knew it was over, but when it finally happened, it happened quickly. The catalyst was yet another school move, when Mum decided I should grow up a bit and go to Randwick Boys High, which was in a completely different neighbourhood (and world, in those days).

Then came the hammer blow. At around this time, Mick was deported to Ireland by his own dad. I think it was due to some of the stuff we were all getting ourselves into, and which his family wanted to distance him from. Mick's departure was sudden and brutal, which, knowing his dad, was no big surprise. Mr Power reminded me of my own father – he had a similar stature and presence – but he was not a criminal and whatever violence he may have had inside him seemed to simmer, not boil.

Maybe the move saved Mick's life, but devastatingly for us three it would be years before he came back. Mick was easily as loose as Terry and me and always up for whatever mad and hazardous scheme we got ourselves into. But where Terry could often be relied upon to take the extra step into Berkoland, Mick had always kept a certain perspective, and I wonder if, had I had the chance to share the details of what I was doing with him, he would have seen that I was taking things too far and advised me to get out. Whatever, I missed him.

Another step on my forced march towards adulthood was that I had by now, thanks to my new reputation as a 'surfer', acquired a girlfriend, Susie, who was a few years older than me. In fact, she was old enough to appear on page three of the newspaper, and in the 1970s this was seen by many as the highest honour a lady could receive. I was very, very proud of her, and utterly besotted. We grabbed hold of each other, partly because we'd both had difficult times with our fathers. Susie's had bashed her regularly and I'd seen the bruises. He was a very violent man. I was able to share with her the mixed feelings I had about Frank's life and death even if I had to omit some of the details.

I never spoke about Mum's career with Susie. I wanted to get closer to her by telling her our real story but of course I couldn't. Where would I start?

So despite my being enraptured, even my girlfriend had to be misled. When she insisted on staying over at our house we would do a delicate dance. Mum carefully avoided the place when Susie was around, but there were times when we all coincided, and then the poor girl simply had to be deceived. Despite Mum's brilliant storytelling, it was not a comfortable way of living.

Once again, Bertie Burwick stepped into the breach and helped out, allowing Susie and me to move into his Maroubra flat, which was conveniently located behind the surf club, just one street away from our old place at Curtin Crescent. It was another step away from my careless boyhood and the friends I had shared it with.

It slowly dawned on me that Bertie was in love with my mum. I don't think he ever even hinted about his feelings towards her, but we just knew. His appearances had become more and more frequent after Dad's death and at some point he had metamorphosed into 'Uncle Bert'. He would appear whenever he was summoned to carry out pretty much any task Mum asked of him. She was visibly repulsed by his stringy six-foot-three presence and long face topped with a perfectly parted and brilliantined reflective black helmet of hair. This didn't stop her from accepting his help in solving some of the many wide-ranging challenges we faced once Baldy was not around to protect us.

Bertie's influence was benign and he never seemed to expect anything in return other than my mum's approval. I think that he genuinely cared about me, much as a real uncle would. It was Bertie who, when Dad bought me that glamorous bright red pintail to charge about on, thought of my safety and wellbeing enough first. Bertie duly went out and got me a brand-new red O'Neill wetsuit so that I wouldn't freeze to death. When all the other adults ran berserk around me, Bertie took care of the practicalities.

Bertie could see the direction in which I'd been drifting and he wanted to help steer me back onto a more sensible and safer course. He knew that I loved cooking and that I wasn't too bad at it, and so he suggested I go and learn how to do it properly. He duly enrolled me in the Marcus Clark School for Chefs in town and I started attending the after-school sessions. I loved the routine and the processes, even if the teaching methods were very different from Nanna's school of deep cuts. One of the very first things you learn in cooking school is 'knife drill', without which no chefs would have any fingers. Nanna's version of knife drill was very different to the one they taught at cooking school.

I hadn't thought very hard about where food might take me, but I knew I wanted it in my life in some way or other. The best thing about cheffing was that it didn't require a charade; it was real, and I didn't have to lie to anybody about it. I think that, for whatever reason, Bertie wanted me to have this gift – a glimpse into a better way of living. It dawns on me that he had given it much more thought than me.

Ψ

Moving out of Melody Street and over the hill to Bertie's helped resolve the delicate balancing of these two worlds, but it also confirmed that I was no longer a child. The assortment of humanity I encountered out in the North Maroubra line-up was very different from anything I might have brushed up against in my old school playground or its surrounding patch of sea. I had surfed here throughout the Coogee Primary years, but then I was just a grom on a plastic plaything. Now I was slowly becoming a local and instead of carefully avoiding some of the piratical inhabitants of the world beyond the North End rip, I was going to have to seek their acceptance.

Steve 'Blackie' Wilson and Tony White were two such pirates. They were part of a crew that dominated the small world of surfers that ran from the North End to the South Maroubra rock pools. I knew Tony especially, because his sledgehammer fists had saved me and the boys one terrifying day under the Coogee pier. These guys, with Kevin Wheatie, Steve Leslie, Davo Davidson and a few others, were becoming the acknowledged rulers of Maroubra, and everyone who wanted to surf there, no matter how good they were, had to honour them and earn their respect.

I didn't know how I could ever break into this group, but then I met a peculiar kid who was to create, and share with me, many of the truest joys of my life. He also became one of my greatest ever friends.

'Fat Larry' Crane was possibly the smartest (in the brain sense) kid in our neighbourhood. He didn't look it – in fact, his round, unquestioning face looked untroubled by any intellect at all, but it was misleading. I think that his brain was just so big that it rarely strained itself enough to crease his calm expression. The volume of fascinating information that whizzed around inside him and came firing out of his mouth had led me to assume that Larry was much older than me, but it turned out we were roughly the same age.

Fat was so clever he was spirited away after only his third day at school and sent to a special school for brainiacs, Marcellin College in Randwick. Despite it all, he was funny, so funny. He knew he was different, brighter than the rest of us, and easily the oddest looking. His way of dealing with his alienness was to wrap it all up in self-deprecating jokes. Referring to his extraordinarily luminous orange hair and eyebrows, he used to say, 'It's hard being a carrot trying to live above ground with all you peanuts.' I think he meant to insult himself and the rest of us. In response to being fat, he made up his own nickname, beating everybody else to the obvious and thereby instantly defusing it, preventing its use against him. He turned 'Fat Larry' into a badge of honour when it should have been an insult. His jokes weren't technically all that funny but his delivery, and the fact that we all knew he was so much quicker than us, convinced us that they were hilarious and that if we didn't laugh it must be because we were stupid.

Of course, Larry Crane, being neither blond, nor thin, nor muscular, and with all his many other differences including real problems being in the sun and the biggest splattering of freckles I'd ever seen, did not resemble a surfer in any way, shape or form. But he gave it his all in the waves and was well and truly part of the top brass of the North End, respected by all the Blackies, the Kevins and the Tonys.

He may not have ripped like the rest of them but he cemented his place in the group with sheer guts (or stupidity). To the point that four ambulances and fire trucks had to rescue him one day when we were cliff jumping from the sky-high overhangs at the end of the Maroubra firing range. Flat days are dangerous because they make for bored surfers. A dozen of us watched Larry leap from the highest spot, attempt a ludicrous backflip and land with a sickening slap on his back, knocking himself unconscious. Larry promptly sank, and his lungs filled with water. It was a time-stopping moment for all who were there, but we did manage to pull ourselves together and fish his well-upholstered but limp body out. My friend was lucky to survive that jump, one that many others have not, but he used up one of his lives that day. Some time later I'd wish he hadn't.

Because Larry was so odd, I felt for the first time in my life that here was someone I could talk to about what made *me* different. You know, my dad, my mum, the fact that I had unusual sources of income and never stayed at one school for very long. It was thanks to his brilliant self-made nickname that the two of us became known as 'Fat Larry' and 'Little Larry'. And this, we certainly were. Big, small. Ginger, blond. Learned, raw. And for a while, inseparable.

Larry loved the pakololo. It was never really my thing but on occasion we would have some brilliant laughs thanks to his never-ending homegrown supply. One day at his place we made some cookies. After twenty minutes of the most exhausting, painful laughter – followed by me having a terrifying near-psychotic breakdown – we both fell asleep and didn't get up for two days. That was more or less the start and finish of my drug-taking career.

Surprisingly, Larry had a relatively normal family. They lived up the hill from the jail in the otherwise uneventful suburb of Matraville and his mum and dad took me in like a long-lost son. Just like the brief episode at Uncle Alfie and Aunty Joan's down in Frankston, in Matraville, I was afforded another glimpse of how families were supposed to behave together. Sleepovers at the Cranes' place gave me treasured moments of stability, particularly when Mum was away doing her thing.

Larry's dad was an avid fisherman and we would often gather for the evening around some huge creature he'd hooked while dodging the ocean rollers that washed over his favourite fishing rock. Trying to get fish out of the sea when you didn't have a boat was a dangerous activity in our old neighbourhood, requiring total concentration in order to avoid being dragged into the ocean and crushed against the barnacle-covered boulders by those sneaker waves. But the rewards were magnificent and we always honoured those beautiful fish in the kitchen. His favourite cooking method was to bake the whole thing in a salt crust that he would ceremoniously crack with the back of a spoon, releasing impressive clouds of fragrant steam.

Larry's brother was openly gay at a time when pretty much every other gay man was hidden in the closet. He took enormous pleasure in pointing out every covert gay man in the neighbourhood and could be relied upon to surprise us with unexpected revelations about the straightest-looking people in politics, on TV or at the corner shop. Sometimes he would wink theatrically at his unsuspecting victims. Naturally, we found this hugely entertaining.

Thanks to new friendships, a steady girlfriend and the relative safety that was possible without Baldy around – and despite my complicated 'day job' – these were golden times. When my home break fired in an offshore breeze with the right swell, the sun sparkling off the water, it was heaven, and as beautiful as anywhere on the planet, even though I hadn't seen much of that planet as yet. But good god, I knew I wanted to.

Those friendships, facilitated by Fat, helped change my surfing, gently nudging my life in a new direction.

Ψ

One day when I got home from a very clean and fun late-winter session at South End, I found Mum in a state. She looked older, pale and distressed. Ominously, there was no half-smile tugging at the corners of her eyes. She sat me down and explained calmly and without inflection that John had been called in for questioning by the police.

At this point, Mum, and therefore I, had two big problems. The Special Investigations Division was keen to talk to her again and get to the bottom of what happened to the proceeds from Dad's armoured van robbery. They suspected she might have hidden the loot or given it to the Texan. I hadn't seen or heard a thing about those green canvas bags since that day four years earlier when I'd stuffed them into a ceiling cavity.

The second problem was the cops now also wanted all the information on the dole scam: amounts, names, dates, the lot. Most of all, they wanted to know about anybody who had any involvement with John. From the expression on Mum's face I knew they had somehow found out we were in it up to our eyeballs. I couldn't help thinking how curious it was that the police never showed the same concern when it came to finding my dad's killers.

At first, Mum did what came naturally to her and tried evasion. One day the police attempted to arrest her as she left our house, blocking off the end of our street. But she saw them first, went back inside, filled a bag with bottles and put on extra jumpers and an old coat. She made a point of rattling these bottles like some old bag lady, limping about at the end of the driveway and down our leafy little side street straight past the coppers. Even I'd been fooled; I thought she'd fallen ill or had suddenly gone mad.

However, the constant dodging and the silly costume acts could not go on forever. The jig appeared to be up and my mother felt that once again it was time to do what we did best – run. Our little family of three was going to have to pack up and leave, more or less immediately.

I'd seen my mother scared before when we were on the run from crooks or cops. It was harrowing but I always believed she had the answers and that we would be okay. Perhaps it was just childish faith fooling me, and perhaps she had actually come close to cracking that night at the Esron without me knowing it. But this situation seemed different; for what was perhaps the first time in the fifteen years I'd known her, she seemed defeated. Due to the chaos in the air I didn't have time to dwell on it, but I did know the moment had finally arrived; the moment when a kid realises their parent is no longer invincible.

Mum came up with some pretty exotic ideas around where and how we might escape, and had already made some loose plans. Coincidentally, at this time, there was 'work' for her in the UK with the Kangaroos. The wider gang had been plying their trade all over the world and there was a steady pipeline of Australian-trained thieves being sent to inflict their skills on the unsuspecting British public. London, therefore, was the answer to everything.

But there was one hitch: I wasn't included in this particular adventure. The conversation veered off course suddenly when Mum dropped the bombshell that she and Kellie would head in one direction, and I would head in another. Apparently, fifteen years on the planet had provided me with all the experience I would need, with the final proof being my resourcefulness in helping out in the dole scam. I was now old enough to fend for myself, and more than ready to quit school and take on the world on my own.

In a practical sense, I guess she was right. I *had* learned to get myself out of almost any scrape. We'd lived apart on and off during each and every one of the crises that had reared up over the years (just not quite this far apart). I'd also saved enough money through my secret career, plus a little tiny bit on top from the millions of phone books I had painstakingly assembled. I could now get on any plane I chose and go anywhere I wanted. When I did my sums, I reflected on how unfair it was that the job for which I had literally bled (from my fingertips) had earned me a fraction of the amount that came out of the other, far easier, but completely immoral activity. The thought didn't take hold for long.

So, as my mother always said, that was that. The only further guidance she gave during this brief passing-out ritual was that all of us had to put as much distance as possible between ourselves and Australia.

Ψ

After the feeling of rejection wore off, I sat down and thought about it properly. What were my ties here in Sydney anyway?

My girlfriend, the beautiful, funny, loyal Susie, had almost had enough of me, or so I believed – we were just too different. This was crystallised one Saturday morning when I was setting off for my cookery class in town. I was looking forward to finding out what complicated French dish the day had to offer: beef bourguignon, riz pilaf, or stroganoff? Or perhaps some sort of consommé.

Susie threatened that she would jump out of the window if I left her in the house alone. She was a grown woman telling off a boy and it freaked me out. I had no idea what to say so I just turned around and walked out. It immediately felt like a wonderful ride was about to end, and that one way or another I was going to be alone again. I'd always felt that Susie knew I was punching above my weight, and she had already started to show signs of being sick of my unusual obsession with tidiness and my head buzzing with superstitions. She'd never shared my slightly upside-down sense of humour or liked all the other ticks picked up during my years of living dangerously with Patricia Blair. My growing obsession with cookery must have been the last straw.

When I got back from classes that day smelling of sweat, onions and garlic, Susie wasn't squished on the pavement in front of our house – she had packed up all her stuff and left. I didn't know what to think, but at least the tie was neatly severed.

Little Kellie was also not going to be a problem. Kell had been getting 'farmed out' for most of her short life because very small kids make for slow getaways when everything is on the line. And because of her frequent absences, I didn't have the kind of relationship I ought to have had with my baby sister.

I regret it now, but at the time it was what it was. I doubted she'd even notice if I left the country.

And so this left Mum, only Mum. I'd miss her fun, her love, her unshakeable confidence in me and her fierce protection. But I knew that she would always be with me wherever I ended up, in spirit and in my veins.

I now realise she was more tightly encircled than she let on, being a person of interest in (or at least connected to) two serious crimes. Her photo must have been on the wall of police HQ for quite some time, perhaps pinned to a board covered with those pieces of string connecting dozens of bad people and their crimes. In fact I bet all those strings crossed over in one place – Melody Street. Mum feared for her freedom but mostly for mine. I'm now sure that above all else she wanted me to be far away, and free.

Underneath it all I felt the same. Having had the unpleasant experience of being locked up in that boarding school in Campbelltown, I was in no hurry to forfeit my liberty and be dragged away from the ocean again. And I did have my dreams.

And so it was decided: the time had come for me to take a Very Long Surf Trip to the most remote islands on earth.

13.

Shaka

What better hideout than a cluster of isolated volcanoes in the middle of the Pacific Ocean.

I seem to have eaten concrete for dinner last night – everything is cramped solid. It could be fear, excitement or nerves. Probably all three. The churning in my belly, and the constant terror of a loud knock on the front door, mean I've barely slept for a week. I just need to get on that plane before the cops come around, and the plane needs to take off.

It occurs to me that Hawaii is a long way from home. Looking at the map, it's a long way from anywhere. But this suits my purpose; not even the keenest enemy – be they cop, robber or murderer – will be able to find me there.

It's handy that Hawaii is also the place I've been dreaming about since the day Dad bought me the Red Rocket. The *Surfing World* magazine covers of transparent waves running across vivid coral reefs that cover my bedroom walls will soon be my reality. But despite the dreams, and the plans made with the boys at Arden Street, I never quite believed it would happen.

But I've got a bundle of ill-gotten cash, four passports, and a ticket to Honolulu on Pan Am. So I'm going and that's that.

Ψ

When you're fifteen, there are a lot of 'now what's?' in life. Those labrador puppy moments when you realise you just haven't thought things through.

And so on that day in 1973, the very day of my departure, it hit me that I'd forgotten to include one important detail. As a schoolkid (Mum and I never did inform Randwick Boys High that I was leaving – it seemed pointless) with no travel experience to speak of except in the desert and a couple of beach towns up and down the east coast, I knew no one anywhere outside Australia – including Hawaii's North Shore.

One person I thought might be able to help was a surfboard shaper called Geoff McCoy. Geoff and his wife, Leah, knew I was a stray from our first meeting at a juniors' surf comp. For some reason Geoff saw potential in me and was supplying me with equipment. He also shaped boards for some of the guys who were competing in Hawaii, such as the great Mark Warren. So I called him and asked him what the hell I should do. In many ways Geoff's gruff answer, consisting of three mysterious words that squeaked out of a crackly payphone, changed my life.

I must have looked quite a sight when Mum dropped me off at Kingsford Smith Airport with a plastic bag and a surfboard wrapped in towels and cardboard. My hair was white-blond, my face dark as teak, but I wasn't all that tall, so I probably looked my age. The flight attendants put a sticker on my

T-shirt that said I was an 'unaccompanied minor' and followed me around everywhere I went until I was safely seated right at the back of the plane. I guess they thought some uncle or aunty would be waiting for me in Hawaii.

During the flight, I sampled a selection of mini bottles of alcohol appropriated from the drinks cart. Most tasted disgusting, especially the sticky dark green medicine that was made by monks, and the bright green stuff that tasted like mouthwash. It was the first time I'd ever been drunk, a not unpleasant experience, and a decent way for a hyperactive kid who doesn't read to wile away ten hours.

After much fidgeting, some snacks, more booze and a long snooze, we were finally circling Hawaii's capital city, Honolulu, where the giant craggy green volcanoes pierce the clouds and dwarf the skyscrapers. Catching sight of Oahu and its surrounding islands, punching up out of the middle of the ink-blue sea like Neptune's fists, left me slack-jawed.

When we landed I wandered about the airport trying to get my bearings. I had to get to the North Shore but no taxi would take me with all my stuff, so I ended up hitching a ride to Ala Moana, where I knew there was a beach and a wave, and slept under a tree. I was bitten half to death that night, but I don't know by what. In spite of this, I had a fairly peaceful night's sleep because I knew that I finally had my freedom. And I was of course still pissed.

In the morning, I went out on the road and waved at every cab and minibus that drove by until a truck finally stopped. When the driver asked me where I wanted to go, all I could do was repeat Geoff McCoy's mysterious words: 'Pupukea. The Colonel's.' And add, 'Please.'

We spluttered through town and out the other side, up the hill, past the never-ending naval harbour full of huge grey destroyer ships and aircraft carriers and out into the pineapple plantations. The second half of this drive hasn't changed at all since those days. You come over a hill and you can suddenly see the entire North Shore stretching out below. Even from a distance of several kilometres, you can see waves breaking far out to sea.

We reached the town of Hale'iwa and carried on past a string of beaches, where I could see dots that were people far out the back but I couldn't scale the waves against them. In places, the narrow, single-lane road was crumbling into the sea. When we rounded a bend and arrived at Waimea Bay, the shore break was pounding onto the sand so hard I could hear it over the rattle of the truck's diesel engine. Then we were at Pupukea, which was little more than a parking lot with a couple of shops. I had no idea what to do next.

I got out of the truck and asked the first person I saw if he knew the Colonel. Of course he did. I got back in and, following the detailed directions, we wound our way up into the hills and along the side of a deep forest until we came to a sprawling little hamlet with rusted out cars in every front yard. I found what I guessed was the right house, knocked on the mesh door and a small and deeply tanned blonde lady in shorts and a singlet opened it.

'Hi, I'm Larry, Geoff sent me,' I coughed.

She said she'd never heard of me, but obviously I was a surfer from Australia and she asked me to come in anyway. This was BB Benson, Al 'the Colonel' Benson's wife, who that very day welcomed me into my new Hawaiian family with barely a question asked.

Ψ

One of the best things about being a surfer is finding yourself in remote, undeveloped but astonishingly beautiful corners of the world. You clock up a lot of kilometres, meet a broad selection of people and come into contact with a myriad different cultures. But there's something unique and special about the Hawaiian islands. Most people are familiar with the beauty, the waves and the landscape, but the real reason that the place is so enchanting is the welcome. There's a warmth here and a peaceful aura that's hard to explain. Luckily for us *haoles* it's been distilled into one simple word: aloha.

The Hawaiian 'aloha spirit' is about tranquillity and nature, a sense of one huge, connected family, history, peace, welcome and good wishes, all rolled into one. The only way to truly understand it is to get on a plane and jump right into it.

For that entire northern winter, I felt aloha in abundance, and nothing else. I was welcomed at beaches everywhere with open arms and a good floppy 'shaka' – the official thumb and forefinger waggle-salute of surfers across the islands. Even the big guys out the back were happy to have me paddling about and getting in their way, at least most of the time. From the moment I sank my feet into the honey-gold granules of sand, felt the clean sea breezes and gawped at the vibrantly coloured stage set, I was at peace.

This was my fresh start, and instinct told me that I ought to keep my head down. You didn't grow up where I did without learning how to detect trouble and cross to the other side of the street. On one occasion, under the rusty Coogee pier that was our childhood HQ, a couple of local heavies started hassling Mick, Terry and me. Tony White, one of the local hero surfers who had always tolerated us out in the sea, wandered past by chance and came to our rescue. He absolutely tore our assailants apart with his fists. I don't know if the intervention was in our defence, or whether he did it just because he could, but it was the first real fight (where somebody might die) that I'd ever been involved in and I'd decided then and there that I'd always avoid them.

Whenever I felt threatened in the surf on Oahu, I'd make a wide-eyed face and flick the hey-how-are-you-today switch that I'd inherited and used so often on the terrace at the Oshey. If that didn't work, I'd skulk off and ride the garbage waves out in the channel. Thanks to this strategy, I kept well away from trouble for the first time in many years, flying quietly under the radar in my new island hideaway. I don't think I got myself into a single argument or scrape all that winter.

Little Larry the schoolboy quickly became something of a favourite son. At beaches up and down the coast, I'd encounter various future Black Shorts and have cordial chats with them all the time. I was even nodded to at Velzyland if I was with the Colonel's son, Fielding, and this was quite something. That place, tucked away down past the cattle sheds and through the woods hidden behind Sunset Beach, was, and still is, the original locals-only surf spot. It's one of those places where, for no tangible reason, you just know in your bones you're not welcome. But for me there were nods, smiles, how-are-you's and grunts of recognition – sometimes my fellow surfers would even hoot at my rides. I felt that I'd found my new home, and I thought it would last forever.

Ψ

About 3500 kilometres north of Hawaii, the Aleutian Islands southwest of Alaska stretch in a long, freezing arc across the very top edge of the Pacific Ocean. Arctic storms sweep across this patch of ocean all winter; each one is a cataclysm of severe gale- to hurricane-force winds that whip the sea up into a confused, diabolical vision of chaos topped with a whiteout blizzard of spray. The fingers of spume streak across the mountains, and frothy waterfalls tumble down from the peaks of the angry breaking waves, filling the air with a pungent hail of iodine. The noise is unbearable to humans, and few ships can survive this hostile stretch of chilled ocean, which boils over all winter, every winter.

The maelstrom then pushes south, taking four or five days to reach Hawaii. During this time, some very strange things happen. The wind dies out in stages, and the clusters of huge wave peaks start to join together into longer, wider, taller, rolling hills of swell up to thirty metres high or more. If you've ever sailed through this you'll know it feels surprisingly peaceful, like a hike through alpine foothills on a summer's day. They call this sea state the 'ground swell'. Because there isn't much wind and these open ocean waves aren't breaking on top of your ship, the sea can feel calm despite the high speed at which the waves are moving.

The swells gather into groups of four, five, six or seven to form 'sets', which share the load of surface tension and gravity as they egg each other on southwards, supporting each other and concentrating their energy by the hour. The monstrous bumps of swell soon combine to make bigger and bigger waves with more and more water in them. The Pacific is very deep, and so there is nothing to stop the march of these giant walls of water until Hawaii's steep volcanic peaks rear up sharply from the seabed and the two colossi collide.

The particular angle of Oahu's North Shore – head-on to the primary swell direction, yet with its back to the prevailing trade winds – creates a winding-up effect, like a fast bowler giving the last flick of the wrist to a cricket ball before unleashing it. The slight holding back of energy till this moment creates a final, mighty concentration of power into the very tight space at the peak of the wave.

Either it's a glorious accident, or Neptune sat down with the best scientists in the heavens to design the conditions for the most terrifying and beautifully violent way for water to behave. This is why nothing can prepare you for your first time surfing the North Shore.

Thanks either to this conspiracy between the gods and nature, or just pure chance, one little stretch of Oahu's North Shore is home to a cluster of some of the world's best surf spots. There are so many world-class waves packed so tightly together here that they call it the 'Seven Mile Miracle', which it is. As beautiful as I found the sight of those waves, I was petrified every time I paddled out during my first few weeks in Hawaii. Leaving the safety of the sand and jumping into the rip was almost always an event.

Everyone knows the waves are big, and shockingly so. They're sometimes tower-block tall. The scale is so different that Hawaiians measure waves using their own special system in order not to run out of numbers. A ten-foot wave in Hawaii is a twenty-foot wave to a Californian.

But it is the thickness, and therefore the sheer volume of water moving inside the waves, that makes them so frightening. On top of that, the water advances on you at twice the speed of a normal wave. As a result, the ocean currents run at high speed out to sea in between each peak like angry river rapids.

The swells that arrive in the paradise of the North Shore are an echo of a terrible tempest that happened in a far removed hell many days ago. But the conditions on the beach are so beautiful that it's hard to imagine. The water itself doesn't travel from the Aleutians to Hawaii, only the oscillations of pure energy. Even a few oceanographers struggle with this, and ocean swells are the least understood of all nature's waves. Just how they join up to get so big has never been fully explained.

Every surfer who visits these islands must, at some point, put fear out of his or her mind and take that leap into the ocean. But when you paddle out through that wormhole for the first time, unsure how you'll get back to land, a new kind of awe strikes you and forever changes your relationship with the sea.

Ψ

The scene of my first North Shore 'experience' was the postcard-perfect, palm-dripping paradise of Sunset Beach. I was just a schoolkid who'd wagged class on a monumental scale, and I should have known I was out of my depth. The day after my arrival I paddled out first thing in the morning. At Sunset there is a wide, fast-running channel in between the main peak and Kammie's reef. This channel makes it very easy to get out past the waves, even on a big day. And that first day was bigger than anything I'd ever seen in my life.

I was transported by the rip all the way past the breaking waves to the outside, way too easily, as if on a drag lift. I wondered if this was why so many skiers die; it's easy for any foolish amateur to get to the top of the mountain. Getting back down safely is altogether different. When I arrived beyond the white, I was greeted by big wave legend Mark Warren, a hero to all of us Maroubra kids. Just like that – confirmation of my arrival in the adult world. I recognised him straight away but he didn't recognise me. Mark was polite and smiling, cheerily saying it was tiny today, which only added to my dread. Four times my height did not seem tiny to me.

I soon discovered that this wave is unpredictable, with sets coming from two different directions catching people off guard, and with a raw power that makes the ground shake. Sunset residents always know when a new winter swell arrives because the houses vibrate on their stilts. The first set that swung in caught me completely in the wrong position. Fifteen feet of water reared up where I wasn't expecting it and collapsed right on my head, driving me down for several seconds. I tumbled around in the foamy depths with no idea which way was up and which way down, or how deep I was.

Eventually I let myself float back up to the surface, hoping not to be hit by my board, but as I was about to gasp for the air my body so desperately craved, another wave crashed on top of me and I was driven down again. For a second time I was like an old jumper in a washing machine but I resurfaced in the end. I gasped and rasped, found my board, pulled it under me and paddled desperately for the shoulder of the wave as if my life depended on it.

When after some minutes I got control of my breathing and I realised that I had survived, the terror subsided and gave way to a strange kind of ecstasy. It bubbled up from somewhere deep inside and fizzed in my brain. I don't know if it was adrenalin draining away, the elation of survival, or just the pure energy of the ocean, but whatever it was, I was hooked.

At the end of this day, I knew that if I could take a beating at ten-foot Sunset then I could survive anything. I'd offer this as a first lesson for anybody dumb enough to want to surf big waves; take a few beatings early on, just so you know you can!

I'm still afraid of Sunset Beach. It might be that first memory, or maybe the shifty back-peakers that sweep in from the west whenever they feel like it and clean everybody up, whether they be floundering kook or skilful pro. That first day I realised that the ocean in Hawaii, while being the very same Pacific that I grew up on, was not really the same at all.

Ψ

There is one Hawaiian wave that sits at the top of big wave surfing folklore. The first and still the most important big wave spot. The colosseum of surfing, where the gladiators are armed with what's known as 'rhino chasers' (heavy, twelve-foot fibreglass surfboards) instead of spears.

Waimea Bay (meaning sacred water) is one of sport's most revered sites and home to the Eddie, the world's oldest and most prestigious big wave surfing contest. Named in honour of the legendary Hawaiian lifeguard and surfer Eddie Aikau, the Eddie isn't held if the waves are not consistently over twenty feet on the Hawaiian scale (about forty-foot faces). At the Eddie, there is no cheating by getting towed in by a buddy on a jet-ski. You have to paddle into your own wave, taking the horrifyingly late air-drop if you want to get it. When the contest is on, the amphitheatre-shaped beach park, the mountains behind and that spooky old church right on the end of the point create an unforgettable spectacle.

The Eddie is to a surfer as K2 is to a mountaineer – you've either climbed it and got the medal, or you haven't. Tragically, too many great surfers have been killed here, even my friend, legendary big wave pioneer Alec 'Ace Cool' Cooke, who was also one of the first tow-in surfers. May they rest in peace.

Waimea, rearing up far out to sea and advancing like an apartment block of black water, is a right-hand wave breaking over a flat reef forty-five feet deep. It requires a board the size of a small boat to attempt the paddle-in. Drowning is a real possibility here as waves that can top forty feet push hapless surfers down so deep that the next wave often arrives before they can come up for air.

If you make it out the back at Waimea when it is big enough for the wave to break, you only have one way back in: to ride the monster. Fast, powerful, seaward-running ocean currents prevent anyone simply paddling into shore almost anywhere on the North Shore when the swell is this big. You can literally be stuck out at sea here, on the other side of that wormhole, with only two awful options available to you: remain out there in the channel or enter the break-zone and take a beating.

At Waimea, time stops when you drop down the face, and the freefall and fade out onto the shoulder of the biggest wave of your life changes everything. I have huge admiration for the tow-in surfers at Jaws (at Maui) and to a lesser degree Nazaré (in Portugal), who risk their lives chasing down massive waves. But in my view, catching a big wave under your own power, without a helping hand from a jet-ski, is a different kind of scary.

I danced around the edges of Waimea for quite a while before finally getting a grip on my fear and taking it on. On that morning a lifetime ago, I hitched a lift down to the beach park and stood on the sandy berm in the corner for about half an hour, watching fourteen- to eighteen-foot (thirty-foot-high faces) sets roll in in groups of four or five. The shore break was typically deadly, six-foot slabs of water sucking up and slamming back down straight onto the dry sand at the water's edge. You have to get past this mini tsunami just to get into the sea, before you can even start to paddle out to the main attraction. It's an awe-inspiring sight in itself and if you time this first part of your entry wrong you'll get snapped.

The plan was to run down the slope, jump belly-first on my board and paddle like hell in between the dumping waves. As I was getting ready, a biggish one rolled in, exploded high up on the beach, and picked me up with it. I was thrown into the air, landing in the scrubby mangrove about twenty feet back from where I'd been. When the water ebbed away I could see my towel and other bits and pieces decorating the bushes all around me. Staggering about picking them up was good entertainment for the passers-by on the road above, but it wasn't a very encouraging start.

I eventually gathered myself, pushed the knotted ball of fear back down and tried again. I stroked, flapped and paddled for miles in the currents, for about an hour and a half, but I didn't get a single wave. I was on the wrong board for a start; the toothpick that I'd thought was too big turned out to be pathetically small. That first sortie may have been a failure, but I did get to gawp from close range at the size and power of the place, and remember that waves always look many times bigger when you're underneath them.

A local lifeguard named Dave had a few words of advice when I finally got out of the water. He'd spotted my distress and been about to paddle out and rescue me, and he didn't want a repeat.

'You need a gun, man,' he advised. 'Go see Barry.'

I needed one of Barry Kanaiaupuni's ten-foot rhino chasers if I ever wanted to come back to Waimea.

BK is a celebrated local shaper, and negotiating to become one of his clients takes months, so the next day Dave kindly offered up a temporary solution. He took me into the lifeguard shed that housed a towering row of glossy wave-riding weapons he and his crew used. He lent me one of his own, so big and heavily glassed that I could barely carry it. But it worked, and that afternoon I rode the biggest waves of my little life to date. And I survived. Dave was very, very generous, considering the stakes for both me and his expensive hand-shaped surfboard. It set the tone for us to become lifelong friends.

Ψ

For now, the Banzai Pipeline was still a phantom. I jammed the car into the side street at Ke Nui Road almost daily that first winter, and ran across the park to look at it just in case it came to life. It was usually an unruly mess with terrifying lumps sweeping sideways across the shore and breaking with an off-putting *crump* into a nasty heap. I didn't get it at all. After about six weeks I nearly gave up. Then one morning Fielding, the Colonel's son, came into my room when it was still dark.

I knew something was up because Fielding hated the mornings. Then he handed me a lighted spliff and announced that today was the day.

'Pipe' is not usually just about size, breaking very close to the tantalising safety of the shore on an inch-shallow lava reef full of cracks and crevasses, and bristling with spikes formed when the molten rock bubbled on contact with the sea thousands of years ago. Pipeline is about vertical drops, speed, power – and tubes.

There are a few reasons why those tubes are the world's best. For a barrel you need powerful waves breaking fast where the water changes depth suddenly. Usually, reefs are needed to do the trick, or very particularly shaped sandbanks. The sudden depth change causes the bottom part of the wave to slow down much faster than the top part can keep up with, and this imbalance causes the lip to throw forward, creating a liquid curtain. For the whole effect to happen in a useful way you also need an offshore wind to hold the face up long enough for the delayed collapse to take place, and to clean up the wave so that it can organise itself into rideable hollow shapes that peel in an even line rather than dumping all at once. Nowhere on earth has a better combination of this power, bottom shape and wind direction, than the Banzai Pipeline.

Here, you can reach a sticky end via a bang on the head as you hit the extremely shallow, sharp, uneven bottom, or get wedged into an underwater lava cave after the wave has forced you down. Pipeline has killed more people than all of the other surf spots in the world combined.

The verticality of the take-off, and the out-of-body feeling of a ride deep in the tube, encased in the stained-glass cylinder that will either spit you out, arms over head, or stuff you into the reef, are the rewards. Pipeline is comprised of three sets of reefs, and waves start breaking over these sets with successive increments in the swell size. As a result you can surf this wave at five feet or at twenty, but whatever the size, it's guaranteed to be beautiful and terrifying. Nobody ever forgets their first time at Pipeline.

On that day when my host dropped me off, the waves were breaking out at the second reef, with swell in the ten-to-twelve-foot range. Small potatoes according to the locals, but I was horrified. Sets of six were coming in from the direction of Kaena Point to the west, sliding across the reef, then suddenly doubling in size. Each wave would throw its liquid load outwards, forming cavernous barrels that boomed like a cannon as the top hit the bottom and squeezed out all the air in between.

You have to time your drop to perfection at Pipeline, and you can't take off from the shoulder. You either take off at the peak and get barrelled straight away, or you don't get the wave at all. You have to commit. In order to make it into the wave you have be in the perfect spot, not a foot out of place either side. And you must take off under the lip because it forms so fast there is no other place to paddle. In other words, there's nowhere on this wave where any sane person would want to take off.

That first session, I saw sets swing in from all over the place and didn't have a clue where to sit. I took a couple of beatings and certainly pulled back on several waves, to my embarrassment. But after a while I finally caught one, right from the slot. The drop is incredible, sending you fully airborne from the moment you start to get to your feet till you hit the bottom. The overhang makes any other position impossible.

So you have to 'knife' the tail of your board as soon as you can and get moving back up the face, under the lip and out across the wave.

I was covered up, hidden in the cavernous and frothy tube for the whole wave, lasting perhaps only four seconds, but it was the most glorious four seconds of my life.

When you come out of a tube at Pipe, there is a boom as a ball of steam is fired out with you, caused by the tube behind you closing up and expelling air and sea foam. It scours any exposed skin like a spray of shotgun pellets, but it means you have survived, and you can add your name to the list of Pipeline heroes.

If only the Coogee boys could have seen it!

Ψ

Fielding and I surfed every spot on the North Shore that winter. We encountered currents, freak waves, big fish and bumps on the spiky lava reef. On this strip of idyllic palm-fringed beaches, I lost count of the number of times I saw people get lost out to sea after dark, dragged in unconscious and loaded into ambulances, or worse, getting hurled onto the reef, knocking themselves out and drowning.

We ventured east and west whenever the winds changed. I was stunned by the beauty of the deserted east coast, where the corrugated volcanic mountains rise up in the hinterland. There's a golf course there where dodging angry players and their balls on the way into the sea is part of the fun, and an island past the ranches and far out to sea where you never see a soul. We also spent memorable days down on the West Side in places like Makaha and Klausmeyers, where it was gangsters not golfers who needed to be carefully circumnavigated.

Ψ

It had been the best holiday of my life, but it soon came to an end. One day after a session at Pipeline, I jumped off my board and jogged up the sandy slope to the top of the steep bank where my towel and stuff were wedged into a bush. A pleasant unknown Aussie tourist came up to me and said he recognised me, which I initially thought was flattering. He then added that I'd been on the news back home and that the police were after me.

I'd completed my Hawaiian apprenticeship, I'd survived my first winter swell season and I knew I'd be back, but it was over for now. The ocean was running out of energy. People who visit the North Shore in the summer months would not believe they were in a surf Mecca; the sea is all Caribbean blues, as flat as a pancake, only good for snorkelling.

It was time to go, but things were still complicated back home. So I thought I'd check in on Mum and Kellie in London. While we'd been apart, the extended family had been busy.

14.

The Kangaroo Girls on Tour

Mum's skills are put to use on the world stage.

My mother's friends could steal anything anywhere, but they were so effective that Sydney ran out of banks to rob. The Kangaroo Gang, which now boasted over a hundred members and associates, had also by now cleaned out every worthwhile jewellery store in town, in the process becoming far too well known. Faces had been seen, drawn and turned into identikit pictures, published in the *Sydney Morning Herald* and the *Telegraph*. The gang knew that if they kept doing business in Sydney – or virtually anywhere else in Australia – they'd soon end up in jail.

So they had to move overseas and find some new victims. Over the years, the boss of the gang had developed a sprawling network of associates across the globe who'd provide information about the richest targets and how to get into the safes, offices and cabinets where the high-value stones or money were kept. Eventually they would become a global supergroup, the world's top jewel thieves, robbing iconic stores and banks, including a $1 million heist at Asprey in London's ritzy Mayfair district.

In Hawaii I was afforded a tantalising glimpse of a very different sort of existence, an existence far away from the world of my mother and her entourage. But the holidays were over.

I flew to the UK via San Francisco, dropping in on an old surfing friend from home, Brian Cregan. He was based in a quirky little motel basement room with twin beds. I'd never been in a basement before so it was highly amusing for me, watching all the different legs going past the window. Brian didn't understand my obsession with the phenomenon of the basement flat. One night I awoke with a fright because my bed was violently shaking. I thought Brian might have been trying to get in with me but it was in fact a massive earthquake. Buildings were toppled and highways torn up right across California. I wondered if this was the beginning of my comeuppance for all those awful crimes. I never told Mum about the earthquake. She would have read something terrible into it, and I probably would have believed her.

Brian would go on to found the Ocean and Earth Surf Company and invent the stretchable polyethylene surf leash, which was a major development in our sport. Before the leash came along, pretty much every wipeout meant a long and dangerous swim to find your probably broken board somewhere along the shore or on the rocks. The number of surfboards (and heads) that this man has saved since 1979 is incalculable. He should definitely be on the podium with Simon Anderson (the thruster) and Jack O'Neill (the wetsuit).

Ψ

After the stopover in California, I flew on to London, where Kellie and Mum were waiting for me. Unfortunately, Dad's scary mate Fletcher was also there.

The trio were billeted in a rambling old townhouse that was four times taller than it was wide, connected together by a creaky old oak staircase that led up to infinity. It was totally stacked full of musty antique furniture, portraits of titled family members and ancient busts, statues and 'stuff'. All of these oddities and pieces of art had different types of dust clogging up creases, settling thickly on surfaces and hanging off edges in wispy tufts. The entire house was permeated with the smell of forest floor mushrooms, seemingly concentrated around the sofas.

Her Ladyship, our host, was an aged party animal who showed no signs of slowing down her drinking and general bacchanalia despite the obvious marks it had left on her face. She smoked approximately one thousand Benson and Hedges Blues each day, with the windows shut, leaving the butts balanced on surfaces and stuffed into corners everywhere, often still billowing out trains of blue smoke. She was beautiful and might not have actually been aged, now I come to think of it, more just worn out, presumably by the town – London, which was as cold and damp as they say, just like in the brochures. I hated the place.

Mum had stuck Kellie in a quirky little London primary school and it was my job to ferry her to and fro every day in the freezing Kensington fog. The poor kid had to wear her hair in a ponytail and a ridiculous tartan St Trinian's-style uniform, although perhaps she was actually at St Trinian's for all I knew. It certainly was an unusual institution, with a shopping list of incomprehensible rules. Kellie did not like me laughing at her Dickensian outfit, at all. But it was all I had to amuse myself and so I taunted her horribly to save my own sanity.

At fifteen years of age, semi-illiterate, with white-blond hair and a ridiculous suntan, I was a schoolgirl sensation (or maybe 'curiosity' is the better word). Everyone wanted to know me because I didn't look like anybody in England, and each week I'd receive crumpled little handwritten envelopes with scrawled love letters inside them, pressed into my palms by my bemused little sister. Of course, they were wasted on an under-developed Ostrogoth. I wanted to be home, jumping into the sea every day and mucking about at Gilesy's with Mick and Terry. This period in London was one of my unhappiest – the 'fish out of water' days – but at least I had Mum and Kell, and we were a great team, but who knows how long anything is going to last? I should have treasured that time when we were together.

As far as 'business' went, Mum was on a roll. After fleeing the law in Sydney she'd dusted herself off and was back to her old swashbuckling, superstitious, superhuman self.

The Kangaroos were all over London, and London was unprepared for what hit it. No department store, jeweller or bank was safe. Mum and her friends were plotting the same kind of organised thievery as before, only with bigger prizes that required more daring. The big difference was the jewellery shops in London were bristling with some of the rarest and most valuable rocks and silver in the world, and they were trying to keep up by installing high-tech (at the time) security. But Mum and the aunties were resourceful enough to keep finding innovative and wacky ways around it. They were on the brink of the big time, and they weren't going to let cameras, trip switches and sensors get in their way.

Fletcher hadn't given a reason for showing up out of the blue. It was weird and just a little bit threatening seeing him without Dad by his side. They'd been like two bull terriers, running around the wild and treacherous park that was Sydney, barking at people and biting anybody who barked back. I was never told about his role in sorting out our troubles following Dad's murder, and I didn't really want to know. I just knew he was absolutely not to be messed with. Back in Sydney, he had seemed protective, wanting to take responsibility for our safety. Mum was always appreciative, and I did suspect that he, like almost everyone, had designs on her, but what the hell was he doing all the way over here in London?

I soon found out. It turned out Fletcher wanted me to become more involved in the elaborate jewellery and clothing thefts, and so he gave me masterclasses on some of the basic techniques. Rolling up cashmere cardigans into a special tubular bag so that they didn't make a bump under a jumper was one of the staple skills, but he taught me many others. I wasn't really in a position to refuse these lessons, and my hopes that Mum might intervene quickly faded. So I paid attention, but had no intention of ever putting the skills into practice.

I didn't feel comfortable around Fletcher. I never had. His nervy examining of his fists, sometimes pausing to give them a nibble or a pick, always kept me on edge. Some people just aren't comfortable in their own minds, and the electricity jumps across to yours. The regular mentions of my dad – what Dad would've thought, how Dad would've done it, and how much Dad would've laughed – didn't make me feel any better.

I was still glowing from my experiences in Hawaii and trying to figure out the practicalities of how to spend my life surfing rather than helping out gangsters. I was resolute, but Fletcher's threatening presence quietly hung over me. I wondered if he'd taken it upon himself to ensure I carried on my father's legacy, or if Dad and he had discussed some sort of succession plan. God, was there some kind of unwritten will? Fletcher had always been our protector, but did his protection come at a price? Were we now in debt to him? And was I going to have to work off that debt by committing crimes?

The mood would always lighten when Aunty Sandy and the elegant ladies of the Tea Leaf Club hit town. These whirlwind arrivals were like Roman triumphs, complete with ceremonial banquets and much singing and dancing. Of course, their visits weren't just for fun; the girls were only there because of some forthcoming caper. There must have been quite a few of these because Mum's brown paper and string boxes were in constant use. By now she was deploying them in myriad different ways:

- Blocking: moving your box or boxes about to stop guards from seeing what the chaps are stealing.
- Dropping: creating a distraction by dropping the boxes on the floor.
- Filling: the boxes, with anything you can steal, via the special hatches.
- Bumping: turning around sharply and accidentally bumping someone you want to distract.

And so on.

I didn't think too deeply about what was going on; it was the usual routine, just in a different location. I knew I didn't want to steal for a living, but Mum's gang was family, and with me being so far from home, they were all I had. I certainly did not have the ocean to turn to. So I shuffled around at the edge of it all, narrowly avoiding getting dragged in, and being sure not to ask too many questions.

I was relieved when it was finally over.

Ψ

After six months or so in the UK, Mum announced that she and the crew were heading to Los Angeles. They were in the frame for a number of notorious London robberies, several in the opulent jewellery and fashion stores of Mayfair. Their exploits started attracting attention in the press – never good news for a thief. And so, true to form, just as things were getting uncomfortable again, they flew away to surprise the hapless police and general population of some other country.

There was an added bonus. A new hunting ground meant that Fletcher was distracted and, at least for the time being, his attention was off me and anything I might owe him. He was off and running, chasing the other dogs.

Mum would go on to pull off some outlandish crimes in America. On one occasion she was running from the police after a major bank robbery went wrong in Los Angeles. In those days banks had no glass screens and each teller had their own individual desk. The girls had done a good job of 'pulling heads' while Gilbert and his panther friend Jerome crawled across the floor, past the manager's office to one of the money stores. They successfully extracted a bag of cash and slithered quietly back into the hall. Each of the gang members then sauntered out of the bank calmly and slowly, one by one. Unfortunately, somebody spotted something and an alarm was sounded, which meant one thing; get into the car fast and disappear.

Mum, always diligent, was the last to leave, and so she never made it to the car and found herself stranded and alone on a busy Los Angeles street. She marched off and made it quite a distance away but police cars were still buzzing all around her. When one came screeching up behind her she jumped over a wall and hid in a garden. The home owner, an old lady, heard the commotion and opened the front door to see what was going on. The only thing for Mum to do was to stuff everything up her jumper and tearfully say that she was pregnant, and that she had fainted.

Half an hour later she was still in this kind lady's living room, having been revived with tea and cakes, chatting away while sirens blazed up and down the street outside.

The next day the *LA Times* ran a story about the brazen Australian 'bandits', even giving photofit descriptions of some of them, but by then Mum and her friends had skipped town with quite a bit of money. I'll bet they had many, many laughs while they were rampaging around America. I'm also sure that she would have driven everybody mad any time they went near a ladder, arranged a pair of scissors at the wrong angles or stole the wrong piece of jewellery.

Ψ

I'm glad I didn't go to Los Angeles with my mum. It has terrible surf, which can be more frustrating than no surf at all. The sea is also cold, green and cloudy. But I had to get out of the UK, which had been slowly suffocating me. I knew that trouble awaited me back in Australia, but I couldn't put it off forever; I made the decision to go home and, in all probability, face the police and be questioned about our dear neighbour John and his brilliant scheme. At least I might get some waves, before or after going to prison.

15.

Down and Out in Darwin

*Australia's back door, unfortunately, is just
as well guarded as all the other doors.*

That kind fellow Aussie on the beach back in Hawaii was right when he said the police were after me back home. I found out that while I was away, there had been numerous arrests, and unfortunately my name was still on the wanted list in connection with the dead man's dole scam.

I therefore decided to take a long and obscure route back to Australia, calculating that isolated Darwin in the Northern Territory might be the least risky point of entry. Surely they couldn't have every airport staked out, right?

Ψ

I had good reason to be apprehensive on the journey home. While I didn't know what the cops would do to me if and when I was arrested, I was petrified at the thought of going to prison. Australian jails may be terrible today but they were more dangerous in the 1970s. I had plenty of evidence of this, even if my parents and their friends tried to keep the darker areas of their lives hidden: no matter how hard grown-ups try, things always leak out. Stories of prison sieges, inmates being stabbed with all sorts of ingenious homemade implements, and all the other miseries and indignities that go on 'inside' had circulated around our family hearth for years. I knew that in prison every day was terrifying, the food was horrendous, bad things happened to your arse, and you could never run away from a fight. I'm also pretty sure there were no swimming pools and the only water sports were a quirkier kind. And you could forget about the sea.

I still have nightmares about landing at Darwin airport that dreadful day in 1974. After we disembarked the plane, I was stopped by two cops in clean-smelling, crisp black uniforms, right there in the arrivals tunnel. They read me my rights then as they promptly arrested me and escorted me onto another plane bound for Sydney. On the five-hour flight south, they took turns to explain in terrifying detail what was going to happen to me. Two years . . . four years . . . maybe *ten* years in Pentridge or Long Bay – all casually dropped into their chatter so that I'd think two of Australia's worst prisons, one where Ned Kelly himself was incarcerated, were my only options.

In my mind I blended what I knew about these horrible places with memories of a dark, dread-filled boarding school in Campbelltown. Teachers were replaced by wardens carrying truncheons not canes, while my fellow pupils all looked and smelled like Dad or, worse, his mates.

These polite yet strangely menacing policemen needn't have bothered with their Stasi softening-up routine; I was already paralysed with fear and totally failed to follow the gangster training I'd received. I confessed to all of it about half a minute after the questions began. It came out in a torrent of pleading (theatrical), tears and groans (both real). I must have cut a pathetic figure.

There were only a few morsels of information that I doggedly held on to. The cops were very keen to know where Mum was, but about that I didn't let on, telling them that I'd been travelling through Europe and had no idea where she was.

I didn't mention that some of those travels had been with Mum, who had taken a detour in between jobs to plot with some rather unsavoury people in Màlaga in southern Spain. I had a pretty good idea where she might be, but no amount of intimidation would have made me give up my best friend and protector. My story was partly true since I had been travelling in Europe. I'd tried to find waves in Spain on my way home, but the board I was dragging about with me never got used. This was mostly because I didn't have my licence and couldn't drive, but also because the Spanish train conductors didn't like surfers and were suspicious of our enormous planks wrapped in giant, filthy socks. Spain was in the middle of a Basque separatist bombing campaign at the time and I think this gave them an extra reason to dislike big packages. Given the number of world-class waves in that country, it's a miracle I never found them!

Mostly, though, the cops wanted to know about our flamboyant, beer-swilling, puppet-string-pulling neighbour, John. I'm proud to say I never dobbed the Big Fat Poof in, even though, and I know we were willing participants, he'd landed Mum and me in an enormous steaming pile of shit. She would not have approved of me snitching on her friend. John was family just as much as the aunties. In a way I should have thanked him; if it weren't for his dole scam, I might have got tangled up in something a lot more dangerous.

Yet again, Uncle Bertie came to the rescue. My kindly, slick-haired fixer of an uncle went and hired a lawyer to represent me. Thanks to his efforts, the police charged me and let me go after a few brief moments of terror and a little time in a cell to think things over. I headed home to the sanctuary of Melody Street, and I spent the next couple of weeks feverishly surfing as if each session were my last, convinced that my freedom was about to come to an end. Apart from this I barely dared to go out; if I wasn't in the sea I'd be home hiding, cooking up whole fish, Irish stews, cottage pies, chicken soups or moussaka in our little kitchenette. I didn't even contact any of my friends and only saw them out in the sea, and I followed Mum's advice about attracting good luck and avoiding curses.

When I did see my old pals I felt shifty, uncomfortable, furtive. My criminal charges were just another confirmation of the chasm between me and many of my mates, even the tough guys that were part of the crew. I'd taken a couple of detours before, but this one ensured our inexorable split was going to be permanent, whether we liked it or not. And I didn't like it; I craved an extraordinary life, but one shared with an ordinary family and ordinary friends. I just hadn't yet learned that these things didn't easily go together.

I think Fat Larry was the only one who I could be even half honest with. He knew when I couldn't spill the beans, and what to do about it if I did. When one such venting happened during the dole crisis and I spewed it out, tears and all, Fat got us on a train up the coast halfway to the border to let nature shield us.

We ended up in a lost forest where a hike to the end of a headland and a paddle across a river mouth led to a perfect right-hand sandbar wave that nobody ever rode, perhaps due to the local bull shark population. It worked. The energy of that lost part of Australia is special. From then on it became our way to get out whenever one of us felt encircled.

My court date duly arrived, and Bertie's lawyer said everything that had to be said for me while I cowered on a bench at the side of the echoey, wood-polish-smelling room. Bertie had instructed me not to say a word under any circumstances. His man would do all the talking. But I'd got so nervous waiting out in the school-like hallway that when I entered the courtroom, I lost control of my face. In spite of the strict instructions, I tried an idiotic quip when I gave my name and date of birth; one of those blurts that happen before you've had the chance to bite your tongue. I mumbled something about my reasons for getting involved with the awful scam and how they were just reasons not excuses but they were real reasons all the same. This is precisely why lawyers don't let their clients speak in court.

After some brief theatre, and a half-hearted, headmasterly admonition, the judge put me out of my misery. I was 'very lucky indeed' to have been young enough to be classified as a 'young, juvenile offender', and to have been helped by a decent lawyer. My confession on the plane from Darwin to Sydney had worked in my favour as well, proving once again my theory that cowardice is often the best policy. As it was my 'first offence', the time I'd already spent in police custody was deemed enough of a punishment and I wouldn't be locked up again. I was placed on a $10 weekly good behaviour bond and was told in no uncertain terms that the authorities would be keeping a close eye on me.

The two cops who had arrested me in Darwin were present in court, and were quite matey with me during proceedings and after the verdict, quipping in a jolly tone that I would 'never be a policeman now'. I don't know what caused their change of demeanour, although I think they may have been impressed that a fifteen-year-old would have four passports. I also don't know if my pedigree – son of Australia's highest-grossing armed robber – was a help (poor little kid, never had a chance, and such a lovely smile!) or a hindrance (once a wrong 'un, always a wrong 'un!).

So after a brief captivity and an hour or so in that courtroom, I was free. The episode signalled the end of my career as an apprentice criminal.

Despite helping me to avoid a prison sentence, Uncle Bertie still failed to get to first base with my mum when she eventually got back from her travels. Ever the gentleman, he kept his disappointment to himself.

I hope that he could nevertheless look at his work with some satisfaction. When I think back I can see that Bertie and Fletcher were living reminders of the hidden differences between the worlds of my two parents, and of why they should never have come together. Bertie wanted me to get away from the underworld and do something honest. Fletcher, the last remaining member of Baldy's dog pack, did not. Bertie wanted me to learn to cook, Fletcher wanted me to steal. Both had a thing for my mum. I thank the sea gods that, among all this confusion, I had surfing.

I never saw John again and I don't know what became of him. When Mum and I were reunited, we barely spoke about him or his crazy complicated scam. All that was left of John were piles of messy, brightly coloured paintings, propped up against walls all over our Melody Street home.

I've come to realise that getting arrested was one of the best things that ever happened to me. Nothing before had terrified me so much. A brief introduction to life behind bars and the chilling fear of being locked up for a long stretch gave me pause to reflect on where I wanted to go in my life and how I wanted to get there.

I had only two solid skills: one profitable, one not, and both dangerous and full of uncertainty. I'd never bothered much with school, mostly because I was hardly ever in the same one for long enough. I therefore didn't have any other options when it came to supporting myself or achieving something worthwhile. These last few months and weeks had given me total certainty that robbery was out and surfing was all that was left.

In the end the decision was easy. Hawaii, Pipeline and an attempt at sporting stardom were my goals, and getting back to those beautiful islands was my priority. As soon as I realised this I felt lighter, and ready for whatever might come next.

How to make it all happen, of course, was another thing entirely. But it turned out that the solution was pretty straightforward: assemble thousands more phone directories, buy a plane ticket, and get a whole lot better at surfing.

16.

In the Jungle with Gerry

Let's take a break from crime, punishment and death,
pack our bags and go on a boat trip to paradise.
You readers have earned it!

I've quit my job as a junior gangster before it even got going, and I've been officially forgiven, by a judge in a court no less. I will no longer be a dirty little crook, and I have my liberty. The only hangover from all the unfortunate events of the last year is the good behaviour bond that has to be made to the court every week. Apart from this I'm free to go forth and try not to fuck it all up again. Without a doubt I am a very lucky young man. All I have to do now is make better choices.

My new career has a much better training regime than my old one: the best way to improve your surfing is to go surfing. Well, it was in my day. On top of this, I'm being given the opportunity to go and do what I love in some of the most inspiring, beautiful and exotic places on our wondrous planet; all this because they think I can ride a wave in a nice way, and my idiotic hobby has started to become cool.

I'm even getting paid a little and my travel and equipment costs are being covered by some of the big manufacturers in the new and emerging surfing 'industry'. In this glorious era of the 1970s, clothing and wetsuit companies such as Billabong, Rip Curl and Quiksilver have arrived on the scene, and they have ambitions to turn this life that we all thought was just a laugh into an actual 'business'. This means that certain people can have 'jobs' in it. *A job, surfing?*

At the moment it's all a bit far-fetched, but many of these companies will soon be turning over billions of dollars and employing thousands of people across the world. They're dragging this niche pastime, that was once only practised by misfits and loafers like me and my schoolmates, up to become an aspirational lifestyle that doctors and lawyers can take part in.

There is also actual prize money on offer at some of the major surfing contests. And some of it is substantial. Two of my old school friends have already started to cross this threshold between pastime and career, proving that it's real. So why not me?

Ψ

When we were growing up, the kids at Coogee Primary and I had surf heroes, and those surf heroes themselves had one superhero who everyone looked up to: Gerry 'Mr Pipe' Lopez.

Gerry was Pipeline Master in 1972 and '73, but this wasn't what defined him. His posture in the wave, arms by his sides, low slung and almost leaning back, was iconic. The mayhem of turbulent spray deep in the pit isn't for the faint-hearted, and Gerry got himself deeper than anyone, but his sheer poise and minimalist movement made it look like ballet. There was a reason why he'd been in more movies, both surfing and Hollywood, than anyone else. Gerry is probably the most graceful wave rider we've ever had and certainly the most aesthetically pleasing to watch.

And so a typical schoolboy dream might go as follows:

Gerry Lopez: Larry, do you want to come with me to an unsurfed left-hand reef break in Java? Just you and me?

Me: Yes, how do you get there?

GL: Well, you take a wooden boat from Bali, and then there's a lot of thick jungle full of tigers . . .

Me: What's the wave like?

GL: They reckon it's the world's longest, fastest left-hander, breaking hard and fast with end-to-end barrels over a shallow, razor-sharp reef. Nobody ever surfs it, it's so remote. If you fall off you're basically done for.

Me: Okay!

And this is, more or less, what happened when I was a sixteen-year-old wannabe pro surfer.

At this moment in my life, my love for home had faded. Mum was overseas again, I had had my troubles, and the stuffy air needed to be changed. I wanted to be as far away as possible. But with the Hawaiian winter swell season many months off, I needed a plan. I therefore withdrew some savings and jumped on a plane to Indonesia.

This beautiful, vast, untamed, illogical, brilliant, chaotic, ungovernable country comprises some 18,000 islands (most uninhabited) and is home to the most perfectly shaped and hollow waves on the planet. The Indian Ocean swell season runs across the other half of the year compared to the Pacific, so this impossible mishmash of islands that calls itself a country was the obvious choice.

Kuta, one of the world's most hectic holiday hellholes, was a single dirt track village in those days. People today who look at photos of it cannot believe their eyes. Kuta Reef and Airports were the only waves anyone surfed on a regular basis; both of them were a stupidly long paddle off the coast, but both were epic, world-class waves in their own right. Uluwatu was just a crack in the cliff with one little thatched *warung* hut at the top where you could get noodle soup from one of the ladies for a few cents. It was all just part of the sprawling forests and farmlands owned by a local legend 'Rocky' and his family, who'd kept it untouched for generations. There was almost nobody out in the surf there, ever. I dare not go back there today as an entire town full of resorts has sprung up, and it would crush my heart.

You can usually see the Bukit Peninsula and its geometrically perfect line-ups from the plane as it comes in to land. When I arrived, Uluwatu had been semi-discovered but it still had a mythical quality to it. I biked down and wandered through the scrubby grasslands to the edge of the cliff. What greeted me was an unforgettable sight: the longest, most perfect wave I had ever seen, swinging in round the corner behind the temple-topped cliff and reeling perfectly for hundreds of metres. The whole thing was one long wall with a perfect cylindrical tube that stayed open from the start to the finish. Before you witness the wave at Uluwatu, you assume it's a lie. It isn't!

On that first trip, I biked down there regularly to surf it alone or with a few others, just us and the sea snakes. It was spooky because some of the best waves were on a higher tide when you had to climb down a bamboo ladder into an underwater cave and paddle out, emerging from a hole in the huge limestone cliffs and praying that the waves didn't stuff you back in. On a big day this was unnerving.

On one occasion, when I was out there alone paddling about in the current, trying to line up the take-off, I noticed a back-lit figure on the outside peak, flowing through every wave he took and racing along the golden, glowing walls in between lengthy disappearances in the tube. Even in silhouette, the unique, leaned-back pose and nonchalant style were instantly recognisable. It was Gerry.

I paddled up to my all-time hero and we were soon surfing one of the world's top waves together, just the two of us. Unimaginable given that today there would be hundreds of other surfers from dozens of countries sharing it with you.

Gerry was open, friendly, down to earth, and he was happy to share waves with a peasant. On top of this, he magnanimously taught me two things. The first was how to pin down the shifting take-off spot at Uluwatu, from where you could pull straight into the barrel. 'Just line it up where the grass meets that bit of cliff, Larry.'

The second was that you could take off on the wrong side of the peak and still make the wave, and that this would all but guarantee you the perfect tube ride if you had the guts and the speed. I want to thank him for this, right here; and I'm sorry that I haven't done it till now. That golden nugget helped me get more tubes in my life than any other piece of advice.

Me in 1978: a colourful 19 years behind me, ready to take on the world. (Photo: Bernie Baker)

My beautiful mum.

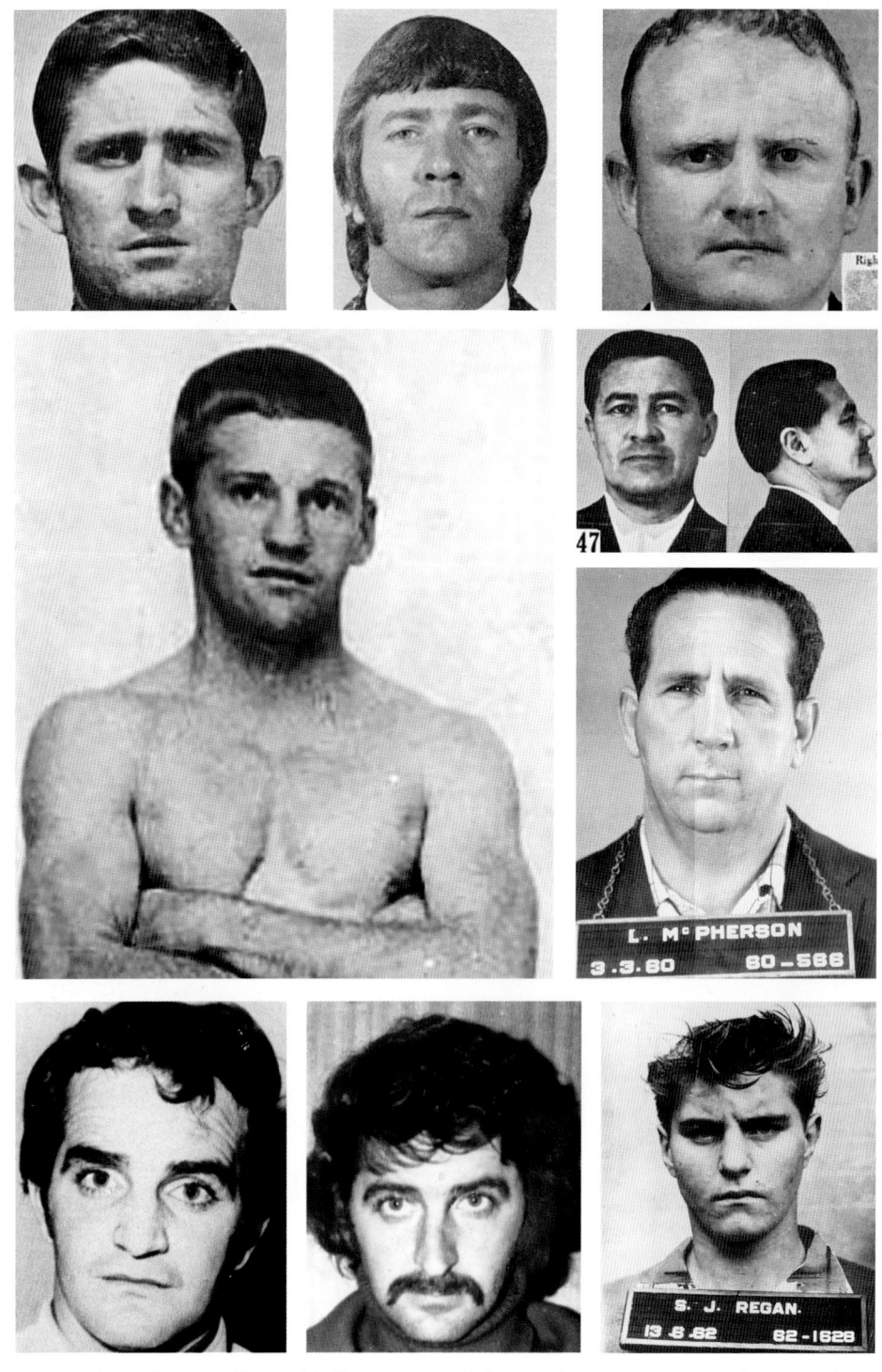

Some of my father's 'friends' (*by row, top left to right*): Kevin Gore, 'Jimmy the Pom' Driscoll, Billy Maloney, Stephen 'the Bomber' Nittes, Leslie 'the Professor' Woon, Lenny 'Mr Big' McPherson, Brian and Les Kane, and Johnny 'the Magician' Regan. None of those nicknames were earned doing nice things.

$587,000 raid: big C.I.B. hunt

WHERE IT HAPPENED: The parking lot at Guildford behind the Commonwealth Bank, and the van that was robbed

POLICE SEEK BRAINS BEHIND VAN HOLDUP

Detectives late last night raided underworld haunts in the city and the Western Suburbs in the search for the three armed men who yesterday grabbed $587,890 from a Mayne Nickless Ltd. security van.

(*Sydney Morning Herald*, 5 March 1970)

THE AGE

THE PAYROLL VAN

$½m haul sets a record

SYDNEY. — Squads of armed detectives last night raided Sydney underworld haunts in the search for three armed men who staged Australia's biggest hold-up yesterday afternoon.

(*The Age*, 5 March 1970)

ANOTHER VICTIM WHO WON'T TALK...
By DAVID RICHARDS

A 70-year-old crane driver was shot in the chest in full view of 100 people on the Melbourne docks last week. But nobody saw anything, including the victim.

Dock vendetta smoulders as police wait for contract killer

Linus Driscoll... reported to be on his way to Australia.

Of the Toe Cutters gang, 'Jimmy the Pom' Driscoll was the most prolific killer. (*Sydney Morning Herald*, 14 October 1979)

The Toecutter Gang

They maimed and they murdered

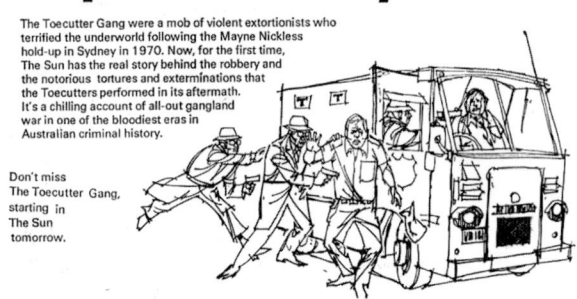

The Toecutter Gang were a mob of violent extortionists who terrified the underworld following the Mayne Nickless hold-up in Sydney in 1970. Now, for the first time, The Sun has the real story behind the robbery and the notorious tortures and exterminations that the Toecutters performed in its aftermath. It's a chilling account of all-out gangland war in one of the bloodiest eras in Australian criminal history.

Don't miss The Toecutter Gang, starting in The Sun tomorrow.

Get it straight from The Sun
You can believe in it.

I'm glad I never read the papers when I was 12! This one from the *Sydney Morning Herald* features a cartoon of my dad robbing a van, and the article goes into rather a lot of gory detail about his demise. (*The Sun-Herald*, 6 February 1977)

'Bandit was killed for share of $587,890'

SYDNEY. — A bandit involved in the $587,890 Mayne Nickless robbery was murdered for his share of the money, it was alleged in Central Court yesterday.

(*The Age*, 11 November 1970)

My mother's jewel thefts made their way into the press all over the world – even our boxes and string got a mention.
(*Calgary Herald*, 20 October 1980)

ABOVE: The Golconda d'Or, Australia's biggest diamond.
BELOW: Detective Sergeant Ted Turner with the fake diamond.

Stolen Golconda d'Or diamond (AP Wirephoto)

Dexterous thieves snatch famous gem

SYDNEY, Australia (AP) — A diamond that drifted over three centuries through the hands of Indian rulers, Persian bandits and Turkish royalty vanished again this weekend when thieves snatched the million-dollar gem from an Australian show.

The theft at the St. John Ambulance Brigade Exhibition of Treasured Possessions lasted less than three minutes, police detectives said. The thieves displayed such dexterity that visitors watching the act were unaware they had witnessed the biggest single jewel theft in Australia's history, they said.

Police said two men and a women snatched the Golconda d'Or, Australia's largest diamond, from a locked display case Saturday and replaced it with a worthless replica before a crowd of about 80 people. One woman told investigators she asked the thieves why they were opening the case and they replied they were repairing the lock.

An armed security guard standing about nine metres from the diamond's display case during the theft, also was unaware of the heist, detectives said.

The theft was uncovered soon after when a woman onlooker noticed the glass replica had fallen over and notified the security guard.

The diamond belongs to a Sydney jewelry firm, Angus and Coote.

The Golconda d'Or weighs 95.4 carats. It is 2.5 centimetres and about 1.3 centimetres deep, with an emerald cut.

The pale gold gem is one of the largest diamonds in the world. It was one of the last precious stones taken from the Golconda mine in India during the 17th century.

Angus and Coote took possession of the Golconda d'Or three years ago as part of their takeover of a Melbourne jewelry firm, Dunkley's Ltd.

They did not say how the diamond reached Australia.

Daring gang nets Australia's biggest diamond

(*The Age*, 20 October 1980)

Diamond gang relied on audacity of theft

The piece of glass used to substitute for the diamond

(*Sydney Morning Herald*, 20 October 1980)

My first-ever magazine cover – how brilliant that it features me, not at the Banzai Pipeline but inside the very stormwater pipe at North Steyne in Manly where they held the 1978 Surfabout finals. The legendary Peter Crawford did the visual pun artwork for this one.

The Surfabout really was a mobile contest format. This particular year, the waves were crap along the whole east coast, so the organisers put us in planes and flew us down to Victoria. Here I am getting beaten at backgammon by Cheyne Horan, who also beat me in the final! (Photo: the late, great Peter Crawford)

Meeting the Lord Mayor of Sydney, Leo Port, for a photo op. I'm not sure who is more out of place, Larry Bertlemann or me. (Photo: Norman Moore)

That 1978 Surfabout was my first real competition, and when Mum and I pulled up for the final we were greeted by the biggest crowd I'd ever seen. (Photo: Tony Nolan)

Shane Stedman handing out the prize for the '78 Surfabout. He shaped my first real surfboard, the Red Rocket that Dad gave me when I was a kid. (Photo: Peter Crawford)

One of the first depictions of surfing, c. 1778.

One of my more garish boards. The volume of water in these waves at Pipeline used to paralyse me with awe. I got used to it for a while, but these days I'm even more scared! (Photo: Peter Crawford)

The inimitable Mr Gerry Lopez, at home at Pipeline. (Photo: Jeff Divine)

I can't believe I actually hustled the great Rory Russell for a wave in the 1978 Pipeline Masters final. No wonder I lost popularity so fast in Hawaii. (Photo: Bernie Baker)

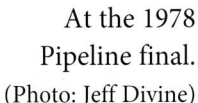

At the 1978 Pipeline final. (Photo: Jeff Divine)

The 1978 finalists: Hans Hedemann, me, Joey Buran, Dane Kealoha, Rory Russell and Gerry Lopez. (Photo: Ralph Cipolla)

The 1979 Pipeline Masters champion is announced. The six finalists (*left to right*): Dane Kealoha, Rory Russell, Tom Carroll, Me, Mark Richards, Shaun Tomson. Today, I can see some dejected faces there. On a positive note, I'm really glad I never caught on to the moustache fad. (Photo: Jeff Divine)

The 1979 Pipeline Masters trophy. Such was the atmosphere that year that I wasn't allowed to keep a copy of the trophy – they had grown tired of this cocky little Aussie hooligan! (Photo: Jeff Divine)

Me giving an embarrassing interview after Pipe '79, and dropping myself in it. (Photo: Simon Chipper)

Mark Richards, Tommy Carroll and me. The other two would go on to win six world titles between them, whereas I just quit! (Photo: Jeff Divine)

Me in my favourite position when Pipeline's in a good mood. (Photo: Jeff Divine)

Oh dear – clothing sponsorships in the late '70s and '80s. There are a lot of these incriminating photographs about, and they will haunt every pro surfer of my era for the rest of our days! Bronzed Aussies or not, we all made fools of ourselves in the early days of pro surfing. This one – with Michael Ho, Mike Benavidez and Chris Barela when we were in the Offshore surf team – possibly tops the lot.

Ah, life as a Maroubra lifeguard! (Photo: Tony Nolan)

Kevin 'Davo' Davidson, Steve 'Blackie' Wilson and me. I would have loved Fat Larry to be in this photo.

At the Pipeline past winners' banquet with (*left to right*) Jamie O'Brien, who took Pipeline surfing further than any of us imagined possible; Tom Carroll; Shaun Tomson; and my co-author, Jezza.

I am lucky to have met my wife, Nyoman, in that Canggu café years ago, and our wedding day was one of the great days of my life.

I love Indonesia for many things: the people (especially Nyoman), the surf and of course the fishing. (Photo: Jeremy Goring)

Gerry was very hospitable, inviting me to his rented apartment, where I experienced air conditioning for the first time in my life. And then one day we basically had a conversation like the one above. I was to go on an exotic and dangerous surfing adventure with the great Gerry Lopez.

Grajagan, in a deep jungle in the east of Java, is one of the best waves on the planet and a sacred spot for surfers everywhere. It is a snarling left-breaker over a table of shallow, pointy lava reef with tubes from start to finish. It's better known as 'G-Land', after Gerry himself, who discovered it all those years ago. I'd like to think I helped a little bit!

We travelled there by boat from Bali and surfed it alone for a few days accompanied only by whales and manta rays, and the backdrop of teeming, shrieking jungle. I don't know if the tigers are still there but they used to leave their tracks on the beach to add a little bit of spice to your surf trip.

In G-Land, through this great man, I came to understand something far deeper about the waves, the sea, surfing, and what it was that continually brought us back. Gerry had an inner calm and a spirit that I'd never been close to before, as well as the effortless ability to exude it while riding the violent tubing sections of a wave. The speed and elegance with which he traversed the huge and fast moving walls of glass made it look as if time had slowed down. I think this was more than an act – Gerry's style, a style revered all over the surfing world – was simply an extension of the man himself.

On that Indonesian voyage I visited more untouched dream islands than I'm able to hold on to in my memory, usually on one of the lurching, inter-island ferries. Every other week one of these hulks would sink, taking all passengers with it. To add to the uncertainty, these boats rarely showed up on time, sometimes departing a whole day or two late. The transport around Indo in those days was high adventure in itself, guaranteed to provide unforgettable drama.

The planes weren't any better. One of the few airlines, Merpati, was nicknamed 'If You Get There' by locals, something I learned when sitting in a Lombok airport lounge next to a smiling, white-collared priest, who told me joyfully about the frequent crashes. When we boarded that plane with its streaks of rust trailing from every joint and bare electrical wires hanging out of the lockers, I thought my travel partner Jezza was going to die of fear right there.

Some of the world's greatest waves can be found off these jungle islands, and I got to surf them with a selection of some of the best surfers of the time. Desert Point, on Lombok, a truly terrifying left-hand tube that never ends, was not even heard of in 1973. Nor Shipwrecks, Scar Reef, and certainly not Grajagan. These places are now household names in the surfing world.

The huge, spectacular fish that we caught – and the sushi, sashimi, maki, roasts, stews, papillotes, curries, wood grills, ceviche, carpaccio, meunière and salt bakes we created – were each an adventure in their own right. Every beautiful creature that we hooked and cooked was another reminder of the glorious majesty of Indonesia's natural world.

In these early days of surf travel, the various tribulations and hardships that went with it filtered out most normal people and drew a curious mix of hippies, wasters, misfits and escapees from life. These weirdos would combine with surf-mag poster stars to create an unlikely and fascinating travelling society. You could bump into the same people in different places, sharing unforgettable moments, some of them life-or-death, without ever knowing if you'd see each other again. Everybody was from everywhere and nobody was from anywhere; all so different, yet all lured by the same intangible thing. You all knew you were sharing something important but you didn't know exactly what it was. Most of all, out here, you were equals.

As for me, I felt like I'd connected with a new part of the family, a far-flung chapter of the Colonel's Hawaiian clan. Drifting around this glittering water-world with this eccentric crew reassured me that leaving the family business and taking up an insecure career like wave-riding was worth the risk. I finally understood that the world beyond the streets, piers and beaches of Sydney's Eastern Suburbs was a magnificent place and, with determination and a little luck, maybe I could have a passport to it.

I don't know if I ever had a coming-of-age period. It could have been when Mum first taught me about the underworld. Or when Baldy turned our lives upside down. But if I could choose one, a moment or an interval that represented a turning point in my life, then travelling the islands of Indonesia aged sixteen would be it.

Ψ

That passport I wanted came within my reach when the world of movie-making collided with our sport. Yet again, my timing was spot-on: the surf move was becoming a thing, and great directors and filmmakers like Jack McCoy and Albie Falzon were making movies that would define the genre. This meant I was invited on all-expenses-paid trips to the very frontiers of world surfing, with pioneer surfers who were already way above my station. I don't think any of us ever returned from these excursions rich, but we didn't starve and we didn't need to take any holiday snaps to show our future kids. Watch me and cringe in any number of these films if you like – they were big news at the time and very helpful to my batting average on the beach, but in retrospect they were pure cheese.

Of course there was a darker side to our postcard sport. Surfing has always been touched by anarchy. There are few rules and in the early days it evolved with no particular plan. With all the travel came a heroin and hash trade that simmered beneath the surface, especially in Indonesia. I knew plenty of people who were digging holes in their boards and filling them with products that reminded me unpleasantly of my father's early career, but thanks to my previous experiences I was more than happy to stick to the straight and narrow.

Every so often, a mate or another competitor would fall victim. My fellow goofy-footer, the stupidly handsome, larger-than-life American Rick Rasmussen, was a regular fixture out at Pipe, where he charged. Rick didn't seem to care about limits, and in our heyday I saw him get deep into enormous barrels – the type that can have consequences. We probably copied each other a bit there, and we certainly egged each other on. Everybody loved him, including me. I'd bump into him in Bali and across Indonesia and he was great company in those remote places where there's not much to do at night.

Rick's recklessness extended into civilian life, and he got arrested on a major charge in Bali (where the prison was a death sentence) but narrowly got off, only to get into trouble back in his home town of New York over a fairly big heroin deal. Shortly after, in 1982, he was dead, shot by dealers in Harlem. The news brought back terrible memories – and not just for me; I had plenty of friends who were sailing close to the wind and Rick's death sent shivers down their spines too.

Regardless of the ups and downs of itinerant life, the new, exciting, globe-trotting rhythm of my mid-to-late teens and the abundance of sunshine and seawater quickly healed my boyhood wounds. I still thought about my father and his murderers, especially Billy Maloney, but with less frequency. I was mending, thanks to this life on the ocean.

Ψ

Us, the old farts, tend to reminisce ruefully about the 'golden days' of surfing. In the late 1970s, most of the top waves around the world were as yet unsurfed. If they had been discovered, they were jealously guarded secrets. But it wasn't all romance and endless fun in the sun. The equipment was truly crap; rigid, heavy, strait-jacket wetsuits and huge, straight, stiff, heavy yet skittish logs were the best you got, and the travel was, of course, not always a pleasure. Yet this was a small price to pay. We were surfing in the best era the sport has ever known.

Today, my fading generation loves to moan about all the changes in the sport, especially the crowds. But the bottom line is anybody anywhere who has ever surfed is among the luckiest people who ever lived. We ought to all just shut up, take a seat and say thank you, Neptune, because that intangible thing that drew us all in when we were young is still the same today. It's nothing less than the healing power of the sea.

17.

The Last Queen of Hawaii

Hawaii is separated from mainland USA by over 3000 kilometres of ocean. For many islanders, it's still too close.

The 'Sandwich Islands', as they were known in the 1700s, were successively settled by Polynesians around 400–500 AD. They employed spectacularly advanced navigation and seafaring know-how to get there, and not a little bravery. The eight major islands and dozens of atolls were independently ruled by chieftains for centuries until King Kamehameha gradually brought the whole lot under one rule in the years that bridged the end of the eighteenth century and the start of the nineteenth.

Soon afterwards, Protestant and Calvinist missionaries started arriving, aiming to 'civilise' the locals. They were accompanied by troops of mainlanders – farmers, speculators, land grabbers – each with their own aims and agendas. It signalled the beginning of the end of the traditional Hawaiian way of life.

Queen Lili'uokalani was the last ruler. In 1893 she was overthrown and imprisoned by a pro-American consortium of landowners and vested interests, backed up by the looming presence of the US navy. A few years later the kingdom of Hawaii was annexed by the US. During the next century, the Hawaiian people's lands would be appropriated, the Hawaiian language and religions slowly suffocated, and 1500 years of history unpicked. There was even a period during which surfing, the traditional sport of the Hawaiian royal family, was banned.

These are some of the things I wish I'd known when I first arrived in Hawaii.

18.

Undercurrent

A stiff shaka. That's how you tell a haole *from a moke. Haoles* make the effort to shape the thumb and little finger just right. But the whole thing is too straight, too erect. If you want to look like a local, you barely bother to lift the hand and you keep your wrist nice and limp – like you don't really mean it.*

After the thievery, fighting, fear and murder of my young life, whether I knew it or not, what I now craved was a pleasant, uneventful decade. If it were me, sitting back in a comfortable chair reading any other biography, I'd want the same. I'd be longing for golden moments among rustling palm trees, sparkling tropical seas making the subject squint, gentle ocean breezes on the skin, lovers sinking their toes into the sand . . .

That interlude is going to have to wait.

When I landed in Hawaii for the second time, Oahu's North Shore was gearing up for a war. The colours of the place were different from home – glittering blues and layered greens replacing the reds, greys and browns of urban Australia – but in some ways the inhabitants were no different.

After the Americans annexed the islands in the 1890s there had been steady encroachment by farmers, missionaries, real estate investors and anybody who saw an opportunity. A lot of people had come and taken from the former kingdom, radically changing the landscape. Anybody landing in Honolulu today can see the impact for themselves. I suppose it's just the way of the world.

But hop in a jeep and take a forty-five-minute drive north on the H2 past Pearl Harbor and the Hale'iwa turn-off to the North Shore, and you'll see something very different. High-rise buildings are noticeably absent, with the old wood or fibro shacks still being the norm in some areas (even if these are being gradually phased out in the face of fierce but crumbling resistance). There are very few restaurants, bars, night spots or supermarkets, only one resort, and virtually nothing outside the drowsy if touristy settlement of Hale'iwa.

But there is the ocean. And in the mid-1970s the North Shore and its terrifying waves were one of the last things on Oahu that a Hawaiian could still call their own. A last local enclave with the violence of the sea acting as its bastion.

Surfing was booming and was on the point of an unstoppable explosion. Air travel was becoming more accessible than ever before and people were on the move. Honolulu and the south coast beaches had already become a tourist phenomenon, driving a bustling economy and creating a reputation for Hawaiian holidays complete with le'is and Blue Hawaii cocktails.

Many surfers came and went, but they rode only the slowly peeling, textured glass bumps of aquamarine on the south side. The vertically mushrooming settlement of Waikiki, with benevolent waves named Ala Moana, Queen's and Canoes, was the centre of gravity. The North Shore, also called 'Country' to the south's 'Town', was terra incognita for most foreigners. Those who dared take the bumpy ride up the highway and through the pineapple plantations usually turned straight back in horror, or got pounded, humiliated, and sometimes drowned.

But when I landed in 1973, the new generation of Australian and South African surfers, headed up by Peter 'PT' Townend, Ian 'Kanga' Cairns, Shaun Tomson, Mark Richards and Wayne 'Rabbit' Bartholomew, were already stirring things up with their new-school performances. They were young and brash and, like all foreigners, not fully aware of the long, proud and sometimes painful history of the kingdom.

These *haoles* were incredible athletes doing things that had never been done on a big wall of water, and they wanted to test themselves in the ultimate arenas of Pipeline, Waimea and Sunset. They were breaking new ground. Their radical manoeuvres almost seemed to disrespect the huge waves, slashing, smashing and shredding the monstrous faces, throwing spray everywhere as if to spit at the spirits of the ancestors – or even the descendants themselves.

Until about 1974, the three or four big local surf contests held at these iconic spots were mostly off limits to foreigners. To be fair, there weren't many of us who would have wanted to take them on anyway. The world championship tour didn't yet exist, and so these contests were the undisputed pinnacle of the sport. Understandably, they became an obsession for the top riders of the time.

With the arrival of the new generation, suddenly the foreigners were starting to tear it apart very conspicuously. It was becoming obvious that their talent couldn't be ignored for much longer. Eventually, they had to be allowed to compete, and when it finally happened, they made up for lost time, going absolutely ballistic.

In the 1975 season all four big North Shore contests were won by foreigners. Not a single Hawaiian took home a trophy. It was a seismic moment, unhelpfully described by one sports writer as a 'coup d'état'. The first contest of the season, at Waimea, saw a foreigner 1-2-3, with Mark coming out on top. Kanga won the next one, also at Waimea (it nearly drowned him; the conditions were horrific, and the wipeouts were awful and chilling to watch), Shaun took out Pipeline and Mark won yet again at Sunset.

It was an incredible achievement. The way in which Kanga and Mark smashed those huge waves, doing beach-break 'hot-dog' moves on twenty-foot monsters, helped to change the sport forever. Every surfing magazine cover for months featured one or other of these prodigies. A single winter season in Hawaii flipped the perception of surfing as much as anything else that had ever happened. It certainly shifted the axis of global wave riding towards the southern hemisphere.

The newcomers' 'smash and thrash' style in the water was echoed by what came out of their mouths on land. They were as outspoken and confident as me, but I wasn't famous. Their way of speaking would have been perfectly respectful back home, but such antics did not sit well with island ways.

We were all tarred with the same brush, and it didn't help that some of my Aussie role models started to hang out in a posse, spending all day at either Pipeline or Rocky Point, dominating the surf. It wasn't just the antipodeans however; there was a *haole* bombardment taking place up and down the coast.

One group that inadvertently became emblematic of the invasion was a sort of marketing initiative led by my fellow Aussies Kanga and PT. PT was the first-ever world champion and an enduring legend while Kanga was tearing it up in the biggest waves at the time. These two men were on fire.

It's easy, with the benefit of decades of hindsight and accumulated wisdom, to understand what went wrong. First, we were bronzed Aussies. But more awkwardly still, the squad started calling themselves 'the Bronzed Aussies'.

Most people who lived through the 1970s can find a few things they'd like to erase, whether it be the flares, the music or the way we spoke to girls, and for me, this little club that I tried so desperately to join (I probably begged) was one of them. The Bronzed Aussies, pasted all over the surfing press in centre spreads wearing high fashion, were marked men. The group was founded on a heady combination of Aussie exceptionalism, media megaphoning and shiny clothes.

And my god did we all like shiny shorts! Even though I wasn't allowed in this club, I literally followed suit with my dress sense (and mouth). Of course, the last place in the world where such a look-at-me attitude could be tolerated was Hawaii.

PT is a humorous, kind, engaging and self-effacing human being. Kanga is a funny, brave, straight-up good bloke. They are two of life's givers, and they were deliberately lampooning themselves. Most readers outside Hawaii would have found their antics very amusing indeed. But in those days our hosts didn't always get our jokes.

Taking into account a couple of hundred years of history, the earth tremors in our sport, and the personalities involved on both sides, the scene was set.

19.

Fast Eddie's Kingdom

*I'm amazed none of us was murdered during the
1976 and '77 Hawaiian winter seasons.*

When major changes happen in a small, tight-knit community, they do not go unnoticed. And the waves of change that were washing over Oahu were being carefully observed on each of the island's four coasts. In the south, it was obvious that so much water couldn't be pushed back where it had come from, and besides, the influx of people here was turning into money, fuelling the economy of the entire state. The rugged and windswept east had no recognised surf at the time and was left mostly alone. The 'West Side' had enough very big men to scare off anybody sane, and not enough consistently good waves anyway.

The North Shore, however, had by now cemented its position as the world's top collection of perfect, powerful waves. The small population who lived on this disconnected rural coastline had at its heart a set of characters for whom surfing was their life. They'd been baptised in its monstrous waves and murderous currents, and they'd had the place to themselves for generations.

The people of the North Shore had many reasons to be unhappy about the newcomers, and now they had a leader. Fast Eddie was a good local surfer and entrepreneur who was respected and sometimes feared both in and out of the water. I think I can say that he was a well-known tough guy, whatever this may mean. With a few friends from the surfing community, he formed a small club, Hui O He'e Nalu (Wave-sliders club), or Da Hui for short. Much has been written, said and filmed about these gentlemen and their brotherhood. Those accounts contain some truth, and perhaps just as much mythology.

Their stated aim was to take back some control of what was happening in their piece of ocean. They would police the North Shore and its iconic Banzai Pipeline, and manage the behaviour of the rising tide of disrespectful visitors. Whether it was intended or not, intimidation would be one of the tools.

Most of this group were quite big men. You'd see them at major surf spots up and down the coast, either sitting in a group or pulling up in their cars, assembling and then paddling out together. I figured that they were kind of a gang from the fact that they all wore the same black shorts at times, and it wasn't long before they became known as the Black Shorts, of course. I thank Neptune that I was never named after any of the ludicrous, sparkly garments that I was squeezing my horribly abused private parts into at that time.

In the 1970s, surfing was still practised in a small world, with so few recognised spots across the globe that you'd regularly bump into the same people wherever you went. And so I'd already met Fast Eddie, surfing the rangy, endless right-handers far offshore at Nusa Dua on the southeast coast of Bali, where the visiting Hawaiians were always charming and polite to everybody. He and I had even enjoyed a few laughs over a stolen camera he wanted to retrieve. (Eddie, of course, did retrieve that camera and I pitied the kid who'd half-inched it!)

I'd also seen him out at my local North Shore spot, Rocky Point, during those first couple of winters. We'd exchanged the pleasantries that come with the vague, disoriented recognition of one person by another that happens when the times and places are far apart. Fast Eddie can be very charming and I saw him as just another local ripper. As a lone teenage school truant I hadn't yet become an annoyance or a threat and I presume that this is why he tolerated me. I also hadn't entered any competitions, let alone won them. And so my first winters on the North Shore were pretty trouble-free, with no terrifying events, apart from what happened among the waves themselves.

But friends and acquaintances soon started receiving beatings, out in the surf and on the beach. Proper, frightening beatings. Some of the fights involved a big group of attackers just wading in with flames in their eyes and picking a target.

Soon enough, it felt like all of us foreigners were fair game. It didn't matter who, and some of the ugliest situations erupted quite unexpectedly. It was even happening between surfers who had thought they were friends, having previously played nicely together in other seas around the world. I was awaiting my turn without necessarily knowing I was in the queue.

In the meantime, the new superstars continued to generate ever more piles of press. Everybody in the media now wanted a piece of them. They were having a moment of unprecedented success, becoming the first-ever media stars in what had been a fringe sport up till now. A *Surfer* magazine piece featuring some controversial quotes received a lot of focus. The article was called 'Bustin' down the Door' and was all about the fresh breed of Aussie and South African surfers taking the world by storm. This was the era of sports superstars like Cassius Clay, whose MO was basically to psych out his opponent by saying how invincible he was. Perfectly acceptable in the US, and positively encouraged in Australia. How were any of us to know that this was not the way they did things in Hawaii?

In hindsight, a lot of it was taken out of context, bouncing about in the echo chambers inhabited by our hosts. If you read most of that surf-mag stuff in isolation, it's difficult to see why you'd take offence; it certainly included plenty of praise for Hawaii and its surf stars. Before some of the stuff was even printed, some kind of vibe filtered through to the islands. And some of the stories, probably read and discussed during the off season when the North Shore was flat and deserted, were like a match tossed into a box of mouldy fireworks.

It's lucky I was practically illiterate when I was young and was never asked to write for a magazine!

While we'd all been back home in *haole* land, people in Hawaii had been simmering, and waiting for us to return. When you added to this background the heat created by the hordes in the water, the trophies in the wrong hands and a century or so of troubled history, it had to blow up.

Our hosts now had a spearhead in the form of the Black Shorts and, for whatever reason, whether it had to do with any magazine articles or not, they seemed to be pointing it at Rabbit. When he landed that winter season, he went out for a fun little flap around at Sunset Beach on his own. Within minutes, the water was quietly cleared of all other surfers, and Rabbit found himself isolated and surrounded by a posse of these black-shorted surfers. He was bashed about the head, held under water, badly wounded and finally knocked unconscious. He came to and somehow made it back to the beach minus his board, which had washed up on the sand and now had a sizeable crowd of big lads waiting for him around it. Rabbit limped off home across the sand. When he reached his accommodation, his host sheepishly told him that they had threatened to burn down the place if any Rabbit was found inside, and reluctantly evicted him.

He hid in a makeshift bush shelter, camping among the scrubby little trees behind the beach for a while, unable to eat any solid food because his front teeth were hanging by threads. A friend eventually found him a more civilised lair at the big resort up the road, the old Kui Lima, where he continued to lie low in fear for his life. It must have seemed like the entire island was out to get him, his mate, and pretty much any other Aussie.

Kanga was also high on the hit list. He'd arrived in Hawaii shortly after Rabbit and had, as the legend goes, promptly been informed that there was a contract out on his life. The pair were now in the same leaky boat. They were under siege in the Kui Lima and it really did seem like somebody might get killed.

One of the most respected families in the islands stepped in at this point, and their desire for a peaceful resolution might well have saved Rabbit's life. Solomon Aikau sent one of his three sons, Eddie, across to the Kui Lima to talk to the two Aussies. His job was to mediate the stand-off. Eddie organised a sort of mock trial for the foreigners at which he called on the mob not to murder the 'offensive Australians'. (Rabbit is one of the loveliest men in surfing, and a living legend. He's certainly not 'offensive'. Nor is Kanga, for that matter. OK, let's just say 'direct'.)

At the 'trial', attended by the attackers and a big crowd of other locals, it was decided that the pair would be allowed to stay in Hawaii as long as they behaved, but no guarantees were given for their safety. That ought to have been the end of it but the tone had been set.

Shaun, who had sauntered in from Cape Town around the same time, also failed to make the right friends. He'd been busy rewriting the book on performance surfing and was destined for mega superstardom. On top of his world-renowned tube-riding skills (it was a joy to watch him surf Jeffreys Bay in South Africa) maybe he was seen as a little too handsome, and that didn't help his cause. After a series of run-ins he bought himself a shotgun and some ammo, which he kept under his bed.

My first experience of the skirmishes occurred one morning out at Rocky Point. I'd been surfing the inside take-off spot, minding my own business. Out the back on the main peak were PT and Kanga, having a whale of a time. That was it. A Black Shorts crew paddled out, surrounded them and told them to paddle into shore. They refused. As a result, a fight broke out, and it had clear winners. I remember PT using his board as a shield at one point, which didn't help much – those two were here for the waves (which they often dominated), not the fights (which they did not).

I couldn't understand why anybody would assault PT, one of the nicest, kindest men around. Kanga was seen as more of a bruiser but PT? It didn't make sense. I'd seen enough fights in my life but they were almost always preceded by escalating voices, shouts and some sort of a dance. This one happened without any preamble. I'm ashamed to say I didn't get involved, but I was relieved that it ended almost as soon as it had begun. I'm sorry I'm such a coward, PT and Kanga.

My second, slightly eerie experience happened a few days later when the Colonel's son, Fielding, and I were surfing a wild and obscure place called (I can't say) on the east side. I'd been there a few times before and even shared a couple of memorable sessions with Gerry Lopez. But this particular day, a Black Shorts crew paddled out and told us to paddle back in. Fielding gave them some chat, knowing everybody individually by name, and they eventually backed down. We both laughed it off, me slightly nervously, but the flirtation left an impression on me.

After another random, violent attack on the street behind the beach, Kanga, like Shaun, went out and bought himself a shotgun, which he kept in his car. He also got a baseball bat, which he kept hidden on the beach when he was surfing. All bases covered. I have no doubt that the Kanga I knew would have gone further than merely brandishing those weapons, had he been attacked again.

Ψ

One thing that most of the main targets had in common was champion status, either of Pipeline or of the world, and so I was in very good company. The trouble was that it was getting harder and harder for me to stay hidden.

My first visits to Hawaii as an unknown schoolkid had gone down without incident, despite my frothy, energetic banter. I'd made friends with some of the local heroes and I felt at home. I assumed this camaraderie was going to last. I was wrong.

It should have been obvious that an Australian bank robber's son with ambitions to win the world's top surf contest was never going to stay out of trouble for long.

I stuck my head over the parapet during that third winter season after a few wins and some good days at Pipe. I was gaining notoriety at the worst possible time, at the precise moment when the animosity between the foreigners and the locals was peaking and Fast Eddie's newly formed enforcement gang was looking for work. At first it was nothing more than some comments on the beach and in the ocean. The process, imperceptible to begin with, was like what it must be like to live in a volcanic zone. Pressure builds along the fault lines. Everybody knows it'll have to be released, but nobody has a clue where or how big it'll blow. Rabbit's terrifying experience had been a mid-sized eruption with very little warning. It was my turn soon. Even Mum's radar was never going to tell me where or when. And that knowledge wouldn't have helped me anyway.

My first taster was delivered one sunny morning at Rocky Point. I'd brought along the lovely Kami from San Diego, who I was falling in love with. I was captivated by her big hazel-brown eyes, and her easy way of being that matched her sandy blonde hair – so I wanted to impress her by putting on a show. When you have minimal education and little to offer in the form of thought-provoking conversation, you let your arms and legs do the talking. My plan had been working up until now.

When I reached the gap in the top of the sandbank I could see there were a dozen or so locals out, their particular boardshorts giving them away, but nobody else. It was clear something was amiss, but out to sea I jolly well stroked; I couldn't possibly reveal myself to be a chicken in front of such a fabulous girl.

As soon as I was out beyond the foam, with barely a word spoken, they surrounded me. I was surprised and confused more than scared. My quizzical 'What, me?' face didn't disarm anybody however, and soon enough, threats were being made. I don't know what was in my mind but I think it was something about Brown Shirts, Black Shirts and Black Shorts – and about fascism coming in the same drab colours no matter where you were, even on a tropical island.

Or did I say it?

Well I must've said *something* – I was swiftly slapped around the chops, which certainly woke me up, and then there was a lot of splashing while one of the bigger boys got some purchase around my neck with his ham-shaped forearm. I bet this would have looked like a childish squabble from the shore, but up close it felt deadly serious. Those arms all seemed to have the largest hands on the end of them, and they were all trying to get a grip on me. I was really in the shit – I thought I was going to drown.

Somehow I wriggled and wriggled and managed to escape (thank you God for the liberating physics of slippery wet seawater). I paddled off very quickly indeed, almost running on all fours on top of the water in the general direction of Sunset Point to the east. Either I was too fast, or everybody thought, correctly, that the job of scaring me off was done, but I was soon free.

The rip that runs out to sea in the channel between Sunset's outer reef and Kammie's reef travels at a freakish speed, especially on a big day when there's a lot of ocean moving around. These channels allow the huge volumes of water brought inshore by breaking waves to travel back out to sea. The bigger the swell, the more water that needs to get back out, and the faster and more deadly the current.

Suddenly, I saw two American GIs right ahead of me, caught in the deadly rip. They were getting sucked out to sea and were panicking. At first I thought one of them had been bitten by a shark, such were the screams and shouts. Panic is the most common cause of drowning on the North Shore; it's the *opposite* of what you need to do when you get caught in a rip. I told them (very firmly, I thought) to grab the tail of my board and relax, then I dragged them perpendicular to the flow, into the whitewater and back to safety.

I wondered, if it had been me drowning, what the Rocky Point enforcement crew would have done. And I never dared ask Kami whether she thought I was a coward (for fleeing the twelve locals with not a hint of a fight) or a hero (for rescuing the GIs). But at least I found out where I was in the pecking order that day. I wasn't nearly as high as I'd thought. My relationship with Kami from San Diego stumbled on for the rest of that season but eventually we went our separate ways.

For now I had got off fairly lightly, but the atmosphere out the back during that 'Year of the Rabbit' was at times unbearably heavy. It felt like I hadn't even left home; underneath it all, Oahu's North Shore was just like Sydney's Eastern Suburbs but with more palm trees and less concrete. And of course much, much larger people; I was astonished and terrified by how tall and thick set some of the local Hawaiians were. It seemed that quite a few of these absolute units had now been enlisted by the Black Shorts.

There were many fights that year, often started with seemingly zero provocation. Whatever the cause, they always seemed to erupt at a time and place nobody could predict, releasing whatever bilious hate and disappointment had been bottled up. Every flare-up left a trail of acrid sourness, each mixing with the previous to form an ever-thickening cloud that hung about the North Shore for years.

And there were weapons, including guns on both sides. When I play those few years back in my mind, I realise it's a miracle that nobody died.

That winter it was clear that something terrible – and very hard to contain – had kicked off in those magical islands. It was a backlash from a couple hundred years of take and hardly any give. It was anger, dispossession, frustration and pride. It was fear of others and the changes they brought. But mostly, I think it sprang from the hopeless feeling that the rising tide of newcomers couldn't be pushed back.

It's fair to say that I hadn't picked the best time and place to flee Australian justice and make a new start. The parallels, and the irony, do not require too much dwelling upon, but I will recap briefly the state of play:

Issue	**Home**	**Away**
Gangsters?	✓	✓
Cops?	✓	✗
Prison?	✓	✗
Guns?	✓	✓
Fights?	✓	✓
Waves?	✓	✓ ✓ ✓

I could have gone somewhere else more peaceful on my crime and punishment gap year and the years that followed, but that simple maths told me I was still the luckiest person alive. I was in paradise, but even the sweet fruits of paradise have some prickles.

20.

The Sunset Stray Dogs' Home

Every mongrel deserves a refuge.

In the early 1960s, Colonel Albert Benson was stationed with the US Army on Oahu, where he eventually retired, forming a lifelong connection with the sea. The Colonel was obsessed with the power and beauty of the waves, and so those who shared the passion became his friends. Al and his lovely wife BB brought up their children as great surfers and the Bensons became a sort of de facto royal family on the North Shore.

The Colonel was a great photographer and cinematographer. Many of his images captured feelings that only those who loved the ocean could understand, but sometimes they transcended surfing and conveyed the magic to a much wider audience.

I first bumped into him on the beach at Pipeline when I was a teenager on my first-ever trip. We'd struck up a conversation because it was me who he'd been filming that day. The Colonel hadn't yet realised that I'd already been living in his house for some time, since the day BB had welcomed me with open arms on the say-so of some surfboard shaper. But this wasn't unusual in the wonderful chaos of that home and its procession of residents. It was the sort of place where you just turned up for a day or two, and the days became a year, with no explanations needed. Which is exactly what I'd done, and we ended up becoming lifelong friends.

The Bensons lived in a rambling two-storey wooden house in the hills overlooking Sunset Beach. Their outdoor shower enjoyed a sneak peak of the ocean in the distance; it became my bathroom and I would gaze out from it on many glorious mornings over the course of the next few winters. BB gave me my own room out the back, which had a lana'i (a verandah), and this was where I slept every night, under the stars.

The Benson kids absolutely ripped in the surf. Blanche and Becky, their two girls, took on any wave anywhere, in the days before girls were supposed to be surfers. Becky mixed it up on the really big days at Pipe and Sunset and was one of the pioneers of women's surfing decades before anyone else. I've seen her casually take off on waves that many of today's pros wouldn't dare drop into. She'd destroy them like they were playful beach-break peaks. Fielding, the Colonel's son and similarly talented, became my surfing partner in crime from day one.

BB cooked us all dinner most nights unless we were out for pizza and trouble. These were banquets for the whole neighbourhood, it often seemed, and any number of hungry itinerant surfers. Luckily for us, we were able to do most of our shopping at the army base, where the Colonel's veteran's pass meant the prices were low. This kept us well fed.

The Bensons had six dogs of different shapes and sizes, from guard dog all the way down to lap. Some were pedigree, some were straight off the street. BB loved them all. It was the same with the pack of stray professional surfers she took in. They came from all over the world, every background, in every shape and size, and every breed from show dog down to utter mongrel like me.

The pack could lose a member without warning from one day to the next, and acquire one or two more just as fast. It didn't matter to the Bensons, such was the warmth and hospitality.

One larger-than-life arrival, and a genuine eccentric, was my great friend from over the other side of the hill in Bondi, Cheyne Horan. Cheyne had a unique, avant-garde approach to everything, especially when it came to his surfboards. He would ride the weirdest-shaped, smallest boards, no matter where, or how big the waves. He even rode these curiosities at Pipeline where the risks are serious.

In Hawaii any board less than eight feet long is described as 'a toothpick', thought unrideable in the big powerful waves, yet Cheyne was charging full-sized Pipeline on a five-foot ten-inch board. Totally and utterly bat-shit mad. At one point he teamed up with legendary yachtie and marine architect Ben Lexcen. Ben was the man who created the famous winged keel that won the 1983 America's Cup for Australia in one of the country's proudest moments. Ben designed and made a miniature version of that winged keel as a fin for Cheyne's boards; once again completely mental and something that has never been repeated since, thank god!

Cheyne is truly one of the greats of our sport, without a doubt, and seeing him around Hawaii always gave me heart. His whacky approach to life – whether it be boards, diet or beliefs – always brought the colour that would light up and lift me out of the darker moments. I love that guy. The world needs more Cheyne Horans.

At the other end of the breeding scale was a proper English Viscount, Edward 'Ted' Deerhurst of Coventry, who was trying, unsuccessfully, to climb up the world rankings after renouncing his title, his family and their sprawling estate back in England. Ted tried his hardest on tour to no avail, but he charged ahead into any size of wave and we loved having someone around who had thrown his whole life away to chase a dream that he must have known he had little chance of attaining. The bloke just loved to surf.

Ted was an early riser, just like me, and I enjoyed his relaxed way of being, so incongruous with his brutal, regimented upbringing in the English private school system. So we surfed together a lot, a Viscount and a robber's son, perhaps the oddest couple out on the water.

The Colonel had one semi-permanent guest in the shape of Larry Bertlemann. Larry had moved from Hawaii's Big Island where he'd been a pig-hunting, spearfishing, skateboarding prodigy. His skating was already famous (he was said to be the inspiration behind the Z-Boys phenomenon in Venice Beach in California), but he was now ripping up the rule book of surfing as well. Larry's approach was totally mad, but he was brilliant company, always just fun to be around. He was a pioneer of the new school of high-energy, radical surfing that was putting an end to the straight-line era of Gerry 'Mr Pipe' Lopez & Co., and that informed everything that came after. Future greats such as Mark Richards (four times world champ), Shaun Tomson (world champ once) and Tom Carroll (twice) would, I think, happily admit to being inspired by Larry.

One reason I enjoyed Larry's company was that I'd once been mistaken for him in the press. After a successful day at the Coke Surfabout, a television presenter made a big deal of the fairytale ending for 'this albino negro from the wrong side of the tracks [me]'. They actually said that kind of stuff in the '70s!

Geoff McCoy, who'd played his part in the creation of this wonderful menagerie at the Colonel's, had his own board-shaping bay under the house. He and his wife Leah also called the place home and Geoff would go on to shape Pipeline-winning boards for me and many others from that little cranny. I have a lot to thank that man for, and I'm not alone.

There were so many champions, lunatics, itinerants and local legends who were billeted with the Colonel. I doubt there's anybody on the list of surfing world champions from 1970 to 1990 who didn't spend time there. The mongrel nature of life on the hill is what made it such a treasured era for anybody who was a part of it. Because everybody was from everywhere, there were no cliques, and in the melting pot that resulted we all felt like we were part of the same shambling, extended family.

For quite a few of us it was the only family we had, and I for one felt more at home sitting on the long grass in the Bensons' backyard with this pack of strays than I ever did among my father's villainous pals in the parlours of my childhood. We had each other's backs and, a few angry surfers notwithstanding, Oahu seemed safer than my hometown. It was also a relief to have someone to paddle out with when the sea conditions were frightening, which was most days.

Ψ

The Colonel had a habit of getting us up at 4 am to film at spots around the island and it's thanks to him (and Fielding) that I got a backstage pass to all four of the very contrasting coasts on Oahu, and to venture out at secret spots where *haoles* were never normally allowed.

These daily dawn patrols usually started with a generous smoke of homegrown 'pakololo', ensuring that the participants were in the right frame of mind. Fielding hated the early mornings and needed that little something to motivate him – I on the other hand knew what my friends were all missing back in Sydney and was irritatingly eager to get up and out into the sea. I didn't need those massive 'hooters' (an old-fashioned term for an XXL spliff, kids) to create a buzz inside my head, but I smoked them with gusto all the same.

Fielding and I became close over the years, and I've probably shared more surfing hours with him than anybody before or since. We had more than our fair share of scrapes, and luckily for me he talked us, or paddled us, out of most of them. In return for teaching me how to behave with the locals, I taught him how to run. His presence allowed me to gain a grudging acceptance among the more protective surfers who guarded certain tucked-away spots, and I'm sure there were many times when I wasn't beaten up or sent back to shore simply due to him being there. There were definitely times in places like Backyards and V-Land when certain groups of locals looked me up and down, looked across to Fielding, and then left us alone, going on their merry way with a grunt.

When conditions were right, we would spend endless days at Rocky Point, a super-fast, super-steep wave where you have to commit everything to the take-off, but the reward is a racy, hollow left-hander perfect for a goofy-footer like me. I gained an awful lot of skills and confidence on that fast and fun wave.

We also spent countless hours out at Gas Chambers and further down the road at Alligators. Next door, Jocko's is like a mini Pipeline and in those days was almost always empty. If you lose your board there you are in real trouble; the currents are incredibly fast, like rivers, and if you do make it in, it might end badly with you getting smashed by waves onto the rocks outside Jock Sutherland's lovely house. We experienced that a lot in the days before Brian Crogan's wonderful leg ropes.

Fielding knew about my dreams and helped me focus the blurry ideas of superstardom into sharp images of winning the greatest prize in the sport. It was he who was the first to tell me I could do it, one day far offshore out at Backyards after I snagged a gaping right-hand barrel that was, he said, the greatest ride he'd ever seen. (I'm pretty sure he was just high.)

I've lost count of how many friendships were forged through Fielding, the Colonel, BB and in that house, but there's a long roll call of pro surfers over many years, most of whom I have omitted, but who owe an enormous debt of gratitude to the Benson family. This hill-top clan probably did more for the spirit of aloha in the islands than anybody before or since. Had I not taken that truck up the hill on my second day in Hawaii when I was a lost schoolboy, I might have had quite a different life.

21.

Take-off

Sometimes the difference between getting trapped by the pounding waves and catching the rip to the safety of the outside is just one stroke in the right direction.

After four years' travelling three of the world's oceans, I've met people from all over, been accepted by some, ignored by others and bloodied by a few. I've come close to drowning more times than I want to remember and my stomach has hosted every strain of toxic bacteria known to humankind. I've laughed and known all the disguises that fear hides behind. I've made and broken friendships, and failed at love, sometimes on purpose.

I don't know what I've learned, but it was fun and now here I am, back home in Sydney.

Ψ

At a very early age, my parents, my aunties and their friends taught me that we could take anything we wanted in life if we just looked people in the eye and dared them to stop us.

More often than not those people did not. This grasping was all I knew. I'd seen it succeed and seen it fail (in the case of Dad, and sometimes myself), but the failures had always been convincingly explained away by my elders. Even those that had awful consequences.

If I'd stuck in one school for more than a year or so, perhaps some diligent teacher might have noticed that I was losing my balance. A well-meaning, but ignorant, selfish prick – this is what I'd become at the age of eighteen. Did this mean I was suited to the world's most selfish sport? Was this flaw an ingredient for success in my chosen career?

In surfing, you turn up, take your waves and go home. It's not a team sport – if there are others in the water they are there to be burned. You do anything you can to prevent them getting the wave you want, whether with a smile, a hustle, a scowl or a sneaky manoeuvre. Much is made of the spirituality of communing with the ocean but a busy day at North Maroubra, Rocky Point or Kirra is often no more spiritually enriching than a queue at a Christmas sale.

Waves are not given by one surfer to another, they are robbed. So what better preparation for this sport than being a robber's son? I wonder if the mean and opportunistic edge that I acquired from my family is what made 1978 such a good year for me.

Ψ

In late April, on my hometown beaches of Sydney, the Surfabout was being run. The Coke/2SM Surfabout as it was formally known was held during an extraordinary period in surfing's history – a time when the sport had as much television coverage as any of the mainstream sports. For two weeks a year, the Surfabout took up a couple of hours of prime time on Channel Nine every night, plus live bulletins throughout the day. When I look at it today some of the footage is extraordinary; the eccentric, other-worldly camera angles are well ahead of their time. Following this annual pageant, glued to the TV, was great entertainment for entire families.

The competitors became household names, especially the favourite and Aussie hero, Wayne Lynch. Wayne was an amazing goofy-foot surfer from Victoria; an avant-garde sensation and an incredible tube rider. When the big old logs of the 1960s and '70s were phased out to make way for the short-board revolution, it was Wayne more than anyone else who led the coup, showing us that snaps, slashes, 180-degree turns and other radical power manoeuvres were possible. The man changed our sport.

Each year, the Surfabout and its camel train of media, supporters, dignitaries and hangers-on would traipse across the country looking for the best waves. The organisers even used a light plane to scour the coast. In 1978, the contest was to be held in Sydney, at North Narrabeen, Avalon and North Steyne in Manly, which often shows itself as a fairly ordinary beach break. For some, it's known more for its crowds and featureless sand-bottom peaks than its crystal barrels. But sometimes, just sometimes . . . The Surfabout attracted almost every one of the world's top surfers, in part because it boasted the sport's richest prize purse.

Three days before the start of the event, I decided in a last-minute bout of bravura and stupidity that I'd jump the fan-zone fence, stump up some money, become a competitor and take them all on. I'd caught a glimpse of the outside and I was determined to catch that rip and see if it would take me there.

Even though I was a nobody (as confirmed in the surf press after my first couple of contests with the line 'always taxiing, never taking off'), I actually thought I could win, and so I filled in the entry form, paid my huge $45 entry fee, and rocked up with a cocky grin. For some reason, perhaps there'd been a drop-out, they accepted me. But I only had access to the trials, where all the amateur kids dogged it out for a chance to go through to the main contest and test themselves against the 'real' surfers.

Mum thought I was mad but she laughed along with me and I think she was proud of my hopeless ambition. And it was about time I did something to put some gloss back on the family name. After several conversations during which I tried to explain the surf contest scoring system, which she did not understand one bit, she eventually became convinced that I was going to lift the trophy.

She wouldn't have known who the 150 or so other surfers were, and to her, the fact that I would have to get past the likes of Larry Bertlemann, Shaun Tomson, Mark Richards, Michael Peterson, Kanga, Rory Russell, Reno Abellira, Gerry Lopez, Michael Ho, Peter Townend, Jim Banks, Bobby Owens, Col Smith, Bruce Raymond, Rabbit Bartholomew, Cheyne Horan and Wayne Lynch didn't mean a thing. To me, however, many of these men were not mortals, they were titans.

Unfazed, Mum came to the beach with me every day and was genuinely excited for her little angel. For this reason, that week holds some of the most hilarious and happy memories, many in our car, driving back and forth over the Harbour

Bridge with Cat Stevens blaring and Mum giving it her all on accompanying vocals. Cat Stevens was perhaps the only artist we could agree on when I was a teenager, except when it came to 'Morning Has Broken', the song Mum would often taunt me with an hour before I wanted to wake up.

'I'm not a fucking blackbird, okay?' I'd wail.

As an unseeded outsider, I had to work my way through dozens of trial heats and 119 other wannabes in order to be allowed into the main event. This was how they made sure that only the top surfers would get to compete, and the TV viewers would not have to waste their time watching flotsam like me.

I toiled through the first few days in the mostly shitty two-to-four-foot slop. I was much lighter back then so I could generate a lot of speed in slow, mushy waves, which allowed me to get little barrels where others may not have got near the right spot. No matter how you surf, barrels receive high scores in competitions. Just ask Kelly Slater, who won eleven world titles thanks to this (and my excellent advice on riding inside the tube. I'm sure he would have pinned it up on his wall). A couple of days in, the show was moved to North Narrabeen, which chucked out a few of its famous left-hand beauties. I slotted myself into a few and that's what put me on top. Somehow I'd managed to get past the hordes of other triallists to come first among mongrels, and to qualify for the professional event where I would come face to face with the best surfers in the world.

For the first time, I had an opportunity to find out whether or not I was made of the right stuff to be an actual surfing professional just like the blokes on my bedroom wall.

When the main event started I scraped through the early rounds, nerves getting at me in the strangest of ways. I wonder if other sportspeople find that their most basic skills are usually the ones that let them down at the key moment. My semi against Simon Anderson was close enough to be a draw and had to be rerun. My heat with Col Smith had seemed a lost cause when I watched his astonishing, almost upside-down manoeuvres. Luckily, that one was abandoned due to poor conditions. Facing Buzzy Kerbox and Larry Bertlemann almost caused me to melt down. I had to chatter constantly and maniacally to myself throughout just to stay calm. My sparring partners thought I'd gone mad.

Looking back at the heat sheets, I seem to have faced most of my childhood idols yet somehow my mind holds on to other trivia. Mostly, the swarms of people dripping off the edges of that sea wall and off the balconies of the huge apartment blocks, hooting and whistling.

However it happened, I found myself in the grand final, where I was to go one-on-one with the current Aussie champ, Wayne Lynch. Wayne was not only an incredibly popular surfer but the overwhelming favourite. It didn't help that he was also my absolute hero at the time and I'd been trying to copy his style all year. But here I was, with a shot at the title. I had no nerves, just pure, frothing, babbling, hopping-mad excitement. Looking back I must have been like one of those warlords chewing amphetamine berries before marching into a village. I'm sure I freaked poor Wayne out with my continuous chants and effluence. In a way I had something to lose, this being my big moment. But I didn't think too much about it and perhaps what made the difference was that he did.

Things started out pretty awfully, in bigger but still fairly unruly waves. I pitied the thousands who'd turned up to watch this ugly non-event. I gave it my best, and tried to shred everything that came my way. I was lucky and caught a few good waves – contest surfing is always part luck because all waves are unpredictable, especially over shifting sandbanks. But towards the end I thought I'd made the better selections, and was convinced that I'd won. I hadn't, of course – it was declared a draw, and with darkness closing in, the organisers called off the contest and decided to run the whole thing again the next day.

ψ

Mum drove me home that night, emphatically announcing that I was the winner and the best surfer out there regardless. I felt deflated, down in the mouth and resigned to failure. I wondered if I'd just fluked those early heats and if my pro career had stalled before it had even begun.

We were up early the next day and were soon driving back over the Harbour Bridge and up to the top of the beach in Manly in my little hotrod. It was a quieter trip than usual. Mum parked up in the back streets of North Steyne and we marched across to the promenade to check the conditions.

It was like night and day.

The surf was absolutely pumping. There'd been no warning, and obviously no internet forecast or webcam. The sea state and the conditions were nothing like I'd ever seen in Sydney at any time before or since. It was six-feet solid (double-overhead), with a perfectly light offshore breeze feathering the tops of the waves. There were cavernous barrels big enough to stand up in, and they were booming out spit, the blast audible from the beach. And word had got around: the beach was packed, from the sea pool carved into the cliff at Queenscliff all the way down into Manly itself. I had no idea there were so many surfing fans anywhere in the world, let alone in Australia. People were standing on walls, crouched on the sand, hitched up on shoulders and clinging to the cliffs.

The contest was now concentrated around the various tents and flags that had been assembled in the middle of the strip, because the best waves were peeling off the banks that sat squarely opposite the infamous 'Manly shit pipe'. This drainage pipe ran through the whole suburb, deep under the promenade and right across the beach to the waterline, where it distributed run-off, sewage, used condoms and any other evil detritus you could possibly imagine. Usually that pipe delivered ear infections, bacterial stomach bugs and sickness, but today it had helped to sculpt sandbanks that were throwing up the most perfect waves that suburb had ever seen. And it would be the centre stage in the richest contest in the history of surfing.

It dawned on me that part of the reason for the crowds must have been me: at nineteen years of age I'd be surfing this glassy, sculpted perfection for half an hour with just one other competitor; the current Australian champion, who until the previous afternoon had never wasted a single thought on this little devotee.

Even better, my greatest ever friend, my most faithful supporter, and the person who had always believed in me even when I was headed to jail, would be on the beach whooping and shouting. Mum never had a clue about surfing but she always jumped up and down with uncontrollable excitement anyway, often at the wrong moments. She was having the time of her life, but also nervously crossing herself, while chanting all of her mumbo jumbo. I hoped this would be a good omen.

Take-off

According to witnesses, I was my usual off-putting, chattering mess that morning on the beach. Up in everyone's face as usual, and utterly unable to be still and quiet. Today's four-letter word is of course 'ADHD' but in 1978 it was probably 'cunt'. The truth is that the conditions were so gnarly that my head was blowing up and my only release was to give a one-man team talk to myself. That babble was in fact a blend of the usual chants finished off with the barrel-riding recipe from my previous winter on the North Shore: Paddle hard and fast. Stop thinking, just go. The later the better. Keep your eyes on the exit no matter what. And so on.

I kept up the muttering out in the water all through the final heat, and Wayne and I were neck and neck throughout. Both of us got shacked a lot, and we exchanged the lead again and again. Every time I caught something I thought was brilliant, he bettered it (I could tell how good his rides were from the sound of the crowd drifting towards us from the shore). The crowd that had gathered on North Steyne Beach was in a frenzy and we could hear them screaming as we each got ourselves into and out of the craziest barrels. Outside of Hawaii it was the best surf I'd ever seen and people today still say it's the best they've ever witnessed in Australia.

At the end, with it all in the balance, a beast of a set came through and I could see Wayne eyeing it up and circling. We both wanted the biggest wave, but I had the luck to be just a little bit nearer to the take-off spot, and somehow I was the one who snagged it. I dropped down the face, angled just slightly, and then pulled straight into a sand-dredging, yawning-wide left-hand keg. It was to supposedly become the longest contest barrel ever surfed in Australia, with (ridiculously inaccurate) estimates of ten to eighteen seconds quoted back to me afterwards. Whatever the numbers, and whether it was ridden well or just adequately, I'm not sure Sydney has seen an individual wave shaped like that one before or since.

Then and afterwards, Wayne was a better surfer, but I'd won the competition, thanks to that one freak wave, right in front of a prime-time Channel Nine audience, a jam-packed Manly beach, and Mum. It was my first professional contest victory and nobody had expected it, especially the ever-gracious Wayne Lynch.

Mum thought it was hilarious that they gave me a cheque that was bigger than me. She said that if it bounced, or if it all went wrong from now on, I could always roll it up like a sleeping bag and camp out under the Harbour Bridge. She did have a point and I felt a bit of a tit when they asked me to hold it up for the cameras. The Surfabout had gone on for weeks, in five different locations and across dozens of heats, many of which were tied. I lost ten kilos over the course of the contest, this before I was even fat, and so I suppose I earned it.

Mum praised, hugged and denigrated me while we cooked ourselves a bowl of pasta at home that night, but I don't think we even had a glass of wine to celebrate. Until I went out afterwards, of course. For three days.

I got her back by using some of the prize money to fit out her miserably equipped kitchen with a fabulous oven, the first one that Melody Street had ever seen. I also paid for a new stove, a monstrous Kelvinator fridge-freezer, a washing machine down below in the cellar and, later, a new house. Nine thousand bucks went a long way in 1978.

In a moment of sweet serendipity, the event's celebrity presenter at the trophy ceremony was none other than Shane Stedman. Shane, the man who had hand-shaped the beautiful Red Rocket that Dad had bought me all those years ago – my first real surfboard. I never mentioned it to him.

ψ

In the aftermath of the Surfabout, the Channel Nine publicity machine ensured that I became a household name. It was mad. Phones rang, letters arrived, people showed up at the house to discuss things, and I was asked to get involved in the oddest of capers. It seemed jeans, milk, soft drinks, wetsuits and surfboards all needed to be talked about by a dumb blond kid who could surf. I jumped at the opportunity to earn a living in this way. It was a turning point; from that day on, I had a new career.

I did many, many interviews. In magazines, TV and even radio. One question that was thrown at me almost every time was about stress and nerves. Was I nervous in the final, head to head against the Australian champion? Did I get the shakes thinking about the enormous prize money at stake? I never answered that question properly because I wouldn't have been able to say what I really thought – that playing in the sea is not stress. Baldy, Pat, their friends and their enemies were stress. Maybe this perspective had helped me just as much as the family voodoo.

In the wake of the contest and all the attention it brought, I started to behave more disgracefully than ever before. I tell myself it was inevitable. It began on the night of the grand final. After our quiet pasta dinner, I hit the town with a selection of Sydney's worst folk and got absolutely written off (me, not my car – there would be time for that). Two days later a magazine editor passed me on the street and called out my name. I didn't respond. Apparently I was still staggering about in a daze, kicking stuff. I believe he thought it was shocking enough, but he may not have realised that I was only halfway through that particular bender.

I continued to learn very little from all this. I drank, partied, shagged and crashed cars all over Sydney, and got more attention than I deserved. I was developing a sort of outrageous alter ego that was designed to hide the real, duller me. My mouth was the main ingredient. As a schoolboy, I had, so I'm told, always created many more words than could fit in that mouth, and as a result I would hop about in front of people while the words gurgled uncontrollably out of me. I imagined myself funny and sometimes I was, which meant I got away with it and believed in it.

The cars had to match my mouth, and each time I wrote off one garish hot-wheels monstrosity I just bought another, making sure it was even louder, brighter and more vulgar than the previous version. Sometimes a sponsor would even encourage me, by buying the new one for me.

I too was brighter and more vulgar than the previous version. My clothing excesses hit new heights, including three-piece suits and some crazy shirts. Success on a big stage was bound to amplify everything I did (or wore), and it sure did. I mostly got away with it, for now, because it was my hometown and it was the late 1970s.

At times the whole thing was slightly dangerous, but it was not a patch on the existence Mum and I had been living a few years before and so I barely registered the carnage that I was causing. As long as I wasn't in immediate mortal danger, I was ahead of the game.

I'd always thought it would be cool to be a womaniser, and this is what I became. I quickly realised that when you are well known, people think you must be interesting, and worth talking to. Assuming that a sportsperson might have a special brain doesn't make any sense – why should they be any more clever than anyone else? If anything, elite athleticism probably hides some terrible character flaw or mental deficiency.

No matter, the fame was working, and the womanising progressed in phases, with the 'porn star period' being the one I remember most, followed by the 'Queenslander period', and then the 'American interlude'. There was a blur of delightful people appearing in my life and then quickly disappearing, none of them living up to the memory of dream-like Tracy from the pier, and I suspect most of them having seen me on TV and probably being quite disappointed at what an ordinary little boy I was when you looked closer.

I hope I didn't hurt anybody but I fear that I did. I ought to have sensed that with this behaviour, my life was turning into a cautionary tale.

ψ

But I was now a pro, goddammit, and I had commitments! Other contests had to be taken on, all over the place. A whirlwind blew me around the country and across the sea to the US, Japan and back for the rest of that year.

For a young, debutant pro surfer obsessed with the perfect waves of Hawaii and Indonesia, some contests can be a chore.

Compared to Hawaii, many of the world's surf spots can deliver a fairly ordinary spectacle unless you happen to be there on the right day. Many of the contests held around our own shores also offer up quite mundane conditions.

But not Victoria's magnificent Bells Beach.

Bells and its little brother Winkipop sit in a nature reserve nestled in one of the most beautiful places in the southern hemisphere. Tasmanian tree ferns, towering gum trees and curvy roads carved out of the forest overlooking the sea create a stunning backdrop. My first sighting left me speechless. Once there, the honey-coloured cliffs and bush with not a house in sight fills you with energy. Pulling into Winki's carpark to check the sea, and getting the first glimpse of those perfect parallel lines peeling into the bay from way out beyond the cliffs, is spiritually uplifting.

When Bells is receiving a six-to-eight-foot southwest Southern Ocean swell, the paddle out feels like about half a mile to the peak. But on the right day it's one of the most perfect long right-handers you could ever ride. I never won at Bells, but I'll never forget the year that Cheyne Horan did. It was the end of my first year as a professional surfer and so I take you on a little jump forward in time here.

The 1979 Surfabout had started in Sydney but the waves had just died at the end. The organisers and TV crews would not let this dampen the final of their big annual pageant. Word came through that the waves at the bottom of Australia were actually pretty good, and so they lined up ten small planes and flew the whole event – cameras, journalists, judges and all the remaining contestants – down to Victoria. And that was that.

After a couple of weeks navigating past every other pro surfer in the world, the contest boiled down to two idiots from Sydney's Eastern Suburbs: Cheyne Horan and me. We shared an epic one-hour final that year, so far out the back that we were in our own little bubble surfing the perfect, long, wonderful walls and pulling into the odd stand-up barrel, me on my back-hand and Cheyne front-side.

Despite my 'ugly ass wiggle' (how the press described my fabulously unco back-hand surfing style), I was in the lead till the very end, but the last wave Cheyne snagged was a perfect bomb, and he totally nailed it. The judges' decision was unanimous. I'd come second. But after that unforgettable hour with nobody but my neighbour from the other side of the hill, I felt like a winner.

I'll never forget the scene down there in Victoria, and pulling into that carpark to lean over the rail to check the sea on both sides of the lookout still stirs my hairy old belly today.

Ψ

Despite the nomadic schedule and the frequency with which I would let myself down in cars, bars and pubs, the to-ings and fro-ings of my late teens and early twenties were actually the first truly stable period I'd ever experienced. The chaos was real, but underneath I was more focused and less afraid than I'd ever been before. I was doing what I loved, surfing was paying my bills, and in time a girlfriend came along who thought I was a polite, neat, nice normal guy.

I met Cathy at the Stubbies Pro at Burleigh Heads in Queensland. Along with Bells and the Surfabout, in its heyday, the Stubbies was one of the big three events on the Australian leg of the pro tour.

For me, it wasn't the actual surfing that made the Stubbies special. Burleigh Heads' wrapping right-hand sandy point break wasn't my kind of wave and featured the added torment of one of the most unpleasant jump-offs of any surf spot. Getting into the sea requires expert timing (aka luck), with a paddle out between squared boulders lurking at just the wrong depth. All the while you're getting pounded by the waves. Watching unlucky surfers stumbling and staggering as the rocks run dry can be funny, until it's your turn. I don't think any regular surfer at that spot has got away without losing some 'bark', as Rabbit (I think) used to put it. I once did this hop off early one morning during a massive cyclone swell, still drunk after an all-night session in Surfers Paradise. It very nearly ended my life when Neptune coughed me out in disgust, tossing me back up onto those angular, hard, unforgiving black rocks and pounding me down into the cracks.

What made the Stubbies such a big deal wasn't what happened out on the ocean – it was the absolute mayhem on the beach and in the pubs afterwards. The event was more a rock 'n' roll festival than a surf contest, and was always a full-blown, beer-hall, piss-soaked prison riot of a party. Queenslanders are simply crazier than us civilised town folk of Sydney. Or they were back in the early days of the pro tour.

For these reasons (the right-hand waves, and yes, the party) I never won that competition or even did particularly well in it. Michael 'MP' Peterson won the first one, the only non-world champ ever to do so. Then Mark Richards, local hero Rabbit himself, Martin Potter and Tom Curren dominated it until they eventually shut it down. I bet they couldn't find a mad enough insurer.

It was at the 1977 Stubbies when I first had a conversation with MP, the year he barnstormed his way to victory. Only a legend is known by their initials and MP was just that. He made his own boards, which often had deep channels cut out under the tails, and which I marvelled at but never dared to try. His brother Tom was an even better shaper, and they were both generous beings who would always stop to offer help to us mere mortals. In his unassuming, almost shy style MP once gave me some simple advice: 'Stop going straight.' He was also the one who first told me to stop farting about and hit the lip. I did as I was told from that day on, not realising that by then he was already trapped by the twin demons of bad drugs and schizophrenia. Like many surfers of my era I am both thankful to, and haunted by, MP today.

But back to Cathy. As usual I was out of my league when I spotted the beautiful, vivacious and incredibly witty woman, who looked and acted like a 1950s movie star. Using all my tricks to woo her, I took her to see a new underground punkish cult sensation called Midnight Oil who were playing a live show at the Playroom over in Tallebudgera. Getting into their gigs, which were explosive and terrifying, was known to be very difficult but I managed to persuade some well-connected fellow surfers to help me out.

The Oils' lead singer Peter Garrett was like a giraffe crossed with an angry and hyperactive Dalek, twitching and convulsing his lanky body all over the stage, spitting staccato obscenities and basically scaring the crowd out of their wits. Fuck that was a gig!

Along with a visit to the new water park and a few surf lessons, my attempts to dazzle got me over the line, and Cathy and I became an item. If I could make this relationship stick, then that would mean that I was properly on track in all areas.

Ψ

In my first couple of years on the pro circuit, I met extraordinary people, I ate incredible food, I did weird TV commercials, stage plays and soap operas. I was given wonderful stuff, I gave interviews in the strangest of magazines and I was flown around the globe. Above all, I got paid.

It's awful to admit, but after that first breakthrough at the Surfabout in Manly, it all seemed so natural and so easy. Sadly, the relentless pace left me little time to reflect on just how brilliant it actually was, and how much it was worth protecting. I wish I'd had the wherewithal to stand back, perhaps at brilliant Bells, and say, 'Larry, this is your job, you're a fully paid-up pro surfer! Go and say your thanks to Neptune, to Mum and to the universe!'

But I never seemed to find the right moment.

22.

A Haunting

Coming home is always sweet. But sometimes it hits us with unwelcome reminders of who we really are.

These are the whirlwind days but nothing seems to stick: my old home – my real home – always draws me back. I love to nestle into the Melody Street back room with Mum and the fake family; that is when they're not away on business. We laugh together like today is the best day of our lives. When they're not around I loiter, roaming our familiar, hilly suburb, where every landmark sounds out a childhood echo.

I still cook and I like to make soup. Get yesterday's roast chicken out of the massive fridge and hack it to bits. Roast it again, with the giblets. Fry it all in the big pot with onions, carrots, celery and any old stuff. Cover it in cold water, add a bay leaf from the yard and simmer the hell out of it. The rest is just details.

Home refills me in between jet-setting, and returning always makes me feel content, even if some of the lingering aromas of my past are stronger than the kitchen smells.

I never for a minute regretted the day I turned off the path my parents had laid out before me. Never even gave it a second thought. My breakthrough at Manly was also the moment when I gave up the hunt for Billy Maloney. It wasn't a conscious decision, but some time afterwards I suddenly realised I hadn't thought about the fucker in months. It wasn't that hard, after all.

I'd made it to twenty, with some prospects, and it was beautiful being able to leave the front drive of our house without fearing a tap on the shoulder from someone who wanted us in jail – or dead.

Ψ

Maybe I'd learned a few lessons after all, if not from the itinerant celebrity life then from some of the sobering encounters that happened in the sea and on the beach in Hawaii. Maybe I was on the way to becoming a slightly calmer and better person with a good chance of staying the course. Maybe my smart new friends, most of whom came from a more wholesome world than I, had helped to smooth my rough edges. I don't know. But back here in the Eastern Suburbs, with the heart tug of Mum's cooking, and the back room overlooking our little garden and its trellis overloaded with bougainvillea and fragrant jasmine, there was a new me settling comfortably back into an old world. What I hadn't given any thought to until this moment was the join between the two.

One afternoon, after a fairly nondescript muck about in the sea, I popped into the Bondi Hotel to meet a pal. Bondi Beach was the place to go when all the decent surf spots were blown out by the afternoon nor'easters. The Bondi Hotel meanwhile was a sprawling, multi-level pub right across from the beach. It was always boiling over with people.

I strolled into the beer garden but instead of seeing my friend, I saw someone else, seated alone, hunched over a schooner. Although I was in a very public place and there were so many people around, I was petrified.

His puffy red face with its rusty wire-for-hair still clinging on was instantly recognisable from the days when Dad was still alive and they'd hung out together at the Oshey. I could also picture his furrowed profile from the plane to Melbourne; when he and his colleague, the blowtorch-wielding psychopath Gore, would have killed Mum and me without a second thought.

It was Billy Maloney.

My body went cold and blood rushed to my face. A decade melted away as if current Larry had never existed, and I was immediately transported back to the other life . . .

I was at Queen Street, Coogee, with Mum shaking me awake. I was getting in that Valiant and driving into the desert. I was hiding with excitable cicadas in tangles of lantana. Dejectedly dragging myself along the grey Frankston shoreline. Stealing from the neighbours in an overheated, fly-blown caravan park. Navigating the sticky beer glasses and cigarette butts in the rancid air of the Oshey. Tugging at $5 notes gripped tightly in those puffy red hands. Looking up at murmuring, pitted and damp faces with halos of fur glinting in the light.

None of it was in any particular order. I was eleven-year-old Larry again, a boy running from criminals but slowly and unavoidably becoming one.

It's one of the worst feelings I've ever had; a cascade of all the thoughts and memories I'd denied for so long. I didn't know if it was a warning from fate, some sign to be heeded, a clue, or something else I should act upon. Thankfully I've never experienced anything like it since.

I could have done or said many obvious things that afternoon – things I've thought about often over the years. I could have called the cops and said I'd located the last Toe Cutter, my father's killer. The man had enough other alleged victims to be of great interest to them. Or I could have called in Fletcher, who had been an intermittent but looming presence in the years after I escaped Sydney, and was always quietly looking for some project or other that he could draw me into. And this would have been just his kind of project.

But I just turned around and walked out of the pub.

It was the last time I ever saw Billy Maloney.

23.

Pipeline Master

*Pipe. Seventy per cent nuts. Twenty-nine per cent skill.
And the rest is luck.*

The North Shore. The Colonel's mountain hideout. Home.

It's been a good year, this 1978. The radio plays toxic screams from the UK all day long but I am back in Hawaii, where they haven't discovered punk yet. Island culture is like that; they'll keep on plucking away at their ukuleles so that we can forget about the real world.

This winter, I seem to be living the life of someone else. It's weird being *almost known*. When people call your name you think it's a friend. But just sometimes it's not a friend. It's somebody who saw you on TV. By the time you realise, it's too late and you've waved back with too much enthusiasm. You then look like a dick, and you're afraid of doing it again the next time somebody shouts across the street at you. This puts you in a quandary, and helps you to become an arsehole. You're definitely better off in the simple worlds of *well known*, or *not known at all*.

I am single again. Cathy has stopped calling after a year of long-distance effort between her home on the Gold Coast and my home, which is spread out across the world. I miss her brilliantly dry observations that I often thought I'd misheard or misunderstood but that would always contain a message.

'Stop all this washing your hair, Larry.' Cathy didn't like my dried-out, lifeless white mop, caused by living in the glare and thousands of hours of salt water. It was also receding apace, possibly getting pulled off my head by the violence of the sea. Cathy thought it was funny that I was being brought back down to earth by the very activity that was turning me into an overconfident and tippy little starlet, and she loved having source material for her witticisms. But it's over now.

As consolation, I've been inducted into the World Professional Surfing Tour, where I am not doing badly (definitely not running last). I have even been given a nickname by the press: the Dynamite Kid. Is it my leg-humping Jack Russell way, I wonder, or an actual compliment? I dreamed that paddling about in the sea would be my job, Mum had agreed, and now here we are. The attention has us both scratching our heads at times, and even though I know she's proud, my career is the subject of many jokes at the Tea Leaf Club. It's going to take quite a few years yet before surfing shakes off its free-ride, draft-dodging, psychedelic-drug aura.

I haven't lost any sleep over my lowly world ranking because 'something rather big' and exciting has happened.

I'm going to fulfil my lifelong dream and compete in the Banzai Pipeline Masters, for the most famous and coveted surfing prize on the planet.

I knocked on the door when I was in Hawaii last year, and the year before that, but it didn't open. I asked my contemporaries, but still no joy. Finally, a letter arrived in the post, just like an electricity bill but without any numbers on it. After I opened it I went down to the beach where the contest director lived, knocked on his door and asked if it was for real. It was.

So the sages of world surfing have accepted me. Crazier still, one of the big clothing companies has also sponsored me – all I have to do is wear their fabulously lurid shorts. The tight, silky little things make me look pretty, although board wax gets stuck everywhere and they quickly lose their sheen. The various girls who I like tell me that they approve of them anyway.

To top things off, the great Geoff McCoy is making me a magnificent quiver of bright sexy brand-new boards. They're being delivered to me right here on Oahu's North Shore, where I'm ready for another winter season.

Ψ

There was a football coach who used to say 'train hard, fight easy'. He stole it from an army general, who got it from Sun Tzu, who probably got it from his wife, who was just trying to tell him he was fat. In any case, when I heard this motto on a TV show I believed it, and in 1978 I trained like an absolute warrior.

Future me would not recognise the Larry of that winter: I was running, stretching, paddling and swimming every single waking minute. I thought I was a Navy Seal for a while, except those guys probably eat more beef – for a while my diet was just a sad jumble of tasteless tofu, literally tasteless bean shoots and limp frizzly lettuce (also tasteless). Occasionally I ate a celebratory avocado and thanked Mother Nature for Hawaii's creamy, rugby-ball-sized monsters, which you can buy perfectly ripe on the side of the road anywhere. The monotony of my diet mushed my brain to the point where I was 'worse company than a lobotomy patient', or so said my fabulous American girlfriend of the time when she dumped me and flew home. But I didn't care; I wanted to be fit and ready for the greatest challenge of my life.

After the events on the beach in Manly back in April, I'd been whisked off around the world on the new professional surfing tour. But I embraced the new direction my life was going in and was determined to do whatever it took to continue. You could say that for one of the first times in my life, I actually had a fire under my tail.

Back on Oahu, I studied the Banzai Pipeline in the closest detail, riding it whenever it reared up and watching its inexplicable mood swings for hours. Pipeline has them all, often in the course of one day. There's only one constant – at Pipeline, waves don't build, they arrive. A blessed sunlit morning of twinkling glass and four foot peelers might call out to you and invite you in, but it can transmogrify into an exploding twenty-five-foot hell's fury in just a few minutes. Getting stranded out there hurt many a time. Today's sirens, thankfully, are hooked up to wave buoys.

Unpicking the fickle secrets of this place takes years. Mick, Terry and I had grown up with posters of it, cooed at pictures of it in *Tracks* magazine, worshipped its heroes (Rory, Reno and the great Gerry), asked ourselves if we'd ever have the nuts for it, and imagined ourselves in it while floundering out at our sloppy little Coogee Point. Pipe was *everything* to us kids on the other side of that ocean, as it was to pretty much every surfer on the planet. I knew I had to give it all or not bother.

So I was doing the physical work but in my head I was woefully unprepared. I had a simple goal and a plan to attain it, but no thoughts about what to do if and when I did. Why would I?

My focus became narrower and narrower the more hours I put in. Breathing. Tofu. Runs. Swims. Stretches. Lifts. All the while, weird things were happening just outside my field of vision, but I wasn't seeing them. Little warning signs, all around me every day. I was unaware that I'd become a blip on the Black Shorts radar.

Despite the Rocky Point incident, I still had no idea how big the bullseye on my back was. It was going to take more than a minor handbag fight for that fact to sink in.

I was so engrossed in my task that I was neither flattered nor alarmed to hear rumours, after just a few weeks back in my old North Shore haunts, that people had been talking about me. All sorts of people. Including the commander of the world's most notorious surfer gang.

I had two shapers delivering me lovely, glistening new boards every week, which created a bit of a scene at various surf spots while I was testing them out. I had a lot of smart clothes given to me by different sponsors, and I maintained absolute best dress code at all times, on Mum's strict instructions. Out of an evening in my spotless new shoes, I looked like a total wanker. I most definitely did not look like a *moke*. I should have known better.

But this place, which was and still is the most friendly on earth, was my second home and everybody was my friend, so why should I feel unwelcome? I was having the time of my life surrounded by the best people I had ever met. I drank with Gerry Lopez, Reno Abellira and other local pals in the evenings up at the main bar in the Kui Lima, sharing stories and laughs. And I surfed all day with the Bensons rather than the other Aussies. In fact, there were only two or three foreigners that I hung out with, Wayne Deane and David Byrne, but they were also well accepted into local life.

But still there were those comments. At first I thought it was just individuals having a bad day, but a pattern began to emerge. Never anything on the streets or out at night; only in and around the water. Slowly, but relentlessly, a sort of border was being drawn, right at the edge of the sand at every surf spot on the North Shore.

In time, comments became warnings and warnings became threats. Soon enough, I was being chased out of the water and threatened by the local enforcers on a regular basis. Occasionally, fists came out.

It's not easy fighting someone in the water – the act of throwing a punch from an unstable sitting position on a surfboard unbalances you and makes the whole show look pretty pathetic. Punch-ups can seem more like a kids' splashy water fight. This is why one of the locals' manoeuvres of choice in those days was 'the choke'. The choke involves somebody with very big arms coming at you without even trying to hit you and simply getting you in a headlock. They then squeeze until you pass out. The worst thing about the choke is that you can't make peace or surrender, because you're unable to breathe or speak. This makes the whole procedure curiously silent and all the more sinister for it.

I'd seen and heard it happen to other interlopers but I never gave it too much thought. I now started to realise I was no longer quite so protected by my local friendships, and staying with Hawaiian surfing royalty didn't offer me immunity. It was going to be my turn soon, one way or another. Maybe I'd been bumped up the hit list because I was now in the main event and starting to look like a chance.

My childhood training, however, was the best a kid could get when it came to dealing with this type of threat. I kept my stupid floppy blond head down, and the flow of filth that normally poured from my busy mouth remained tightly sealed in. For once, unbelievably, I was acting with some wisdom. When that wasn't enough, my twitchy feet exploded into action, and I ran and disappeared like a ghost crab into a hole. I told myself that I only had to last three months, to make it to the Masters before they got me. And in short, somehow, I did. I'm pretty sure that during the '78 winter swell season, despite many near misses and the odd glancing blow, I wasn't beaten up one single time.

As the time flowed by, and despite all the distractions on the shore, I became more and more obsessed rather than less. I recalled all the events that had got me to this point and none of the memories invited me to go back. I think that the awful fear of returning to my old life was probably the spur in my side; it certainly allowed me to put any playground insults and fights into perspective. Yes, I would always run (and fast), but I am not sure that I was ever actually afraid of the ogres I was fleeing. Certainly not as fearful as I'd been when I was a boy.

And then there was Mum, my X factor. She told me I was going to win, I believed her and, as she always said, that was that. What other competitor, be they Lopez, Kealoha or Tomson, had that sort of secret weapon? Looking back, I'll never know if she was messing with me or just trying to support me in her own special way, but her confidence somehow found its way into my head. During her travels, she had picked up a golden Buddha with jewels for eyes, on a thin gold chain. This was my Lucky Buddha. It had become a permanent attachment around my neck, a portable little piece of her magic. I'd started holding it while repeating all the usual ridiculous incantations.

Ψ

In that late November of 1978, the northwest Pacific swells started to appear, building in size and intensity. Somebody somewhere out at sea was very, very angry and the catastrophic storms that resulted were sending bigger and bigger waves our way. Pipeline duly started firing like a cannon, and the Masters preliminary heats were announced. The waiting was about to end.

Whilst I still didn't know how to prepare mentally for such a huge event, on the eve of the contest I drove down to Ehukai to gather my thoughts and check out the waves. They were sweeping in menacingly. After a three-hour practice session I ran out of the sea, up the sandbank and across the park, where I spied one of the enormous posters that had been plastered all over shops and on telegraph poles across the North Shore. These garish makeshift creations listed all the competitors as if to remind me who I had to beat. Most of my heroes were competing, and I remember scribbling some quick calculations on a piece of cardboard in the car:

Who I gotta beat . . .

- Local legend Rory Russell, Pipeline winner for the last two years in a row.
- Gerry Lopez himself, winner 1972 and 1973.

- Mark Warren. No comment.
- Dane Kealoha, Pipeline hero and local favourite.
- Michael Ho, godfather of the North Shore, Pipeline winner, five-time finalist.
- Larry Bertlemann.
- Mark Richards.
- Wayne Bartholomew, current world champion.
- Shaun Tomson, 1977 world champion, 1975 Pipeline Master.
- Reno Abellira, Kanga, PT and another twenty-three of the world's top surfers.

I reminded myself that I was only nineteen years old and these gods would not look down and see me coming. Who's going to worry about a kid like me? That was it, my pre-contest routine for the biggest and most dangerous event in the sport.

I hopped in the car and Carl Douglas's song 'Kung Fu Fighting' came on the radio. A good omen or a bad one? I didn't care; that dumb song with its silly martial arts intro and its whooping and yapping helped break up the tension I felt.

Humming away slightly madly out the car window, I raced back up the road to the Kui Lima, my temporary digs for the duration of the contest. It took about fifteen minutes, enough time for the sun's last glow to give way to darkness. In another sixty I was showered, fed, tucked up in bed and fast asleep.

Ψ

The next day, I rose early and was on the beach by 6.30 am. The waves were mercifully small by Pipeline standards, but they were dredging off the reef, hollow, clean and perfect. The good barrels were opening up wide enough to put your hands in the air without getting knocked off your board.

I watched the first two heats, witnessing Dane Kealoha absolutely smoke his way through the first. The current champ, Rory Russell, won the next. It was clear the two local favourites were at the top of their game. When you see somebody make six-to-eight-foot Pipe look easy, you know they're going to be hard to beat. The pair looked right at home.

Then it was my turn, in heat three. The waves were perfect and I found myself as fired as I was scared. Somehow, by getting as deep into the barrel as possible, I won it outright, ahead of Shaun Tomson and Larry Bertlemann. It was a turning point – I'd been a cocky kid on the way into the water, but on the way out I felt like a contender.

This qualified me for the next round, where I faced five other formidable surfers, including Gerry Lopez himself. I've never been totally convinced that Gerry is human, and so the idea of beating him in a competition was something totally far-fetched, with or without the power of voodoo. This belief was reinforced as I watched him play with everyone, getting the deepest barrels in the prelim heat after mine. Luckily I only had to come second in this one to reach the next stage. Gerry's presence towered over us all and he duly mesmerised, floated and glided to a graceful win. I don't know what was going through his head as he swatted the rest of us aside, but did anyone, ever? It didn't matter, because we were now both through to the semi-finals.

Another surfer running frighteningly hot was Honolulu local Hans Hedemann, a Hawaiian up-and-comer almost as fresh as me. I'd been watching him rip up the waves hoping

I could avoid him in the heats, but thanks to the convoluted mathematics of the running order I ended up facing him in that semi. Hans smashed it, with me second and Rory third, and the top three of us went through to the final act.

And that was that. Flushed along in a current of adrenaline and made-up confidence, I had made it all the way to the final of the Pipeline Masters. I was sixty minutes and a few good rides away from the prize I'd been seeking since I was a little boy on a plastic toy. It was all flowing in my direction, and if I kept performing, I was going to go all the way.

Then the sea god pulled the plug out. Kona (westerly) winds blew in, the waves disappeared and the organisers put the event on hold. The stoppage would end up lasting almost two weeks.

$$\Psi$$

It's 6 am.

I don't need an alarm clock. Finally, today's the day. I am already up and about, and getting into a car full of surfboards. Every few years a couple of fellow Aussies and I club together and purchase a rusty old new vehicle, and this is one of the worst we've had, drinking up more engine oil than most cars get through petrol. The black sticky gunk oozes out of its every pore, often leaving translucent yellowy-brown stains on our board shorts and T-shirts. The whole car stinks of it, but the boards do fit rather well.

It hasn't been an easy fortnight kicking my feet, the fickle weather and stuck-still clock reminding me that nature doesn't care about us, or surfing, or human ambition. For nature, the complex mysteries of the mind and of the movements of the air and ocean are problems already solved, and it is only us who are still trying to figure them out. Too much time with too little to do always makes this worse.

I've spoken to home a few times from the greasy grey phone in the hall. Not Mum, unfortunately, who is still running about overseas, but at least I had a chat with Fat Larry. To my horror he congratulated me in advance, saying he was double bluffing to head off a jinx. Then he told me he was the only one who had never believed I would actually get this far, and so it would be fine if I lost and proved him right. For him this was all very funny – the more anxious I am, the happier he is.

I pull out of the Kui Lima carpark and take a right onto the Kamehameha Highway. A few minutes later I'm passing Sunset Beach, where I can see it is absolute carnage out there. There will be nowhere to hide today, no fluke is going to get me through the first three rounds of this contest and into the final.

Soon I've parked my car and removed the finely curved Geoff McCoy gun I'll be needing. I've trotted across the beach park lawn and emerged through the naupaka scrub at the top of the bank, and I'm staring at it: eight-to-ten-foot, perfect, barrelling, clean, full-power Pipeline in all her spitting majesty. And she truly *is* majestic. The high-energy waves are breaking so close to the shore you can feel the shockwave through your feet each time a tube collapses on itself. Spray is firing out of every imploding cylinder with a *whoosh* and a *boom*. I stand awestruck and watch for some time. Till 7 am.

As usual I ask Mum for help, taking care to say 'bread and butter' three times first. Mum isn't actually here, but I see her face laughing at me and I know she's listening, wherever the hell she may be, and sending me luck through the ether. If anybody has the power to help, it is her.

Ψ

The finals of my first Masters were held on a fickle, wind-affected day, where skills came first but the shifty peaks made it so that luck ran a close second. But I still had a bit of luck. When I'd made it to the final, nobody except me was expecting it.

Here we all were, ready to go. Kealoha, Lopez, Russell, Buran and Hedemann. And then there was Little Larry from the 'Bra. A party of six. Dane had a shot at the world title that year, and I think this was why he had lava bubbling up inside of him. Gerry was Gerry, the current champ, and there was no time to chat about our times in Indonesia and our other adventures over the last few years. He wasn't at all impolite, but off in his own elegant world; it was probably easier like that. Thank god for another foreigner, hot shot Joey – always fizzing with stoke, and one of the rare breed who couldn't help showing how much fun this caper was.

After the long wait, by the time of the grand final the contestants were as ragged and jittery as the waves – I think we all wanted to strangle each other by that point. And the format – six blokes on one peak fighting it out with almost no rules for a full hour – was perfect for that.

My plan was clear – to get barrelled, sure, but to be *different*. And I had the gear for it. Surfing was at a crossroads with new equipment and attitudes to match. Carving and straight-lining were being replaced by bigger manoeuvres, or just more of them. Accordingly, I was going to wiggle my way to victory.

Ψ

And this is basically what I did. The Hawaiians surfed beautifully that day, more beautifully than me. And they got tubes galore. Joey and Hans thrashed and smashed with verve and panache, and also managed some very good, high-scoring barrel time. I tried to do both, but with the added wiggle, making sure to spend more time in the deepest, nastiest caverns of the tube. Those deep rides in the barrel were made possible by the 'backdooring' technique I'd learned from Gerry Lopez all those years before out at Uluwatu and here I was using it against the legend himself in his own backyard. The counterintuitive move involves taking off on the wrong side of the peak, so that you are speeding towards the advancing lip at first, rather than flowing with it. It feels like suicide but it works, and I needed it on that last wave. The thing was an angry, beastly near-close-out barrel from start to finish. I really didn't think I had much chance as I fell down the face of it, barely connected to my board or to the water. I don't know how I ducked my head under the falling weight of the lip without being driven through my board, but I somehow stayed on, pumped back up the face, hung on and made it out the end of that thing with an inch to spare.

And that was that. The best day in my career. I stood in the honey-coloured sand of Ehukai in front of the Colonel and his entire family, plus half of Hawaii and thousands of bikini-clad, screaming tourists. I was the newly crowned Banzai Pipeline Masters champion.

I have no idea what went through my mind. I believed Mum's prediction, perhaps, but I was still an Aussie nobody and I was as shocked as everybody else. The surprise blew all the other emotions out of my head. I wish I'd stood back, looked to the sky, thanked Neptune and taken it all in, but I didn't.

After the trophy presentation, the hand-shaking, the interviews and the speeches were done, I jumped in my car. Dire Straits' 'Sultans of Swing' was on the radio and I drove back up the Kamehameha Highway drinking in Mark Knopfler's sweet singing guitar. Soon enough, I was back at the Kui Lima for beer and whisky with my fellow heathens.

Ψ

A surf contest in Hawaii is daunting for many reasons but one of the strangest is American girls in bikinis. At the warm-up contests there are thousands of them and they all seem to want to talk to you or yell out suggestions about what you should do with various body parts (theirs and yours). I've never had any swagger and in truth I find it quite frightening. A large number of these new 'friends' arrived at the Kui Lima where Wayne Deane, a bunch of other Aussies and I have the solemn duty of entertaining them. Which we do, giving a good account of ourselves, or so my imagination insists.

Next morning, once again I'm up early. I'm not entirely sure about my behaviour last night, but am fairly certain I offended everybody. At one point I dressed up as Gary Glitter, which didn't help, even if none of us knew he was a paedophile back then. I don't think I'm the king of the world anymore. I'm back to being an anxious, ragged tuft of Aussie tumbleweed.

I know what to do. Everybody is asleep so I grab my seven-foot pintail, get in the car and drive back down the Kamehameha Highway. Past the cattle sheds, across the beach at Sunset (where I can see and smell from the wafting clouds of iodine that it's pumping even though it's barely light yet) and straight past the school opposite Pipeline. A fleeting glimpse at Rock Piles, where the beach is taking over the crumbling road, confirms that it's on today. I'm feeling better already.

Despite the hurtling there's time to dream. Only one thing has been missing in the midst of the pageantry: Mum, far too tied up to be here. I know she would have moved everything for yesterday if she could – she always loved the idea of my pointless passion and was eager to facilitate and witness it wherever I went.

I remember a trip up to the far North Coast years ago with the musketeers when she had agreed to drive us in the Valiant, that shiny brown sardine tin, boards roped onto the hard top. The boys had freaked when they realised after a few kilometres, with the Valiant speeding down a hill squealing like a tortured pig and the transmission getting molten-hot in second, that mum didn't know how to change gears.

She had been so committed to helping us get exotic waves that she'd refused to allow this small detail to get in the way of all our fun. Mick and Terry had to spend the rest of the 800-kilometre trip up one of the world's most dangerous and twisted highways operating the gearstick for her, telling her when to push the clutch down and when to release it. The boys were quite amused but mostly terrified and I think they only tolerated it because, like everybody, they were smitten with her.

A few corners later I pass the Waimea bend, up the hill and down again, and arrive at Jocko's where I park in the tiny lay-by opposite the beach, still dazed and drunk but not yet hungover. My organs are as desiccated as the piles of leaves crunching underfoot. Some lovely left-hand barrels are flaring far out to sea, visible over the top of Jock Sutherland's rocky backyard, and I get that feeling again in my beer-and-whisky-scarred stomach. Doubts vanish.

I run across the road and jump into the rip, half paddling, half getting dragged out to sea, ducking my head under the waves and letting the sea refill me from the outside in. All around, my life is perfect as I ride the six-footers alone in the pale amber light.

24.

At the Peak Looking Down

On the days when the sea is brightly lit you can see oncoming waves more clearly, but they cast darker shadows.

A life seen from an older age can often be divided into parts. For mine, the separation between 'before Pipeline '78' and 'after Pipeline '78' was the opening up of a deep crevasse. Me being me, I gladly leaped across this crevasse without even knowing it was there. Only when I landed on the other side did I realise that I couldn't get back. Things had to change after winning surfing's big prize, but almost every part of my new existence would become unrecognisable.

I knew there'd be way more sponsors, trips and attention than in the aftermath of Manly, but becoming known as a 'Pipeline Master' created reverberations I could never have expected. The first thing I found out was that success opens the door to great adventures, but not usually to friendship.

As that unlucky sea captain discovered in 1778, Hawaiians give most visitors the warmest of aloha welcomes. Sometimes they even elevate a foreigner to god-like status. But I was about to learn two hundred years later, such adulation is always temporary. Like the captain of the *Resolution*, I had had my deification on the beach, but I was now outstaying my welcome. Entering a run of local competitions and making a decent showing was one irritant. My dress sense, general manner and loose mouth combined to create another. I'd be dicing with my own destruction if I were to win the Pipeline Masters again. I might not meet my death gloriously, surrounded by my troops on the beach, but I couldn't rule out being choked or just smacked over the head by any number of people who my presence had offended.

Immediately after the 1978 contest, I was in a blissful shock, blinded by an avalanche of attention. On the one hand I felt uncomfortable – I wasn't used to mingling in polite society and I also had something to lose for one of the first times in my life. On the other, out in the sea I was starting to feel invincible. I'd only entered two major surf contests, by chance the two highest paying in history, and I'd won them both. The competition tour of the US and Australia that came soon afterwards delivered adulation and cheering on beaches everywhere. I didn't have a manager saying, 'Look out' or 'Calm down.' My mentors on the rung above me were equally inexperienced, and the example they set just egged me on even more. And there was all the magazine stuff. I guess it was bound to fuck with my head.

Well, that's my excuse for letting the horrid, yapping inner Jack Russell even further off the leash.

At the time it seemed perfectly natural to strut about and talk myself up like I did. In my past, especially as a teenager, I had learned how to handle new situations and to hide my nerves and fear. That method, the tried and tested way of the outlaw, was to go on the attack and display total confidence, even if you did have half an eye on the exit. This MO had stood me in good stead for most of the tricky moments in my life up until now. It had also probably helped me win when the chips were down. Sudden success and adoration (both false and real) had only fuelled it. So why not trust it?

But it turned out that all this was a terrible recipe for handling overnight fame. Especially in a proud country with a deep heritage and a troubled, isolated history such as Hawaii.

On top of all that, new opportunities following on from my newfound celebrity meant that I had started the process of going truly soft. While I was away from Hawaii over that summer season, I had played Sir Andrew Aguecheek in an acclaimed (the show, not me) theatre production of Shakespeare's *Twelfth Night* in Sydney, prancing about drunk in tights opposite Sir Toby Belch. I'd been studiously honing my art at drama school as well as hanging about with various theatrical types. At night, I was usually at home in Coogee cooking riz pilaf or chicken cacciatore from Nanna's little notebook. That lady always grew her own herbs and so I always went to enormous pains to seek them out fresh, and I would be peeved to distraction when I couldn't find them.

When I did go out I was often a well-dressed man-about-town – not a hard man on the steps of the Oceanic or a surf nazi looking for trouble at the North End bluff. That ridiculous dress code was always strictly followed, in particular with regard to my feet. Fauntleroy was back in town! If everybody else was in thongs, I was in freshly unboxed brogues. If they were in singlets, I was in a polo shirt. And instead of ripped denim shorts, I got around in neatly pressed chinos.

I even sported the odd knitted cardigan or a pastel-coloured cashmere jumper perfectly draped over my shoulders. When shorts were essential, for example, on the beach or in the surf, I still had options, including those shiny little metallic numbers from my sponsors at Offshore.

I was definitely not hanging out with hardened criminals anymore or fighting under the Coogee pier. All in all, the nine months spent enjoying life around the world after the wonderful events of 1978 were a disastrous preparation for the next season on the North Shore.

Ψ

Soon after I returned to Oahu for the 1979 winter swell season, the sinewy, vinegary self-styled Black Short lieutenant who I called 'the Rat' issued a very odd warning. I'd been surfing an uncharacteristically small and messy Pipeline, testing a quiver of five new boards that Californian Brian Buckley had just shaped for me. One in particular was sprayed in a gloriously fluorescent series of rainbow stripes that yelled 'Look at me!' to everybody walking past on the narrow strip of beach. The waves were garbage that day but I scored an awful lot of them, which probably annoyed all the other surfers out there – if there was any chance I hadn't been noticed, Buckley's luridly pretty specimens would have made sure of it. I was still in warrior mode however, getting ready to defend my title, and so I didn't give it any thought.

Over the off season, I had forgotten about the undercurrents, and the trials and tribulations suffered by all my fellow imports. I thought my return would signal a fresh start. I was the champ, after all. Perhaps everyone had missed me while I was away.

My wonderful de facto godparents, BB and the Colonel, were on the beach guarding my gear as I came and went to collect and test each board. After a couple of hours, I was pleased with myself and got a wave that ran all the way through to the beach, where I bellied in and sat contentedly next to my lovely sparkling new toys.

The Rat, attracted to all the colours and with incandescent hatred burning in his eyes, strode up to us and, without warning, stabbed all five of my brand-new surfboards with his own one, like a spear. I'd been wrong about fresh starts. It turns out that on the North Shore, there is no forgetting.

I'm wary of anyone who's shorter than me; the two other short people in my life, Dad and his mate Fletcher, were two of the most violent men I've ever known. I've also never been one for fists if they can be left down by my side; by age twenty I already knew what awful things could happen when they were raised. And so I didn't offer up too much fight that afternoon on the beach. It was a shame that, surrounded by my beloved surfboards and my dear friends, I couldn't just run away. Knowing my position was hopeless, I just stood there, looking at him. Then after about a minute of silence, one of the behavioural ticks that I'd picked up via Mum's friends at Melody Street slipped out. Without doubt that living room full of thieves and their silly pranks and jokes had permanently warped my sense of humour and so, for no good reason, I started to laugh.

The sorry little scuffle was over pretty fast and without too much blood except for a dribble down my cheek. BB especially was horrified and I felt awful for her – she was the most kind-hearted and generous lady I knew and a magnanimous host to all of us *haole* jetsam. I think the Colonel himself was just speechless. He would have seen many real fights in his time, but none as plain silly as this one. The Rat marched off swiftly without any further aloha, except to let me know that I would 'never be safe in Hawaii' even if I was a guest of the Colonel.

I'd never seen the board-spearing ritual before. Perhaps my assailant invented it there and then, just for me. Perhaps he and his boss saw themselves as doing their bit to protect local waves from invaders and the sight of so much glistening new hardware on display sent him over the edge.

The theme continued throughout that winter despite me keeping a low profile (by my standards). I was here to surf and win contests, not get hurt.

Alas, that day's board-stabbing and fisticuffs was only the start of it. Some of our antagonists had guns, which were used on occasion. I occasionally stayed with my dear friend Dave, whose father had a house right on the peak at Pipeline. Dave's lifeguard patch, running from Pipeline to Waimea, is probably the toughest in the world. To jump in and prevent people drowning along that most dangerous of coasts with its massive swells and turbulent currents, you have to be more than a good swimmer or an expert surfer. You have to be that thing that transcends all of it – a 'waterman'. In Hawaii, being a waterman is more consequential than any surfing honour.

Dave had befriended me against all odds when my Hawaiian adventure was just beginning. That's the way he is, always ready to extend the hand of friendship to anybody who needs or deserves it, no matter the cost (and the cost of befriending *haoles* could be high during this time of bitterness), and without expecting anything in return.

A shadow had passed across our friendship once – those days were always more confusing out of the water than in it, especially when it came to our relationships with girls. Dave and I never really knew when the other was serious about a girl and it was during one of these tangled periods that we each slept with the other's girlfriend. I was in love with Rebecca, who I'd met at a surf contest in Australia. So much so that I took her to Hawaii. I left her there when I had to go to the US mainland and do my duty by some sponsors by competing at the Katin Pro in guady Orange County. Before I left I gave her a diamond ring.

When I got back to Hawaii, I found out what had happened immediately. Dave basically admitted it. I was devastated and blew up in his face, accusing him of 'premeditated murder'! I had a completely childish fit, partly because I'd recently noticed, while we were getting changed for a surf, that Dave had a bigger nob than me. To be fair he was also quite tall, extremely handsome and of course a supreme lifeguard.

Given that I'd shagged his girlfriend back in California, he just laughed at me, became annoyed for a second, but then laughed again. He had things in perspective whereas I briefly hadn't. Dave forgave my petulance and thanks to him our friendship survived and flourished. It's another mark of who he is as a person. Rebecca never gave me back that diamond ring.

But even Dave, a bona fide local hero who was saving dozens of lives each week, was not immune from the troubles. One of the tough guys apparently had a row over a girl with him one day, and he was shot in the face. An old friend from my home town who witnessed it told me Dave only narrowly survived.

He was incredibly lucky that the bullet went in one side of his jaw and out the other and miraculously missed his brain or any arteries. Who knows whether the near miss was intended or whether murder had been the desired outcome? The bullet took quite a few teeth and a bit of jaw with it though, and his face had to be wired up for some time.

I don't think Dave ate any truly enjoyable food for several months during his recovery, but he did recover fully. Somehow, he still greets me with a lovely aloha smile whenever I see him. I sometimes wonder if it was his openness during a time of intolerance that made him a target. Whatever the reason, the incident demonstrated that nobody was safe in those days, local or not.

And of course it rocked me. After this, the Rabbit Bartholomew incident and my own various scuffles, I was becoming wary. I knew that I had to make use of my childhood experience and turn that radar up to its most sensitive setting, to detect and avoid trouble at the slightest blip. Maintaining that setting is tiring; it makes you irritable and you start seeing everything differently. Connections are made when they are not always there. I don't think it's paranoia – not quite. Lucky for me, living on the best island on earth prevented me from dwelling on this too much.

I also had my heart set on winning a second Pipeline Masters and to do so I obviously had to avoid being maimed. The need to keep a low profile was in direct conflict with the need to practise and get good waves at the power spots, especially Pipe itself, which meant that I was in a race against the clock.

This is why I started buying into the Colonel's early morning surf sessions, waking up the long-suffering Fielding earlier and earlier each week, to a point where I believe he actually hated me and started to feel ill every time he heard I was around. My body clock – and slightly manic zeal to win – was starting to affect his pro career by exhausting him mentally and physically.

I was lucky that underneath all that gangster bravado I was a runner-away, not a fighter. In the family business, I'd spent years learning to spot danger and make swift exits, and I was fast both in and out of the water. Perhaps that was my own superpower: speed and controlled cowardice.

I don't know why these huge tough guys ever bothered trying to chase me once we got onto the beach, because they could never get near this terrified little rabbit once those legs got going. They must have been crazy – or slightly stupid – not to have realised the futility of trying to catch me after so many attempts (definition of madness and all that). Eventually I would get caught and when that happened, it wouldn't end well.

One other useful concession to fear meant that I stayed in an awful lot and cooked. This isn't too hard on the North Shore where there are few bars and the ahi (yellowfin tuna) is the freshest on the planet. Preparing Hawaiian raw fish salad (poke) and sashimi for the family on the hill was all the night-time excitement I needed, with the only requirements being a very sharp knife and a few condiments.

Cooking had always interested me but now became central to my life. It was psychotherapy, relaxation, safety, and a handy pastime to discover at a point in life when you find out that your big mouth is really only a disguise for insecurity. I was starting to see that I was only comfortable in three places: the Melody Street back room, out in the waves, and in a kitchen surrounded by knives and produce.

Thanks to Nanna's cooking lectures, I bet there will be a few fabulous ladies out there who know that they only stayed with me more than a week because of the food I made for them. Watching some guy paddling about in the sea is not a great way to spend your time, and it definitely isn't worth it if he gets back home with nothing else to talk about but tubes and take-offs.

Despite all these strategies, it was hard to stay out of the thick of it. In surfing, you have to get waves, and at Pipeline there is only one shifty little take-off spot, about two feet by two, with fifty surfers (these days over a hundred) all wanting to use it. It's a miracle that there aren't even more fights and serious accidents.

To add to the challenging atmosphere, some of my fellow blow-ins behaved pretty badly, perhaps because they thought they could get away with anything, being so far from home, but mostly because we were all so young. The main reason for the aggro was quite fundamental; in the early days of surfing, it was not a cool sport. Doctors, lawyers and tech people did not surf. In fact, people with actual jobs did not surf. Surfing was the refuge of the misfit. The majority of my fellow wave riders came from weird, broken, abnormal homes just like me. Most of us had nobody in our group of elders to tell us how to behave. In essence, for quite a bit of time we were tarring each other with our own brushes.

This didn't help me in my attempts to stay away from trouble, but the art of running away did, and after that initial blip and a few very minor hand-slappy disagreements, I made it more or less intact to Pipe '79.

Ψ

As the winter rolled on, like all surfers on Oahu, I waited and waited for news that Pipeline would be on again. Surf forecasts in those days consisted of looking at isobar charts on the back page of the newspaper, seeking out closely packed lines in the north of the Pacific, and measuring the distance and angle between the centre of the storm and the coast. From this, you could work out when the swell ought to hit (usually by adding three or four days) and match it up with local wind and weather forecasts to see if that would mean anything good. You could be right, and you could be off by days, which is why I never bothered.

But Randy did, and soon enough, in early December, it was announced that we were in business. Randy, Rarick and Fred Hemmings were the oracles of competition surfing in Hawaii; they also invented the world championship tour that we see on TV today. So after their much-awaited announcement, a ripple went around the North Shore.

Ψ

The finals day itself started in an unpleasant way. In fact, it nearly didn't start at all. Early in the morning, during the Masters warm-up period, I was mucking about out the back in mid-to-solid ten-foot surf trying to find my feet, and to get into the competition groove. After all, I was the reigning champ and was meant to be a professional. Without doubt I was minding my own business.

Suddenly, Dane appeared from out of nowhere and dropped in on me, just like that. Dropping in means paddling into somebody else's wave from a wrong position away from the peak, a bit like an offside in football. This practice is the cardinal sin of our sport, and usually results in a fight or at least some verbal handbag waving. So I was taken by surprise. I hadn't heard the new North Shore locals' rule, which was: 'Every wave that comes in belongs to us.' And it sure was a lovely, clean, well-shaped little wave. Tempting as a warm meat pie on the lips, ready to be bitten and swallowed.

And when you're about to bite a meat pie, no seagull is going to swoop in and stop you. Therefore, instead of conceding the perfectly shaped beauty to the local hero like a polite holiday maker, I asserted my rights and took off right behind him. It was a mistake. At waves like Pipe this can be dangerous, leading to high-speed collisions. Never a good thing when big men and sharp, heavy boards are involved. I dropped down the face and held my line, meaning that Dane had to eject and give me back my wave. I immediately realised that this was going to become an incident. Dane Kealoha was, as I knew well, not the person you wanted to have a disagreement with. Not just because he was huge, but because he was an emerging legend of the North Shore.

My next memory is of being knocked off my board, clubbed in the head by his two very large fists, and my Lucky Buddha charm with its silver chain being ripped from my neck and sent to the bottom. I was stunned. I surfaced, clung to my board and stared at him speechlessly. My heart started beating faster and faster till it reached three times the normal speed, and my breathing shortened to a dog-like panting. I don't know what he said to me, it was probably just a glare, before he paddled back out to sea.

It took time and effort to slow down all my bodily systems and try to relax and focus, and even longer to let the cold chemicals drain away, but life went on, of course; this was the North Shore.

When you are a runner-away, it is usually a bad idea to stay and fight, and so this was not a good start to a finals day.

Ψ

A few hours and a number of heats later, I somehow made it into the final. I was within sight of the peak, and all I had to do was catch the best waves and ride them better than the five legends of surfing who had also made it to this point. We were to tussle it out together, every man for himself, with very few rules other than that he who gets the best ten waves in the hour and spends the most time in the tube, wins.

Hardly a recipe for fair and sportsman-like competition!

The beach was absolutely packed. Ehukai Beach park is a natural amphitheatre; the sand slopes steeply down to the shore break and so everybody has an uninterrupted view. The waves break so close to the beach you can see the expressions of the surfers and hear the noise of the spray flying off the tops of the waves themselves, and the occasional *boom* as a barrel spits somebody out. It's the best place in the world to watch the surf and the perfect setting for a competition.

The pageantry is ad hoc, natural, provided by the place itself and the crowds that are barely contained by the thin strip of sand squeezed in between the bushes at the top of the slope and the waterline. Every so often the surge will run through the crowd, taking baskets, towels and the odd child back into the sea as it retreats. I haven't been to any sporting event anywhere in the world that compares to the extraordinary vibe that you get here at Pipeline every December.

I had hoped that Mum might be able to come but she was doing her thing somewhere, and I suspect she was in full flow keeping the police forces of the world on their toes. Instead, I was surprised by the sudden, unannounced arrival of 'Fat Larry' Crane, with both parents in tow. My lunatic friend from Maroubra, with a smile so deep it split his face clean in two, had appeared on the beach and announced that he'd flown all the way 'from Sydney, Australia!' to be my head cheerleader. Larry was possibly the only person from my childhood with whom I shared no bad memories at all, and so he and his family were a brilliant substitution.

By now the surf was about ten to twelve feet (eighteen- to twenty-foot faces). Not huge, but big, and easily enough to snap you in half or stuff you into one of the lava caves under the take-off spot if you got it wrong. The crowd was hooting every barrel and oohing every wipeout as if they were out there themselves. I imagine the Colosseum once had a similar ambience. Their favourite gladiator was clearly Dane, who had a lot at stake because a win here would leapfrog him into a narrow lead for the world title with only one contest remaining.

My five co-finalists and I mooched on the beach for a while, waiting for the signal to paddle out and start the heat. I made no eye contact with Dane. Maybe I exchanged a few words with my fellow Aussies MR and Tom Carroll. Larry Bertlemann was doing his routine, which was very little indeed, being the coolest surfer on the island (planet?), and Shaun Tomson was meditating quietly.

As for me, I was babbling the usual word-minestrone to myself. Bread and butter, bread and butter, and so on. I added some fervency, out of necessity since Lucky Buddha was at this moment drowning in a lava cave and unable to be of much assistance. I considered him a lucky charm and with good reason – after five years of travels with the little golden one, I was still here and therefore clearly still alive against all odds, and he was the common factor.

Finally, we were told it was time to head into the sea and out the back to await the starting hooter. (Why does that word get a new meaning every decade?) At this point, Fast Eddie intervened. He and his crew had been given the job of water marshals for the duration of the Pipeline Masters, as was the (inexplicable) custom. I felt it was like engaging the Hells Angels to police a rock festival. It meant that Eddie could sit out the back with all the competitors, supposedly to help anybody who was drowning or to retrieve a lost board. Unfortunately, it also enabled him to be a little bit mischievous, greeting me with an ironic smile as we all arrived in the zone for the start of proceedings, and using his position to subtly distract me as I paddled back out past him after each ride. He may not have meant to distract me, but I was distracted.

The heat was bloody chaos. On some waves, all six of us went for the peak, elbowing each other like jockeys. I saw Tom go for a seemingly legitimate take-off at the same time as Dane, only to get pushed off his board by the much bigger man, who took off across his free-falling body in the opposite direction. Dane was smoking it, getting back-hand barrels that drew *oohs* and *aaahs* from the crowd thronging the beach and spilling over the water-line. He soon had nine waves and his last must have been a heat winner because the packed amphitheatre reacted with an ecstatic roar. He was way out in the lead, and retired to the beach having filled his quota. Everyone thought he had it in the bag.

My second to last wave, however, was something really quite bizarre. I don't think it was a sign from above, or any kind of intervention of fate, but crikey that wave was one of the strangest I'd ever ridden. I took off from second reef straight into a full-bore barrel, was blinded in the foam and became lost deep in the pit for a few seconds, before being ejected by the rasping spit out onto the shoulder. But the ride wasn't over yet; as I started to lie down on my board thinking of the desperate paddle to safety, there was suddenly a *new* section of the wave forming, a sort of dessert wave . . . I got back to my feet and rode the weird little afterthought, which delivered me into a second barrel. It caused an uproar on the beach, and I was sure it had earned something close to maximum points from the judges going by the whoops and shouts. It was definitely game on now between Dane and me.

I needed a ten on my last available wave to win, nothing less. Once out the back again, Eddie, who must have seen the momentum swing in my favour, was smiling at me and chatting away from his handy marshalling position. I couldn't hear everything he said because I was in deep concentration checking for the next set and jockeying with the others to try to occupy the ideal spot, but I assumed it was not 'may the best man win' or whatnot.

This constant chatter seemed to me unusual behaviour during a competition. Kind of like being heckled by the head ball boy at a grand slam tennis match. But in this case the ball boy was an orc who would beat you up without a second thought. It's always unsettling when somebody who normally wants to bash you in the head starts smiling and chatting like you're a friend. And to be fair, Fast Eddie always had a very nice smile.

I put him out of my mind and went for one last wave, pipping the remaining surfers to the take-off and free-falling down the on-rushing mountain. When I hit the bottom, everything shook as I absorbed the force through my knee and hip joints, but I kept just enough control and latent speed to climb a couple of feet back up the face and under the heavy lip. I kept hidden deep in the liquid cathedral until its blizzard of spray ejected me onto the open face and over the back of the wave.

It felt like another full points haul in my humblest of opinions (I know how that sounds), and the crowd was going quite mad because, like me, I don't think they believed I was ever coming out of that thing. The hooter signalled the end of the heat, and as I bellied back to shore I was sure that the day was going to be mine.

When the judges announced my win and I collected the cheque, and a massive, heavy wooden block that was under attack from metal fish with a glassy blob of spittle on top that was actually quite beautiful, Mark, Shaun and Tom shook my hand warmly. I think they were happy for me, and they knew they were going on to have great futures. Tom seemed just stoked to be there even if he'd bought it horrifyingly on a couple of contested take-offs. Larry Bertlemann was just Larry, living undisturbed in his own parallel world and taking whatever came his way while probably dreaming up skateboard designs in his head.

But I hadn't noticed Dane, head thrown back and face covered by his hands as the announcement was made, and then smouldering behind a gracious façade. This was the second year he'd been denied the trophy. It never even crossed my mind that not winning today might have cost him the best chance he'd ever have of a world championship.

25.

Over the Falls

Seeing is mostly a hallucination – the brain telling the eye what to see and the eye confirming. More signals speed away from the brain towards the eye than come back the other way. This explains a lot.

Back-to-back Pipeline wins should have been the peak of my career, opening up a mountain range of opportunity. But at the one time in my life when I needed to keep my busy little mouth shut, I did exactly the opposite.

I knew that people were angry about the local favourites being beaten in their own backyard again. And by now I was well aware that many of us newcomers had made ourselves unwelcome on the North Shore. Yet I was still making the same mistakes as the rest of us, the same noises. Sometimes my musings were even worse.

Today, it amazes me. PT, Kanga and Rabbit had blazed a magnificent trail, and I'd followed it. It had given me great success. They had made their youthful mistakes, which I've dwelt upon in these pages, mainly in order to try to justify my own. But I didn't learn from them when it counted, that is, while all this great stuff was happening. I just *copied* them and added some cream on top.

My first error was an interview in *Surfer* magazine right after the 1979 contest. I managed to get it all wrong, starting with actually believing what the biggest magazine in the surfing world had called me ('The new king of Pipe'). They'd also cooed about me being the youngest-ever winner, to add to the swelling hubris. Then I, a two-time winner from nowhere, was asked about what my plans were for the future. My mouth has let me down many times in my life, spitting out things that I thought were funny because at Melody Street they were. Or channelling American footballers and boxers, as many of us did back then.

What I said next, however, broke new ground. It was that moment when you see a huge set wave looming up ahead. You're nervous but you think you have it nailed – you're going to make it – and so you paddle casually up the face only to get sucked backwards, headfirst over the falls, downwards in the tumbling whitewater to your doom.

Grinning away like a child, I said I was going to put five (correct, *five*) Pipeline Masters' victories to my name. I wanted five but three would do. I said it with no pride or swagger but because it was simply what I thought and since they asked . . . But it was utterly idiotic – a disaster class in post-match media management. And just like the others before me, it was going to cost me dearly. I'd made many mistakes, all contributing to my downfall, but this was the best.

Ψ

By the time the *Surfer* article was published I was long gone, having nonchalantly jetted back to Sydney. In Australia, my big mouth was not seen as a character flaw, but rather as an endearing quality. The battling Aussie mongrel and all that. Yap, yap!

I spent the year all over the world, lording it up in Japan, America and Indonesia and god knows where. Life was the best and certainly the easiest it had ever been. People gave me yet more stuff and I had yet more time in front of camera crews doing adverts and rubbish TV, both of which are a guaranteed way to give a person an even more skewed sense of their own worth.

I also drank more, crashed more cars and spoke with alarming confidence to more ladies than ever before. I was called 'rambunctious' in the press, and I didn't know what the word meant. I was also too lazy to look it up. I should have.

Fat Larry and I tore up Sydney, writing ourselves off at the surf club and staggering about town insulting grizzly men and complimenting horrified women. At least I didn't get involved in any crimes*.

It didn't help my character development that I was also spending quite a lot of time in California, both competing and carrying out a growing job sheet of sponsorship missions. This brought me face to face with people who were not always from the same background as me, and whose feet had long been as disconnected from the ground as mine were quickly becoming.

In those days all surf towns had a place where pro surfers hung out, stayed or outstayed. The pro tour birthed and encouraged these halfway houses, which brought surfers together with a procession of whatever curious folk the town in question might feature. In Hawaii it had been the Colonel's, and in Los Angeles's South Bay it was the Doc's. Another stray dogs' home.

Doc Ackroyd – and he was a real doctor from Minnesota – had a sprawling den in the affluent suburb of Hermosa Beach which fulfilled this function for years. Doc welcomed me in even though he didn't really surf. His other regular guests included Shaun Tomson, Dane Kealoha, Rabbit Bartholomew, Clyde Aikau (Eddie's brother), Montgomery 'Buttons' Kaluhiokalani, and many more. For a while it kind of felt like home, just like the house up on the hill on the North Shore.

The Doc's friends Chris Barela and Michael Benavidez, alongside Michael Ho and me, formed part of a branded surfing team sponsored by Offshore clothing, and so groups of us hung out together quite a bit, often at Montezuma's Mexican Restaurant on the Hermosa Pier. As well as the surfers, the Doc's entourage included a rotation of actors and musicians. At the upper end of this scale was the sandy-haired, fun-loving and permanently luminescent Debbie Tate. Somehow or other Debbie and I hit it off and for a short time were inseparable.

In the late 1970s, the surf spots of Palos Verdes just south of LA were a closely guarded secret and became legendary for all the wrong reasons, as local gangs beat up any visitor simply for being there. Localism is one of surfing's ugly secrets, and can rear up anywhere, but the Doc's neighbourhood spots of Haggerty's and Lunada Bay set the template for the rest of the world. Having Debbie by my side gave me a pass to ride the waves and thanks to her I never got necklaced (or whatever bizarre punishment du jour was in force at the time), even if we did have to get helicoptered out one day in the floods that ran rivers down the steep hills.

I was in town for the Huntington Beach Pro-Am, and on contest day Shaun Tomson beat me into second with Tom Curren coming third. Debbie had been barracking for me on the beach and I'd probably disappointed her, but she had a big heart and forgave me. Debbie had an enormous, canvas-topped safari jeep in which she took me on a consolation ski trip up to Big Bear in San Bernardino County. It was not just the first time I'd been on skis; at that point in my life I had actually never even seen snow. I felt like a child refugee on that mountain – a feeling I often had when mingling with the wonderful folk of eccentric, illogical Southern California.

Debbie and I also took in Sun Valley, which sticks in my mind as one of the most wondrously beautiful places I have ever visited. Debbie was smart, immaculately dressed, and she oozed glamorous nonchalance. To my eyes her family were Hollywood royalty and I couldn't fathom why she would take an interest in me. Perhaps it was because I was from such a different world.

I remember one day visiting her mother and enjoying a delicate bone china pot of tea at the elegant hair salon she owned and ran over in Redondo Beach. The salon walls were covered in framed photographs of Debbie's sister, Sharon, whose stellar film career had been tragically cut short when she was murdered by members of Charles Manson's cult in the summer of 1969. The murders had shocked the world and Debbie and her family never really got over it. They had faced unimaginable grief with dignity and to my eyes the salon was like a sort of sacred shrine.

ψ

In what was becoming a bit of a pattern, Debbie soon tired of my itinerancy, one-dimensional focus on surfing and raw fish. Sadly, ours wasn't to be a long-term relationship. After this blurred year spent bouncing around the world instead of thinking, the time came for Pipeline 1980, which I, like half of the world outside Hawaii, was absolutely convinced I was going to win.

But when I arrived back on the islands, I was not presented with a le'i.

The ugly atmosphere was evident from the moment I paddled out for my first surf. Whereas in the past, aside from the 'incidents' with the Rat et al, the worst I'd copped was a bit of backchat. Maybe a few slaps here and there. But now there was a noticeable and nasty darkening of the mood. Last year I was the enemy simply for winning stuff and being foreign, but I still had my friends. This year, I felt hated. Possibly, I deserved it – I was an excitable wave-hog and they hadn't forgotten me mouthing off in that *Surfer* magazine article. Possibly, I did not. But I never got the opportunity to sit down and talk it all out, to find out what I had done wrong, or to try to correct it.

Even the surfers I knew best were now blanking me or giving me weird looks. Michael Ho, godfather of the North Shore and a close friend of the Bensons, was inexplicably (it seemed to me) cold. It puzzled me that just a few months ago Michael, Chris Barela and I had been on the same team at the Huntington Beach titles, with no hint of acrimony, and everyone knew how much I revered Michael. All of a sudden past friendships and collaborations counted for nothing, and any bonds formed off the islands had a clear and incontrovertible expiry date.

My favourite and most convenient Rocky Point haunt was now a regular stop-off on morning Black Shorts patrols.

It was Fast Eddie's surf spot anyway, but it felt like his minion, the Rat, had it in for me. In hindsight, I think the man was a fringe player who was singling me out for special attention in the hope that he might be taken a bit more seriously by the big boys if he gave me the odd slapping from time to time. I wasn't exactly the most intimidating target.

Either one of these two would bring six or more of their huge mates, often including the colossal Squiddy, a native Hawaiian and local legend who seemed like an oak tree, out into the surf whenever they saw me it seemed, and literally chase me from the sea. Sometimes the group would follow me to the next spot down the beach and repeat the routine until one of us gave up.

In 1980, it was made clear that I would never win another Pipeline and the powers that be were going to do everything they could to hinder my preparation. I tried what I thought was diplomacy, I hung out in the channel taking the lesser waves that swung in wide, and I generally kept away from other surfers. I even did that face with the eyes and the open mouth. None of this had any effect, and if I wasn't harried out of the ocean, the enforcement crew would deliberately drop in on me or snake me for waves. If a wave was mine, any regular within striking distance would circumnavigate me and take it. Often this would come with the expectation of a fight that I would not provide, to everyone's disappointment.

Ψ

With a third straight Pipeline title in sight, once again, I retreated even deeper into my little crab hole. I was a winner. The champ. Some people still patted me on the back and even called out my name as they passed by and so this must surely mean that underneath all the other chatter, some people still loved me. At no point did any of the managers, TV producers, clothing sponsors or contest officials ever sit me down and say what I needed to hear. 'Larry. Stop being such a little prick. Be quiet, be humble, apologise to everybody in Hawaii, and change those awful shorts!'

I don't know if it would have made any difference, but I regret not seeing clearly what was happening right in front of me all the same. I could have put in the effort, the thought, but on the North Shore I just looked down into that honey-gold sand, deployed the 'Larry filter' and saw only what I wanted to see. And that, of course, was lovable little me just making the jokes and smoking it in the waves. Taking this narrow view ensured that I failed to deal with the angry undercurrent.

When the 1980 Pipe finals day arrived, I made another fatal miscalculation. Pro surfing was by now a TV sport, with major sponsors, substantial prize money, professional judging panels and an entire industry sprouting out from it. Some competitions staged the same kind of glitzy production as American football, complete with rows of scantily clad ladies and grandstands heaving with boozed-up teenagers. It was easy to get carried away with it all.

I didn't understand that out in the water, even during a professional contest, you were still on Oahu's North Shore and the waves were not the only threat.

The man-on-man heat system hadn't been introduced yet, nor had the interference rule, so it was still possible for competitors to hunt in packs of three or more to surround and pick off stray mongrels. It should have been obvious that an impolite half-criminal from Down Under who dressed up and was up for his third straight win would be the primary target. I was, after all, the idiot *haole* who'd told the world that he was going to rule the waves for *a decade*.

It started pretty well and I won a few heats, sailing into the semi-finals feeling like it was going to be my year again. But that's where it all changed. I was hounded and chased off waves in that semi, sometimes by three or four other surfers, and even more hurtfully, not just Hawaiians. At some moments, I felt like a seal hunted by orcas. This is a disqualification offence today but it was within the rules back then. It turned many of the heats into a sort of medieval battle, where alliances held sway over individual skill. I crashed out of the competition barely taking a wave.

Mark Richards won the contest in the end, heralding the beginning of one of the most illustrious careers the sport has ever seen. MR would go on to become world champion no fewer than four times in a row.

People still say that I was running hot, nailed on for the title and that I was robbed that year, but the fact is that I'm lucky to have survived Pipeline 1980. As well as the aggression among the competitors, the waves were massive throughout the entire competition, breaking way out at third reef. *Tracks* magazine described the conditions as 'the day surfing went to war'. On most waves it was purely a question of chance whether you pulled into a perfect ten-point barrel or got smashed by the lip and driven into the seabed. Bodies and boards were broken, and some of the wipeouts still make me feel sick when I replay them in my mind. Two of the worst, by the hard-charging young Tom Carroll, can still infiltrate my nightmares today.

On both occasions, I thought he might never resurface, and either one of those drillings could have ended the career of many other surfers. Not Tom, as his amazing successes subsequently proved. These days when it's breaking like it was that week in December 1980, you get towed out onto the waves by jet-ski. I've never dared watch any of the videos from 1980 but I guess I know the ending anyway.

After falling at that second-last hurdle and missing out on the final, I got in my car and disappeared back up the Kamehameha Highway on my own-some. I felt like a little boy robbed of a lolly. Being chased around by groups of surfers I knew I could beat, instead of being allowed fair one-on-one wave riding, right in front of the judges, said to me that it was a system rather than a person that I'd been up against.

A few days later, in the depths of my self-pity, I pulled into the parking bay opposite Jocko's, and Supertramp's song 'Crime of the Century' came on the radio. I loved Supertramp, but this felt like a slightly sick joke. Not only did it ruin my favourite song of theirs for good, it kicked me in the guts while I was already on the floor.

Ψ

After tasting 'stardom' and getting paid to tour the world's most exotic surf spots, I gave up serious competition surfing. I was bruised by the manner in which my run of success had ended and I actually felt sorry for myself. It was pathetic. I couldn't deal with the fact that I didn't win that contest. I just wanted to go home.

The truth is that in 1980 I lost. Fair and square under the rules of the day – I simply hadn't studied them hard enough.

And I did not rise from the ashes or stirringly turn adversity into triumph. I just quit, age twenty-two. The irritating swagger that had helped me win had become my Achilles heel. It had made me a target. At the time I thought that evil and darkness had won the day, but looking back, I could have found ways around it, by taking a look at myself and making a few adjustments instead of blaming everyone else. Fellow surfers like Tom Carroll, Mark Richards and even Shaun Tomson certainly did.

It helped that I had other interests. I had already been weighing up the two possible careers: acting and surfing. In hindsight, I lacked the skills for the first, and the drive for the second. Perhaps it also worked against me, having the knowledge that failure in one always came with the safety net of the other. Perhaps this dulled my hunger and made it too easy for me to give up and run away.

I also had that other pair of distractions – drinking and womanising – and I had become rather good at both. I did love the booze – an intense affair that had started on a Pan Am flight to Honolulu years before, and that was now flourishing. And I continued to take advantage of the whitewashing effects of being a pro sportsman, where faults are overlooked and you gain an entourage who are happy for you to believe that you're a little more special than you really are.

I had briefly enjoyed all the advantages I'd been handed after half a lifetime with Patricia Blair, like the naughty and opportunistic little boy she had brought me up to be.

But ultimately, I squandered them.

26.

Return to Melody Street

Mum is up to her old tricks.

The blood is everywhere. Dripping off me and onto the floor, dribbling off the knife and onto the table. I can't seem to stop it, and the drops are so big I can hear them splashing on the tiles. I didn't even feel it slice into me. I put my hand to my mouth and it tastes of old nails.

It's bolognese night at Melody Street and my brand-new, viciously sharp Victorinox has been in use for the first time. It'll never be this sharp again (having been blunted on one of my knuckle bones), and I'm running my left middle finger under the cold tap, trying to staunch the flow.

Mum straps me up while shooting me one of her looks and we're ready to go again. I've finished dicing a mountain of teeny, perfectly even cubes of onion, and I'm now crushing the cloves of a whole head of garlic under the flat of the blade. My eyes are stinging and weeping so I breathe through my mouth to clear the vapours. Mum meanwhile is grating two slightly soft and monstrous old carrots.

'You're in the wars there, Larry my love! By the way, the girls and I are doing a little number next week. They'll probably be going on about it tonight.'

I've finished mincing the garlic and I'm onto the celery, cutting it into half-inch pieces. Mum's tearing some bay leaves and has opened two rusty old tins of plum tomatoes.

She continues, 'There's an exhibition on at the Town Hall. Biggest diamond ever seen in Australia, Larry.'

'Hmm, okay, Mum, ha ha.'

The side of my mouth droops as I contemplate what she might be planning. I heave the dented aluminium stockpot out of the cupboard by the sink and plonk it on the red-hot ring. Mum glugs a stream of oil into it and the mix is soon throwing up curls of blue smoke.

When my mother laughs, she laughs properly, but she has a way of squeezing witticisms out between contractions so as not to waste any time by pausing.

'I liked you in that Levi's advert . . . How on earth did you squeeze into those jeans . . . Am I not going to get any grandchildren now?'

'Ha ha, Mum. They paid me a lot for all that pain. And it was bloody hot! Did you know they shouted at me in the surf? The guy waved me in and told me to stay out of the barrel 'cause the cameraman couldn't see me! Seriously.'

I'm tossing little balls of glistening, fat-streaked pork mince into the pot and they're blowing up, spitting angrily alongside some chunky pieces of streaky bacon. I want it as brown as possible so I let clumps stick to the bottom as long as I dare, while chopping a few fresh tomatoes on the side until the fat renders and makes little pools. Two scrapes and the clumps are turned upside down for an all-over tan. By now, the kitchen is in a thick fog and I can barely see Mum; the open window's not helping at all.

When the meat is a golden-brown with the odd deliciously crispy dark patch, in goes some tomato paste and the onions, which spit and bobble about. We're going to let them sizzle and brown for a fair old while.

Mum and I are gossiping and giggling about all her silly friends. I'm full of stories too, about failed auditions and drama school. And the fact that I'm about to head back to Hawaii for another winter season. Mum jokes that I live in winter and run away from Australia every time it gets hot. I've given up trying to explain to her how proper waves only get made in winter storms.

When the onions have softened into a deep golden mush and the tomato paste has been tamed, in go the garlic and the celery, just for a couple of minutes. Then a huge slug of yesterday's basket-covered bottle of dodgy Chianti, which fizzes and hisses into a cloud of sweet and sour grapeish perfume.

'We've got to deglaze this properly, Mum.'

The liquid helps me unstick all the thick meaty liquor from the bottom of the pan. When the wine has evaporated I can chuck Mum's carrots in. Like Nanna before her, she swears by them for texture and thickness. Mum then splashes in a bit more wine of course, and the tomatoes, which plop in and splash the stove and the both of us. Good god it smells great already!

Some dirty cheating stock cubes, two crumpled and torn bay leaves and plenty of warm water later, we can stir it a little bit more and then leave it to simmer for the rest of the afternoon.

The other chopped tomatoes and a few herbs all go in at the end once everything in the pot has made friends, amalgamated and thickened.

It's ladies' night at Melody Street, and everybody's coming round to discuss their latest madcap plan.

Ψ

After the sourness in Hawaii, I fled home and found time to stop and reflect on a decade that had started with the worst moment of my life (Dad's murder) and ended with the best (the success I'd always dreamed of, and not being in jail). It seemed like half a lifetime, and it was.

Yet the new decade had already started to disappoint.

It had started with the chilling realisation that sporting success isn't handed to you on a plate. You have to work for it just as hard as people work for success in the real world.

So I decided to give that real world a go. Sort of.

It had all begun with a conversation on the way to the beach one day, a few years earlier, when I was still a kid celebrating my freedom. Fat Larry announced that he'd landed the lead part in a TV commercial. He then suddenly and loudly started singing an incredibly annoying song in front of everyone getting changed in the carpark:

The Milky Bar kid is blah blah blah
And only the best is blah-di-blah
And so on

Over and over again.

Larry's unruly mop of ginger hair and alien face had, once again, been the ace card as it was exactly what the chocolate bar company had been looking for. They wanted a head that the viewers would never forget, and Fat Larry had exactly that.

'Little Larry,' he said to me, 'it's really fun, and it's fucking easy. You stand about for three days and try to do as you're told, then you get paid.'

I wasn't particularly impressed. But Fat was undeterred.

'There's more, Little Larry. You, mate, are doing the next one with me!'

At age not-much-teen, Larry had single-handedly persuaded the casting director to hire me as a singing extra. Apart from some free chocolate, I don't think I actually did get paid, but it was quite fun, and it ended up as a useful entry on my résumé. My time dressed as a little cowboy running about with a toy gun would eventually help to launch me into a whole new career – the only downside was that I developed a taste for those sugary, fatty little bars, which became another long-term addiction, only supplanted by booze and cheap Indonesian cigarettes.

Now, years later and with a little help from pro surfing, I landed some decently paid work, doing Coca-Cola commercials. Milk brands also seemed to love my outdoorsy appeal. For a while you couldn't get away from my face on the TV, on bus shelters, and leering at you from containers of Big M flavoured milk. Fat and I did many of these commercials together, sometimes by coincidence and sometimes with me returning his favour of years before and shoeing him into whatever I was working on. One such gig was a series of adverts for the *Sunday Telegraph*. We both found this funny because page three was the only part of any newspaper either of us had ever read.

Whenever we were on set together it was hard not to wet our pants laughing at each other and at the stupidity of the situations we found ourselves in. I mean, here we were trying to act, surrounded by clever and accomplished people who appeared to take us seriously even though we were useless frauds. Visions of Fat Larry firing a gun dressed as an Indian or the pair of us drinking cans of fizz wearing nothing more than ridiculously tight Levi's can make me lose it even today.

The ads led to a number of embarrassing appearances in absolutely terrible but very popular soaps and drama series. My first attempt was as a walk-on 'cool dude' (that's what it says in the credits) in *The Restless Years* – truly one of Australia's worst-ever television programs. In another, *The Young Doctors*, I was in bed for a full year playing a patient, Brad, who'd been crippled by a surfing accident and whose mother was a famous actress. In the series, my stage mother would refuse to come and see me, being too busy with her career. My main job was to moan a lot. It became difficult when I'd turn up on set terribly sunburned – awkward when playing somebody who's been bedridden for months on end. I was awful of course. It almost killed me both on the screen and off it.

I was so bad at acting that one of the producers made me go to drama school for a full year, no doubt to try to make me see the light and give up. It was a terrible experience. I had to read Shakespeare in front of our class, which was as traumatising as a big west set bulldozing through the line-up at Sunset Beach. I also had to act the part of a pea by rolling into a ball and squeaking. Mum, who didn't think much of my new job, always said it was a shame that there weren't more plays or films about vegetables.

There must be many talented performers out there who never had the right opportunities to realise their dreams. I was blessed with those opportunities, but they were wasted on someone who didn't have the talent to grab hold of them. Not so for many of my fellow cast members on *The Young Doctors*, who went on to have long and brilliant careers. Russell Crowe certainly did – his stint in 1977 was a springboard to wonderful things, including buying the Rabbitohs rugby league team that was based near the end of our street. I on the other hand did not go on to have a long and brilliant acting career. When they finally realised I was never going to make it, Brad was miraculously healed and released from hospital.

Ψ

I had never told my mother who I saw that day in the Bondi Hotel beer garden. She'd made it through a decade of danger and fear without losing her optimism or her ability to lift all of us by making us laugh at the absurdity of life. In fact she seemed more radiant than ever. Who was I to pour cold water on that? The fear we'd shared for so long had lost its grip and her old self-assurance was back. She fussed over me as always, showering me with new clothes and shiny leather shoes, taking me out to swanky places and making time for me even though it was clear she had an awful lot on. At times I felt like I was twelve again and I allowed myself to sink contentedly into the comforting routine.

There was no sign or talk of our lovely neighbour John, even though I tried indirectly to find out what had happened to him – and his ingenious dole scam. Mum seemed simply to have shaken it off like it had never happened, and I didn't want to confront her about that either. It seemed as if, somehow, we'd got away with it. But I'll simply never know. I was something of a returning hero, and questions about my season on the pro tour overrode everything else. Ignoring the past and embracing the glorious present was fine by me.

Mum's present certainly showed no signs of slowing down: in the Melody Street back room they were still discussing robberies and other elaborate ideas for stealing things, and it seemed that not a lot had changed while I was away. I wished they weren't still crooks, even if some of their conversations were very, very funny. And I had missed something; during those few Hawaiian winter months Mum had moved a rung or two up the criminal ladder. It appeared she was flourishing.

She was still a fun-loving tea leaf, don't get me wrong. The house was still littered with Waterford crystal, beautiful bone china, jewels of all types and fancy clothes still in their wrappers. But she was now revered in the underworld. Her head-pulling skills were in demand everywhere, no doubt thanks to that sixth sense of hers, which had extricated the Kangaroos from a few sticky situations while they were on tour overseas.

Crime bosses across Australia were now turning to Mum for help, relying on her special powers to smooth out the unexpected wrinkles that came with the many different kinds of robberies they were attempting.

When Mum and the aunties got back from their worldwide shopping trip, while they found that the local heat had died down, it was still a lot more challenging for the gang to steal from banks and jewellery stores as they'd done in the old days. Some of their previous escapades were notorious and so their faces were still too recognisable. But the biggest challenge was the modernisation of security systems and police databases, no doubt in the wake of some of the embarrassingly lucrative jobs my mother and her friends had carried out over the years.

And so with the help of Mummah's imagination, the Kangaroos and other associated gangs were trying all sorts of new and crazy operations in unusual new places where their pictures had not yet been circulated in those pre-internet times. One of these in particular brought special joy to our little Coogee nest. Mum and her friends were planning the biggest and most brazen jewel theft in the country's history.

Ψ

In 1739, the Persians sacked Delhi and confiscated a 130-carat Golconda diamond from the local mogul. It was eventually passed on to the Ottoman sultan and finally fell into the hands of Turkey's founding father, Kemal Atatürk, who sold it off in some kind of austerity drive in 1909. The diamond was named the Golconda d'Or after the area near Hyderabad where it was originally found and because of its extremely rare and peculiar golden hue. It found its way to Australia in 1962, having been stripped down to 95 carats, and is still one of the rarest diamonds in the world. It's so rare, in fact, that today, nobody knows where it is.

When news came that the gem was to be the headline act at a display in the Town Hall right in the middle of Sydney, Mum was ecstatic. She simply could not miss the opportunity to add herself to the list of proud owners of the 'Glonda', as she and her friends had clumsily renamed it.

Stealing the magnificent diamond was to be a broad-daylight operation. Head pulling experience in banks and shops around

Sydney was central to the plan, but this was clearly not going to be enough to get the job done; the jewel was the main attraction in a major exhibition and there would be way too many heads to pull.

The girls and two of the blokes went down to the Town Hall to take a look at the exhibition and devise a strategy. The huge diamond was displayed in a glass box with a sturdy metal base on a tall pedestal slap bang in the middle of the room. There was an access hatch underneath, secured by a chunky looking padlock. It was all rather visible. One of the chaps would need quite a lot of time to pick that very prominent lock. Clearly he would need a lot of cover and a lot of head pulling.

Something new, surprising and very subtle had to be conceived, and after days of frenetic debate between Mum and the ladies, it dawned on her what they had to do . . .

It was time to bring out the trusty brown paper and string.

A cardboard box would be made up. Much bigger and sturdier than the old gismo she'd often used. I would assist in making it look like a large parcel on its way to the post office, with the usual wrapping, stamps, address and string. Just like in the shoplifting days, although we wouldn't be filling the box with gourmet foods on this occasion. It was hoped that this ridiculous contraption would provide enough cover for the lock picker to work his magic.

I kept my involvement to a minimum – I was no longer a child and I had my acting career (and my liberty) to protect. I had rejected the criminal world in a juvenile courtroom years ago and had tried not to look back. But the nostalgia of the moment, the egging on by my mother's ridiculous gaggle, and the sheer stupidity of the scheme tempted me. Teamwork with

Mum always involved precision, meticulous organisation and, of course, superstition. But entertainment usually came first, and it always made her schemes hard to resist.

The group quickly realised that getting into the display case was going to take far too long, and the amount of time required to get past that lock couldn't be reliably predicted. There was a fair bit of debate about how to deal with this imponderable. Somebody eventually came up with the idea that it might be faster to get in via the light fitting on the top of the cabinet, if only that could be reached.

This is when the 'Big Bertha' was dreamed up: a second box, even bigger than the first, and very sturdy, that the head thief could stand on. This one would have to be made of a very particular type of lightweight plywood. Unfortunately, what they would gain in time, they would lose in discretion. The elected operative would be embarrassingly visible to the fifty or so onlookers, especially with his striking looks and particularly lanky body. The original sight-blocking box would therefore have to be as big as the Big Bertha. Stand on one, wave the other about to block people's view . . . perfect.

Of course, a plausible story would be needed when bystanders asked the inevitable questions. If it came to it, people would be told that the Glonda was having its daily pamper, needing to be freshly polished to bring out that special sparkle. The last part of this cleaning routine, which included putting it back into the glass case, would not actually happen. At the end of the performance the Golconda d'Or would be replaced by a plastic fantastic. A replica.

As usual, attention would be diverted by Mum and the ladies of the Tea Leaf Club.

Yet more boxes and props of all shapes and sizes would be needed to create a sort of waltz, moving around the room with perfect timing to block the lines of sight of the numerous staff and guards. This could be carried out using simple geometry and, at a push, bumping the kit into anyone who was getting too interested in the show in the middle of the room. This elegantly choreographed operation was something they'd done on a smaller scale many times, but on this occasion the angles would have to be perfect. Not everybody would buy into the diamond-cleaning act and certainly none of the security people would be fooled for too long. Once the job was complete, everybody would then leave one by one, very slowly, heads held high, as was the custom.

The discussions about this absurd and complicated theft made for days of excitement and sniggers at Melody Street. As usual it didn't seem like a crime was being planned at all. It felt like Mum & Co. had all gone slightly mad while I was away earning an honest crust on the surfing world tour.

When the big day arrived, the gang of five or six prepared perfectly; as usual the ladies were all incredibly well turned out from top to shiny toe. Mum and the aunties had the job of bringing the boxes and they made a hell of a sight departing Sandy's place that morning, dressed like film stars on the way to the post office.

They split up and arrived at the Town Hall in pairs. When they entered the Hall, there was a bit of a moment; they had expected forty to fifty people but there was a crowd of about eighty excited onlookers, pressed up against the barriers to catch a glimpse of the priceless diamond.

The flirting and chatting went ahead just the same – and with the same success. They were not kids anymore, but my aunties were all beautiful, elegant ladies. Mum coordinated the movements of each of her accomplices, which were carried off to Royal Ballet standard. I wonder if her synchronised swimming days had contributed to her great choreography skills and the clever moves they'd come up with.

The ladies managed to get one of the key staff members to turn his back on the display area. Two blockers equipped with the big boxes set one up by the stand for the boss, who being a circus freak was quick to hop onto it, lean over the display, unscrew the light fitting and remove the diamond through the hole. The other big box was momentarily held up as planned, more or less creating the required screen.

More or less. Mum said that at this point, there was an awkward moment when some nosy bystanders asked this gentleman thief what he was doing. He stuck to the cleaning script, wiping the stone with a flourish of a table napkin, and replacing the diamond with the fairly sad little copy, which bore no real resemblance to the real thing at all.

And that was that. They left the Town Hall one by one, stopping for a chat with whichever staff member approached them, until they were safely away.

My most vivid memory of the Golconda d'Or episode was the triumphant debrief meeting back at home. There were the same beautiful smiles, in the same old back room, talking and giggling about the same old things. But I was no longer a twelve-year-old running errands and making the tea. It clicked in my mind that this scene was an echo of my past, albeit one I could smell and hear. It felt like I was physically present in my own childhood recollection but this time the adult in the room was me, herding this ridiculous group of unruly schoolchildren who it seemed never intended to grow up.

Ψ

The fun was short-lived. By Monday morning it was clear that Mum's friends were never going to be able to shift this unique jewel. There was only one diamond that had its particular tint in the world. The thing glowed yellow-orange because of some sort of rare mineral trace only found in that one particular mine in India. It was also huge. It was and still is the biggest jewel ever stolen in Australia.

The robbery was in every newspaper and on the news, with pictures of Mum's fucking yellow rock everywhere you looked. On top of this, the jewel had been on loan to Sydney and so our town's 'good' name was on the line. The place already had a reputation for tea leaves and horrific crime in general, and the theft of a priceless diamond was not a welcome addition to our civic rap sheet. The police chief even staged a public re-enactment of the heist in the Town Hall to try to get to the bottom of what had happened.

Various crime bosses were arrested, two of whom had actually been spotted at the scene at the time of the robbery. But all were later released due to insufficient evidence. An awful lot of names were in the hat it seems, and the main thing they all had in common was that they were friends with Patricia Blair.

There was a lot of friendly competition about this job due to the high profile of the prize. I do not know which others had played a part on the day, but there was a theory that two other top dogs had tried to steal the rock but were beaten to it by Mum's team. In the end nobody went to jail, and so I don't suppose we'll ever know the full story.

My mother was never arrested or questioned. That miracle was, in my view, just more evidence of her special powers. She would have had to use them to disappear and stay hidden from everybody after this most public of escapades.

In any case, they were going to have to find another way to extract some kind of profit from their efforts. Mum said that the girls went to the police in the end, who were so embarrassed about the news reports of the brazen theft that they offered a small sum to hand the diamond in and forget about it. But the diamond was never officially recovered, and is still listed as missing.

The silly escapade would be tea-time conversation at Melody Street HQ for the rest of the decade. Sometimes it would be me passing the teas through the hatch, just like when I was a kid at Coogee Primary.

Sadly, my mum, my baby sister Kellie and I never became super-yacht owners after the heist. That's how I know that this was not a profitable job. My aunties have always shied away from answering too many questions about the robbery, and about what ultimately happened to the Golconda d'Or. Two of them died recently, taking the details of the diamond's final resting place to the grave.

I sometimes wonder if Mum decided it was 'bad luck' and tossed it out of a window, just like she did with my precious, beautiful opal from Coober Pedy.

One detail reported in the *Sydney Morning Herald* was especially amusing to everybody in our Melody Street back room. Frustrated police had searched the Town Hall several times for clues. The only evidence they could find, which would be theorised on for many years to follow, were a couple of empty plywood boxes covered in brown paper and string.

Ψ

When something life-changing or era-defining happens to a person, family or in history itself, nobody ever truly sees it at the time, least of all the subjects.

Mum was particularly magnificent that week of the robbery. Assured, radiant, joyful; she had visibly come back to life while I'd been floating about in different seas around the world. For Mum there was a feeling of a new, brighter decade beginning, the 1980s, with all the shiny possibilities that it could bring. I think Mum's newfound sense of self blossomed after she realised she'd overcome everything thrown at her, and that she was still defiantly standing. The diamond heist was proof that she could flourish on her own terms, whether or not she got to keep the proceeds.

My beautiful mother died a few years later of a brain tumour, aged only forty-eight. She never stopped laughing and making everyone laugh with her. Sitting here now writing this section of my life story, I think the Glonda was the high point of her mad, dangerous, hilarious and utterly incomprehensible career. Her Pipeline.

Epilogue:
Floating Back to Shore

Most of the interesting things in my life happened when I was young and stupid.

Many of the people who were around me at the time in this story were kids like me and might come off badly in this account, which often fails to predict the wonderful people they would become when they grew up. I thought it best to be honest about how I saw things then, to paint what I saw without adding the gloss that comes with time.

After the difficult events of the late 1970s and early '80s, for example, most of the protagonists and antagonists grew up, shook hands, had a beer together and a hearty laugh about how dumb they'd all been.

I've had to change a few names – and leave some out altogether. Many of the people in my early life, my forefathers, elderly relatives and 'babysitters', are deceased or in jail, but some of their stories just have too many warts. Those who are still on the loose wouldn't want to be dragged into my life story, even after all this time. Many have always refused to talk about those days, and some might still have their guns. So I've kept them out of this because underneath all the performance, I've always been a runner-away.

Not once did I hint at my past in interviews with magazines, newspapers or TV, or even to my fellow athletes. I have never understood it fully. Even when I'm alone today, with time to think, I don't know what to make of my boyhood as a thief's apprentice, let alone my moment as a young offender and a participant in a terrible scam. I must have known it was wrong, but it was also all I knew.

I think a few people will be shocked about how little they knew me back in the day and I apologise to them; I had my reasons.

Despite all the lies I had to tell, I formed lifelong friendships in those early Maroubra and Coogee days. It was always a riot meeting members of the 'Bra crew years later in the most unlikely places, whether on the pro circuit or on one of the many sponsored surf trips to the ends of the earth. I occasionally see the other two musketeers of Coogee Point, Terry and Mick, and have come to realise that these boys adjusted to adulthood much better than me. Half a century later I still carry regrets about how I failed to be open with them about who I really was.

'Fat Larry' Crane was the exception. At the time of Mum's big diamond heist he was in his heyday as an actor and man-about-town, and always had the best stories. Now, for once, I had something to top them. Celebrating the madness of life in 1980 with that lunatic genius might have been my life's high point.

It may have been Fat Larry's as well. Things started to become more and more complicated for him after that year. For one reason or another, the acting gigs were not covering his expensive tastes and like so many other surfers in our orbit, he got involved in messy stuff. It wasn't long before he was found dead behind a garbage bin in Kings Cross, chased down and kicked to death right there on the pavement by two nightclub bouncers.

I've never quite gotten over the devastation of losing my friend. He delivered some of the best, funniest moments in my life and, apart from my mother, brought me more joyful madness than any other human being. He knew he was smarter than me but we found each other unnaturally funny, which was something I had previously thought impossible. That alien knew why I was me. And then he was senselessly taken away.

Everybody felt Fat Larry's loss deeply. Whatever it was that he had been up to in that club, he didn't deserve to die for it. At a local community meeting shortly after his death, money was chipped in for the scolding [sic, I guess the term is a play on words] of his two killers, but the punishment didn't make anybody feel any better (especially not the killers, who were held down while boiling chip fat was poured all over them, and one of the pair subsequently took his own life).

As if things did not seem bleak enough, shortly after Larry was killed, his father was washed off the rocks by one of those sneaker waves while out fishing during a big swell. He'd been doing what he loved, they said, but who actually loves sliding off a rocky ledge to a certain death? Larry's fantastic mother Joyce had also lost her only daughter at around the same time.

In Maroubra, where I became a lifeguard, I was allowed to keep the other half of our nickname, 'Little Larry', even if it became quite ironic later on in my life as food took over from surfing, and the effects of it meant that I changed shape and had to be renamed.

I've been forgiven by many of the girls with whom I shared parts of my life. Cathy and I are still old mates, and I occasionally enjoy the wormholes into the past offered up by phone calls, pots of tea or unexpected meetings with people I shared it with.

Hawaii represented a fresh start for fifteen-year-old me, even if I made some of the same mistakes there too. Most of us arrived on those islands as kids with minimal education and short, chequered pasts. We were not well travelled. Few of us had finished school and many of us had seen family tragedy or come from messy homes. Pro surfing hadn't been invented and there was nobody to tell us how a professional athlete should behave, let alone how to handle the dizzying spoils of success. Certainly none of us had done our Hawaiian history. So yes, I regret some of our behaviour, but I can't blame any one of my compatriots for their exuberance in those exhilarating times.

Wayne Bartholomew must have come close to quitting Hawaii after the events of 1976, and maybe even dropping out of pro surfing altogether, such were the threats to his life. I can imagine how rattled he must have been. But he stuck it out and went on to win the Pipeline Masters and a world championship. He surfed with real style, underpinned by a steely determination to succeed. After his surfing career he became president of the ASP world professional surfing tour, and today he's one of the most influential people in the sport. He was a prankster, joker and hell raiser in his youth because his family life was a little bit like mine, but he never lacked drive or ambition. In 2009 he was awarded an Order of Australia medal for public service.

Peter 'PT' Townend, the first-ever surfing world champion, went on to become a huge success story in the surfing industry and sports media. He is kind of a big deal! It clearly runs in the family; his son Tosh is a world skateboarding champ. But PT is still modest as hell, funny and very willing to take the piss out of himself. He's always stepped forward to help anybody trying to make a go of it, and anybody who needs it, including me.

Ian 'Kanga' Cairns is still a bruiser, a proper Aussie who went on to be incredibly influential on the contest circuit and in the formation of pro surfing. He's living it up in California these days, but don't be fooled by the gentrified environment; nobody who saw his wipeout at Waimea on the way to winning that 1975 contest will ever forget it. I don't even know how he got back in the water after that.

Mark Richards went on to win four consecutive world titles and countless major contests, becoming one of the most successful surfers of all time and earning the right to be recognised only by his initials. MR also lit up the world as a surfboard shaper, inventing a twin-fin design variant that had an incalculable impact on the direction the sport took, allowing previously impossible manoeuvres to become commonplace. The incredible thing about Mark was how low-key, personable and humble he was, despite being such a fierce competitor. I wish I'd followed his lead. Whenever I surfed with him out at Jocko's, he would encourage me when he didn't have to.

Tom Carroll went on to win two world titles and earn a reputation as one of the most hard-charging and fearless surfers the tour has ever seen. I'll never forget the first time I saw his explosive trademark snap one day out at Rocky Point. Something about the audacity of it told me he would soon become unbeatable. Even after suffering some terrible injuries he always came back stronger and fitter. He became the first ever 'million-dollar surfer', signing a historic sponsorship deal with Quiksilver at the end of the 1980s.

Shaun Tomson won a Pipeline Masters (on his back-hand) and a world title, which surprised nobody. He took competitive surfing to a whole new level. Shaun also founded Instinct Surfwear, which became an iconic brand of the 1980s and '90s. He was the consummate athlete, bringing a previously unheard of level of dedication and determination to the sport. He even found time to moonlight as a Calvin Klein model, and had a later career as a motivational speaker. Despite all this Shaun will stop to chat with any mere mortal and has always been one of the great ambassadors of our sport.

Tom Curren went on to win three world titles and cement his name in the surfing hall of fame. He occupies a god-like status in the wave riding pantheon.

Cheyne Horan just kept on being Cheyne. I always enjoyed hanging out with my friend from over the hill in Bondi and we had many, many memorable sessions together at our respective home breaks, where both of us ignored the petty localism that could flare up from time to time. Cheyne was runner-up to the world title four times but never won it. Most thought he'd been short-changed. I did, and I wondered if his board design rebellions had rubbed judges up the wrong way. Yet I never heard him complain. In 1999, Quiksilver ran a Masters event at Lafitenia in southwest France, inviting just about every pro legend who's ever lived. Cheyne blitzed through the field of superstars and won hands down – it was the most popular contest win I've ever seen. I was privileged to be there (I came about last, blaming the croissants, oysters and vintage hams).

Cheyne's exploits with the laser zap board design are a key part of the history of our sport but today he remains a fun-loving madcap icon, representing everything that was crazy and free-spirited when surfing was at its best.

Viscount Ted never went back to his old life on the country estate and never got to swap his landed title for surfing one. He passed away tragically young having never won a major surf contest but maintaining a place in the heart of every pro surfer he ever shared a patch of ocean with. I didn't give too much credence to the suggestions that his death had been in some way connected with the undercurrents on the North Shore.

Gerry 'Mr Pipe' Lopez, my first and biggest surfing hero, won two Pipeline Masters, and was hugely successful designing both surfboards and snowboards. He still surfs deep in the barrel today; he also snowboards, does yoga and is a living advertisement for the spiritual way of life.

The Colonel and BB Benson passed away but their kids continued to tear up the waves of the North Shore for decades after. Colonel Benson's flavoursome photography still decorates secret corners of Oahu today. You'll know when you see one of his works – they are unmistakeable, even fifty years later. Whenever I spot one of his little vignettes in a magazine or on a café wall I am instantly transported to a time and a place that, before I know it, causes a knowing smile to creep across my face. There's nothing I can do about it.

Dane Kealoha never did win a world title, having possibly been denied by events at the '79 Pipeline Masters. He deserved one – he was a trailblazer and the most aggressive and competitive surfer I ever faced. He did go on to win at Pipe in '83 and may have been just about the most popular victor ever.

Thanks to his unusual stance in left-hand barrels, he's credited with inventing the 'pig dog' style of back-hand tube riding, which made it possible to ride deep when going the wrong way. The rail-grabbing, body-twisting stance is still in use all around the world today and could be said to be Dane's legacy.

I'll always regret that we never sat down together and properly reconciled. I would have told him that, even though we were the same age, I saw him as one of the gods. We were both just kids in the days of our brief rivalry and I was the stupider of the pair. He was one of the true greats and passed away in 2023 at the age of sixty-four, far too young. He was a waterman and true Hawaiian legend, and he was loved and respected by all throughout his life, which probably proves that it was mostly me and my mouth that were in the wrong.

As for Fast Eddie, he's a successful entrepreneur these days and still a senior figure on the Hawaiian surf scene. That club of his matured into a respected surf-wear brand and a society supporting locals and promoting the aloha spirit. Nevertheless, we're all still scared of him. His kids absolutely rip in the surf, and we're scared of them too.

I've been brutally honest in this account about how I saw him during a fleeting period in time when we were so very young, which means it's hardly likely that I've got him right. In truth I'm not sure anybody has; extracting a man from a myth is not easy, and that man and his club still hold their place at the very heart of surfing mythology today, almost a half century on.

In hindsight I don't think I was ever one of his main targets; I was just a tempting little morsel for the wannabe Black Shorts who wanted to impress him, and the Rat was one of those – a runt of the Black Short litter. Perhaps chasing me around the coastline was part of his attempt to earn the respect he craved from the rest of Eddie's pack.

I hear that the Rat himself has rounded the edges over the years, just as we all have, and is now an upstanding citizen and pillar of the surfing community. In the 1970s and '80s it seemed to me he was a total demon, and I probably built him up in my mind into something far worse than he actually was. He was an outsider, just like me, and he'd had real tragedy in his life too, so I had two reasons to feel for him. But his pain seemed to have morphed into bursts of hatred, whereas mine became a sort of comic fatalism and that was the difference between the pair of us. Perhaps we could have compared notes on our ridiculous lives, but that opportunity never arose.

I didn't blame the Black Shorts for wanting to take back their idyllic part of the world and its incredible waves. Whatever it was that happened between us all those years ago, it never dimmed my absolute love and respect for Hawaii, its seas and its people. They never invited the hordes of blow-ins, of which I was one of the noisiest. Throughout the 1980s, as surfing became more and more popular on mainland US and beyond, the number of visitors to Hawaii exploded, dwarfing the modest crews of visitors that had seemed so shocking to everyone in 1975. And it only kept on growing. Surfers were like a virus, their population increasing to a point where they almost started to eat each other. The situation must have been horrific from the point of view of a native Hawaiian, born and bred in that unique five-kilometre paradise strip of the most powerful, beautiful waves on earth.

I knew how 'situations' like I experienced would have been dealt with back in my home town. In fact, I'm not sure what would be more flammable: a big session out at Pipeline, an afternoon at the Oshey with Dad's friends, or a busy day in the surf at Maroubra's North End.

Those guys and their small army of exceedingly big men were a product of a unique set of circumstances, an unrepeatable time in the history of both Hawaii and of our sport. I for one believe that the right outcome arose out of their actions, both good and bad. Visitors to the islands now know very well that the first thing they must do is show respect to the place, its traditions and its people, both in the water and on land. Much of this is down to the efforts of the Hui O He'e Nalu and their Black Shorts.

If it hadn't been those guys and their brotherhood doing the policing, it would have been others. There were plenty of gritty, angry characters about back then, some of who were far more ready to let fly than Fast Eddie. If I bumped into any of them today I'd probably offer them a nice cup of tea and maybe see if they wanted to share a bowl of my excellent eight-hour pork mince bolognese.

And of course I'd apologise. Not a false apology in expectation of a 'never mind' reply, but a sincere one. For misunderstanding, at the time, the incredible and long-standing heritage of Hawaii. For confusing being a good surfer with being a waterman, and for failing to grasp the fact that the latter is a true vocation, and so much harder and more worthwhile for it. I guess, in short, I'd apologise for being an arsehole.

Then, after me getting smacked in the face one last time, we'd probably settle in for some great yarns.

Ψ

Only a few of the players in the first half of this book are still alive. Of the few who are still with us, there are fewer still who I can talk freely about, and some who will never come clean about the events surrounding my mother and father. Cryptic clues have been left for me over the years, trails of breadcrumbs that lead nowhere or to a paradox, but many secrets have been, or are being, taken to the grave.

You can see many of these people in any of the various films and television series that were made about my dad and his world. One film about my father's career and demise – *The Money Movers* with Brian Brown – was said to be the most violent film ever made in Australia, so gory that not many dared go see it.

I never had a face-off or a moment of parting with my dad's mate Fletcher. He was my uncle, protector, mentor and minder at various times, but I never understood what he expected of me, or what our relationship was supposed to be. Fletcher probably saved our lives yet I never thanked him because so much was unspoken in those desperate times. I'm pretty sure that one way or another, perhaps by being so different from Baldy, I disappointed him.

He was as much a shadow as Billy Maloney, even if they were on opposite sides of the war, and he continued to pop up from time to time, getting me out of scrapes in the most unlikely places around the world. I fought for years to keep both of these men out of my life and out of my head and I am happy to leave them in the past.

Good old Bertie Burwick – Uncle Bert – died decades ago. He was one of the few elders who wanted me to have an honest career and a normal life, and I'm lucky that he persevered with me. He helped me to veer off a shit course and onto a good one, and he helped me equip myself with the tools to stay on it. I don't think that the Berties of this world, the givers, often receive the rewards they deserve, at least not in this life. I owe him such an awful lot.

Jimmy the Pom spent time in jail for the murder of Billy Maloney's brother but was later retried, released and eventually deported to England, where he continued his contract-killing career for the Kray twins in London's East End. He was never tried for any Toe Cutter activities. I believe he died in the late 1980s. The police seemed more interested in him being a transvestite than a murderer; Roger Rogerson investigated him for quite some time and seemed to become slightly obsessed with this. The detective sergeant was one of the few cops of the time who actually faced justice, although he had to shoot somebody dead for it to happen.

Detective Sergeant Kaiser, who had been deeply mired in everything surrounding the death of my father and our subsequent pursuit by the Toe Cutters, would eventually come quite close to getting punished for his decades of corruption. But not close enough. He stood accused of receiving stolen goods, distributing counterfeit money, extorting abortion clinics, recruiting customers for prostitution, fixing trials, framing alleged offenders and murder. Instead of facing an investigation, however, he was one of several officers who were allowed or encouraged to take early retirement and claim their pensions instead. A small number of his colleagues were eventually sent to prison but I'd rather it had been him.

After his police career, Kaiser popped up as a private investigator and security consultant. If you mention his name in certain circles in Sydney's Eastern Suburbs today, please stand well back from the cloud of flying spittle that will fill the air. Even if all the old crooks who are still alive are now quite frail, they more than make up for it with the amount of anger they feel towards this copper!

Billy Maloney fled to the UK and never faced justice for my father's murder. The police over there interviewed him about all of it, at which point he more or less confessed. He is written into criminal folklore for his founding role in the Toe Cutters.

Having chased Mum and me around Australia for months on end trying to squeeze the location of Dad's loot out of us, I'm guessing he can't have missed my cheeky face all over the television a few years later. I often pictured him looking at me in Coke adverts, mouthing off at surf contests, lying in bed performing miserably in a woeful soap opera, or staring out from his milk container when he pulled it from the fridge in the morning. Billy never faced a reckoning in court for what he did, but did my cheeky mug haunt him? Did he think about what he did to my dad? Did he wish we were all dead? Or were there simply no thoughts at all about us inside that fat ginger head of his?

Very few members of my mother's little club of tea leaves are still with us. Even so, I had to fiddle with their names in this memoir. Those very old ladies don't like to talk about Mum, the Kangaroo Gang or their escapades. In 2013, a 76-carat Golconda diamond of an average hue fetched €16.9 million at an auction in Geneva. Nobody talks about the Glonda, but wherever it is, it would be worth about $25 million today.

A few of the other crooks are still around, and every so often I'll encounter a frail old man somewhere about town, a tottering white-haired crim released after a long jail sentence. He was once a somebody but now he's stuttering about the suburbs, happy for any company. He'll have a coffee with me, chat about Mum and Dad or Unc, and share a trivial story that I didn't know. He'll eagerly tell me about a random shooting he did, where somebody died for a minor lie or over a woman. There'll be not a hint of regret and perhaps even a giggle. It helps me to feel better, to hear it confirmed that this was just the era and the place we all lived in.

Ψ

As for me? I've had a brilliant life based around the simplest of pleasures. Food, family and always the ocean.

I was brought up in a vastly different Sydney, one that doesn't exist today. This is generally for the better. I know that gentrification has rendered the place smug, and too expensive for many people to call home, but you've always got that glittering sea, and, apart from the joggers, it is safe. Anybody who lived there when I was a kid knows this is a fair price to pay.

Over the years, I haven't reflected all that much on my parents and their peculiar careers. In my childhood it was all I knew, and so their activities didn't shock me at the time. People have asked me why I never spoke to anybody professional about what happened to my father and I suppose that my decision to ignore it was just another act of running away. We all grow up in the shadow of our fathers, but Frank 'Baldy' Blair's wasn't the dappled shade of a leafy tree, ever-present and dependable. It was the hard-edged, cold darkness that overcomes you when a fast-moving storm cloud passes over. I don't know what else I would have to say about it if I were lying on some therapist's couch.

Dad corralled me into a world that few get out of in one piece, whether in body or in mind. But he also gave me the tool that ultimately helped me escape it. Did some part of him know this on the day he decided to take the long drive over the Harbour Bridge all the way down to Manly to buy me that shiny new surfboard? I'll never know.

Mum, on the other hand, always knew everything. I'm sure that her support of my ridiculous idea to become a pro surfer, a decade before such a profession existed, came from a prescience and wisdom that was unique to her. Whether she thought surfing was a realistic aim or just a step towards something else doesn't really matter, she knew it was a route out of the sordid place in which we were stuck.

I had no regrets about quitting professional surfing at such a young age, even if I did feel a little cheated when I didn't win certain contests. I always had plenty of other interests, lack of talent notwithstanding. I loved food and drink, I enjoyed acting, girls were always a wonderful distraction and, above all, I adored getting into the sea and grabbing a wave. I still do. If I'd had a coach or a manager, like today's surfers, I honestly don't think things would have been much different.

We all have to learn that life is unfair at times, and with my particular set of circumstances, I did too. But I was still living a dream and, frankly, I came to realise that while I had all the lip and all the bluster, I never really had that drive and uncompromising disregard for fun that marks out the true champions from the mere mortals. It's terrible to have to admit that I got over almost every contest loss I ever suffered within a half hour and got on with the business of having an epic life.

The distractions that helped me to live with the failures would almost become my downfall. Especially the booze, which I struggled with for a decade. I reckon I was trying to drown a whole cast of demons in the stuff, but they'd always swim back to the surface whenever they wanted. I eventually came to my senses and gave it up completely. These days I don't drink or smoke, which is incredibly boring for me and worse for the people around me. Even more sadly, I also gave up the Milky Bars.

After my pro career came to a sudden, early end, I carried on competing on and off for a while, picking events where the waves were going to be good. I may not have given a great account of myself at the Pipeline Masters of 1981 or '82, but I did get to ride the world's most radical wave for several hours with just a few mates for company. That's unimaginable today. And I still had some sponsors supporting me, with invitations to go on tour or make fabulously naff surf movies in exotic locales.

I continued acting (badly) for a few years but I always knew it wasn't my passion, and that I wasn't very good. Mum, usually full of thickly laid-on encouragement, was honest with me about this. The gigs therefore gradually dwindled through lack of interest on the part of both actor and director.

Outside of surfing I only had one other safe place – cooking. So I became a chef and a providore of fabulous food for fancy restaurants. Both careers were facilitated by Uncle Bert, who used his clout to put me on the inside track at the Sydney Fish Market. It was hard work but fun. I am still meticulous (read, fucking annoying) about processes, ingredients and recipes today, thanks I'm sure to Nanna and Mum. The main reason I never made it stick as a professional was probably laziness.

I still travel to Hawaii and Indonesia to get waves, and when I'm there I sometimes bump into the characters from the second half of this book. Most of us have long forgotten our childish behaviour from half a century ago, and what seemed to be high drama at the time now only serves as reassurance that you can grow out of any youthful stupidity. We were punks back then because we had no education. These days, we look back, laugh at ourselves, have a drink together and toast those who are dead.

Today, as an adult, I don't think I'd take on many of the North Shore waves during a full-blooded winter swell. I've been back five or six times in recent years and have been terrified most of the time. Something always goes brilliantly wrong in the seas of Hawaii.

Those swell-chasing travels are how I met my lovely wife, Nyoman. She ran the café at Bali's Canggu Beach in the days before there were any other cafés or even a town, and she's a better chef than me. We have two fabulous children together. I don't deserve any of them.

Throughout my mixed-up little life, I've always found myself drifting towards the outside of any activity I pursued, loitering on the fringes of the cliques that each one created. I was never part of the Bronzed Aussies, the Free Ride generation, or at the heart of the pro surfing tour as a full-time contestant. I was never in one acting job long enough to become indispensable, and I remained detached during the various phases of my food lover's career, never truly buying into any particular part of it. It always felt safer to hover out there on the fringes of things.

If my parents and their friends impressed one thing on me, it was to be ready, willing and able to run. And when you're on the outside of a crowded place – rather than in the thick of it – it's much easier to do that.

Surfing has been the greatest gift. Even if it can also be a curse. With most other sporting passions, you can pretty much rely on the fact that the court, footy field or whatever will be nice and playable every time you visit. Not so with surfing. For good surf to happen, you need a fine balance of elements to fall into place. Most of the time, one or more of those elements are missing and conditions are rubbish. Wrong wind, wrong tide, no swell, too much swell . . . It seems like something is always wrong for us frustrated wave riders. So there must be another reason we keep coming back. What is it that captivates us?

For me, it's about escape and connection. Leaving everything behind and coming face to face with new people, nature, places, or sometimes just ourselves.

It can happen in your own backyard when you find yourself on one of those perfect, clear offshore mornings when nobody else has bothered getting out of bed and you're out the back on your own, wrapped up in the glory of Mother Nature. That first duck dive, when your head gets wet for the first time ducking under the waves, prepares you for the encounter by resetting your mind and opening it up to whatever's waiting for you on the outside. It works every single time.

It can happen in Hawaii, where swells can jump from four to twenty feet in minutes, your survival requiring such intense concentration that all worldly cares have to be put on hold. You are disconnected from your daily anxiety by the very act of survival, by the immersion, and by the distance from land.

And it can happen in the places that you might never have heard of if you weren't a stupid surfer, where you're forced to rub up against places and cultures you never would have dreamed of. Like the tiger jungle at Grajagan, the pythons of Sumbawa, the forest shamen of Siberut, the smoking volcanoes of West Java, the machete wielders of Sumba, the man-made pandemonium of Padang, the crystal-cold, seal-infested waters of the Outer Hebrides, the Avalanche of France, the shark-infested Tunnels of Kauai, the Backyards of Oahu, the Three Bears in the west, the shark-infested Trapdoors in the north, the shark-infested Cactus down south and finally, much closer to home, my own equally shark-infested Maroubra South End.

Another much simpler way to say it is this: it's usually the stuff that happens when you're not actually riding a wave that makes surfing, surfing.

This has been the unexpected blessing bestowed on me by a surfing life. But that's just me. In the same way that everyone who stares at the beach will see their own special flecks of colour in the sand, you will find your own particular meaning out there in the surf. It won't be the same as mine I hope, but you will find it.

Co-author's Note

Larry and I spent over twenty-five years travelling the world's most obscure places, looking for perfect waves. Together we got sick, lost and terrified in swarming jungles, dusty deserts and on remote coasts. When there's no internet and no pub you talk an awful lot, and it was during these moments that Larry's extraordinary life story just came out, revealing itself in random instalments.

Eventually people encouraged Larry to write it all down as best he could, or get involved in film projects, but the man absolutely hates writing; he didn't have the most consistent schooling, after all. And perhaps he wasn't ready to talk about every detail of his early life anyway, which he'd kept to himself for decades, even among close friends. It can't have been easy, given the attention he received.

It took a while to realise that what Larry had told me about his early life and his parents was not only accurate, but barely scratched the surface of an extraordinary piece of Australian history, at the centre of which he, his mother and his father squarely sat.

Larry's memory is like mine, full of holes. And his elders didn't always report events accurately to anybody, let alone document them, with good reason. The few who are still alive are often reluctant to revisit the momentous events that shaped Larry's childhood. As a result the process has been archaeological in places with all the uncertainty that can bring when trying to pin down exact dates.

I've done my best with it, and failed in parts, but I hope you've enjoyed reading it. His really has been an extraordinary life.

Jeremy Goring

Acknowledgements

Our eternal thanks to: Jeff Divine; Bernie Baker; Norm Moore; Tony Nolan; Peter Crawford, RIP; Justin Crawford; Ralph Cipolla; Colonel Al Benson, RIP; BB Benson, RIP; Sean Davey; Luke and the team at *Tracks*; Matt Warshaw; Ben Macartney; Bert Kidd; Mick; Nyoman; Adam; Dave; Brandon, Shané, Rod and the incredible team at Penguin Random House Australia; and Tara at Curtis Brown.

About the Author

After the events in this book, Larry Blair left the acting and pro surfing worlds and became a professional chef and providore of fine seafood. When Canggu, the bustling resort town in Bali had just two cafés on the beach, Larry met the daughter of the owner of the better one and he is still married to her today. They have two brilliant young children. He has kept out of trouble between Indonesia and the NSW North Coast ever since, apart from when he's being chased by sharks.

Powered by Penguin

Looking for more great reads, exclusive content and book giveaways?

Subscribe to our weekly newsletter.

Scan the QR code or visit penguin.com.au/signup